O B — A M B — 824

Give a Little

Give
A LITTLE

~~~~~~~~~~

HOW YOUR

small donations

CAN TRANSFORM

our WORLD

Wendy Smith

HYPERION

NEW YORK

While the author has made every effort to provide accurate telephone numbers and Internet addresses at the time of publication, neither the publisher nor the author assumes any responsibility for errors, or for changes that occur after publication. Further, the publisher does not have any control over and does not assume any responsibility for author or third-party Web sites or their content.

Library of Congress Cataloging-in-Publication Data is available upon request.

ISBN: 978-1-4013-2340-0

Hyperion books are available for special promotions and premiums. For details contact the HarperCollins Special Markets Department in the New York office at 212-207-7528, fax 212-207-7222, or e-mail spsales@harpercollins.com.

FIRST EDITION

10 9 8 7 6 5 4 3 2 1

This book is dedicated to my brother,

Kevin Christopher Smith

(1966–2005),

who inspired me to appreciate

and make the most

of every day of good health.

CONTENTS

part two

hunger

part three

health

part six

giving, lending,
AND clicking for good

INTRODUCTION

With open hearts and open hands, we gave what we could,
and a little became a lot.

It was the worst natural disaster in recorded history. For years, two colossal slabs of rock, the Indo-Australian tectonic plate, supporting the continent of Australia and the Indian subcontinent, and the Eurasian tectonic plate, supporting Asia and Europe, had been moving against each other, the Indian plate sliding beneath the Burma plate of the Indo-Australian plate. On December 26, 2004, the Indian plate slipped about 20 meters under the Burma plate causing an earthquake of 9.1 on the Richter scale and unleashing pent-up compressional forces equal to *23,000 explosions of the nuclear bomb that decimated Hiroshima.*[1]

In addition to causing the great earthquake, the sliding of the Indian plate beneath the Burma plate displaced ocean waters, creating waves that rushed toward coastal areas surrounding the Indian Ocean at hundreds of miles per hour. When the nearly undetectable waves hit shorelines, they grew to monstrous heights—some nearly 100 feet high. They pushed inland as far as three miles like concrete walls of water, destroying everything in their paths.

Nothing stood a chance against the dual forces of the quake and the waves. Virtually everything that took a direct hit was annihilated—humans, property, the environment. Approximately 230,000 people died that day. Twelve countries bordering the Indian Ocean reported a total of over $10 *billion* in damages to infrastructure, services, and industries.[2]

We'd never seen anything like it. With twenty-four-hour news coverage from cable television, we saw it all, almost immediately. It was unbelievable. It was horrifying. We were overcome by sorrow and sympathy.

We jumped into action like never before—governments, aid agencies, you, and me. We knew what was needed. Everything was needed. The agents of relief and reconstruction needed cash. Immediately. So, we gave. And gave. According to the United Nations Office for the Coordination of Humanitarian Affairs, as of January 2009, governments and civil society around the world had contributed a total of $6.2 billion.[3] Nearly two-thirds of that total came from the United States. The U.S. federal government provided $841 million in aid.[4] That's 13.6 percent of aid from across the world, a healthy share of the whole.

What I'm going to tell you next, however, will seem unlikely. Maybe impossible. Yet it's true. It just didn't get any news coverage.

Together, foundations, corporations, and individuals in the United States gave $3.16 billion.[5] The first surprise is that American civil society gave *3.7 times* the federal government's contribution to relief and reconstruction following the tsunami.

If that surprises you, this will shock you: $2.78 billion of the U.S. share, or *45 percent of total giving from around the world*, came from ordinary American citizens. U.S. corporations gave $340 million, and foundations gave $40 million. But you didn't hear reports about the tremendous generosity of everyday citizens—only the large donations made by individual companies or foundations.

And there's more. According to a study by the Center on Philanthropy at Indiana University:

> **. . . Despite the highly publicized million-dollar gifts from corporations and celebrities, most of the giving to the tsunami relief efforts came from gifts of less than $50 made by millions of Americans across the country,"** said Patrick M. Rooney, director of research for the Center on Philanthropy. "These giving patterns are very similar to the charitable response to the September 11, 2001 terrorist attacks and what we believe occurred after Hurricane Katrina."[6] (Bold added by the author.)

One-quarter of all of the 106 million U.S. households in 2004 donated to tsunami relief efforts.[7] The median donation was $50, while the average donation was $135.[8] Everyday Americans sent a second tsunami of $50 donations to repair a corner of the world 15,000 miles away.

That's how it works. You've heard it takes a village to raise a child. It takes all of us to fix the world. That means you and me—doing good, lifting lives, remaking the world.

WHAT TO EXPECT FROM *GIVE A LITTLE*

This book is going to change the way you think about charitable giving. I'm going to show you that there are organizations *using small contributions from everyday donors* to address four critical issues related to poverty: (1) hunger, (2) health, (3) education, and (4) access to tools, technology, and infrastructure. I'm going to describe those organizations and the value of their work in ways that you may not have considered before. *Give a Little* cuts through the muddle of hyperbolic language found in fundraising letters and gives you straight facts—facts you can rely on that will empower your philanthropic decisions.

You'll find it's not the size of the contribution that matters; what matters is the outcomes your giving produces. I'm going to describe the outcomes created by your gifts from a variety of viewpoints, including simple economics, basic science, and stories straight from the sources—beneficiaries, donors, and founders of organizations. You'll see how you hold the power to transform the world by improving the lives of those living on the furthest margins of daily life—"the bottom billion" among us.

While researching the organizations and stories for this book, I was inspired over and over again by the wisdom and determination of people living in desperate situations and by those creating new opportunities for them. I was also inspired by *you*. Specifically, your concern for the well-being of folks you'll never meet, living in faraway places, and whose lives would be unrecognizable next to your own. I congratulate your optimism and determination that everyday citizens can improve those lives.

I share that optimism and determination, and I'm going to tell you exactly how each of us can afford to transform the lives of folks halfway across the world or in our own communities. Together we're going to help end extreme poverty. We're going to treat and control the spread of HIV/AIDS, tuberculosis, and malaria. We're going to build bridges; ease asthma so children can go to school; help mothers give birth to healthy babies and survive their deliveries; get irrigation pumps to millions of subsistence farmers and help them create commercial enterprises; give families goats, bees, or llamas to make them microentrepreneurs; provide clean drinking water that is accessible, safe, and affordable.

This book tells stories from many places: heroes persevering in the face of unimaginable deprivation; people called to action by an encounter, an idea, even a photograph who founded an organization or a movement in response; services and technologies that produce tremendous impact for mere pennies. There are tales of transformation: of futility changed to hope, of families moving from barely surviving to thriving.

Ultimately, this book's story is simple but profound: There are many ways that you can make a real, lasting, and meaningful difference in the lives of people who need only the *opportunity* to achieve prosperity. You can afford to provide that opportunity.

YOUR PERSONAL GIVING ADVISER

When wealthy folks want to make substantial charitable donations, they often turn to professional donor advisers who help them define their philanthropic interests and the causes and organizations that match those interests. This brings to mind a couple of issues: First, research shows the majority of total giving by individuals comes from households with incomes *under $100,000*;[9] and second, every donor deserves access to information that maximizes the meaning and effectiveness of his or her donations.

That is where this book and I come in. Think of me as your personal giving adviser and this book as a guide to changing the world from your kitchen table armed only with a checkbook and a pen. Together, we're going to make big things happen without emptying your bank account.

IMPORTANT NOTE

Give a Little emphasizes giving that can help eradicate cyclical poverty in the United States and in developing countries around the world; however, I know there are many other causes worthy of your support. I am not advocating for you to redirect the charitable donations you are already making to your favorite causes and charities.

The local animal shelter, program for developmentally disabled adults, children's hospital, United Way, literacy program, mental health center, public radio station, and so many more nonprofit programs NEED YOUR HELP! They are doing critically important work, often right in your backyard, and rely on your continued generosity to sustain their efforts. Most of these programs are relatively small and have very limited budgets for fund-raising. You may need to seek them out in order to fully appreciate the breadth of the services being provided right in your community. I recommend going to your community's Web site and taking a look at the list of local social services providers. They are already producing change, often one person or family at a time, in ways that make your community stronger and a better place to live. Many provide our country's social safety net, and most of us, at some point in our lives, will require a service that relies at least in part on charitable donations.

Instead of redirecting your donations, I would urge you to *add to your current giving with a few modest donations each year.* In this way, Americans will realize the full potential of their collective giving power and *change the world*.

Give a Little reveals just the tip of the iceberg that is effective charities doing good work, but you'll learn how to identify other nonprofits that will make good use of your donations. You can get more information and descriptions of programs by visiting me at www.givealittlenow.com

how AND *why*
we give

~~~~~~~~~~~~~~~~~~~~~~~

chapter 1

Doers and Donors

"Few have the greatness to bend history itself, but each of us can work to change a small portion of events, and in the total of all those acts will be written the history of this generation."

—ROBERT KENNEDY[1]

HOW A DOER CHANGES THE WORLD

In 1990, twenty-five-year-old Jim Ziolkowski was trekking across Nepal when he entered a remote village and encountered an inauguration ceremony for the village's new schoolhouse. The school had been built with the help of a group of British mountaineers. The local residents' joy and the obvious importance of the school moved Jim deeply.

When he returned home to the United States, Jim took a job with GE Capital as a member of the Financial Management Program, ready to embark on a long and lucrative career; however, his heart was still in Nepal with the villagers and their children celebrating an opportunity taken for granted in the United States—to go to school, to learn to read, to improve their lots in life.

So, Jim did what any highly motivated, visionary, but penniless, twenty-five-year-old would do. He quit his job, recruited his similarly broke brother, Dave, and friend, Marc Friedman, and launched buildOn, a nonprofit organization with the intention of building schools in developing countries.

Jim's magnetic personality, optimism, and determination rallied hundreds of additional volunteers, donors, and major investors, such as General Electric, which partnered with buildOn and continues to donate all the organization's office space and information technology. Seventeen years later, buildOn has constructed over 300 schools that have provided educational opportunities to over 100,000 children and adults in developing countries. It also operates more than 100 after-school programs in the United States that engage high school students in local community volunteer service, global education, and fund-raising to support school construction overseas. buildOn has grown from a kitchen table enterprise to an international movement to empower youth to improve their lives, their communities, and the world.

Jim's is a story of singular dedication and self-sacrifice in order to make a real difference—to markedly change the world. But, Jim's total immersion isn't the only meaningful approach to creating change. In fact, Jim couldn't have realized his dream without the thousands of ordinary individuals who opened their wallets and created change another way: *by making affordable donations to his cause.*

LET'S FACE IT: WE'RE NOT ALL JIMS

The vast majority of us will not quit our jobs, leave our careers, and risk all of our large or small personal fortunes to make a difference. It's not that we're not caring. Far from it, we would love to help make the world a better place. It's simply that we aren't all called to incubate and grow a new enterprise. We have other dreams and talents. But, we can partner with people like Jim by contributing to their efforts financially. And amazingly, none of us has to break the bank to make it happen. When enough of us write checks, the checks need not be large.

I used to think the only way to make a difference in the world was to get into the trenches—to work directly with those I wished to help. I believed that I had to be hands-on to get the job done.

I was naive.

I've worked in the nonprofit sector for more than twenty years, about half of that time operating programs and the other half raising funds to keep programs operating. When I was on the programming side of the equation, I felt tremendous satisfaction helping to transform lives. For most of those years, I helped run a child care and early learning program for primarily low-income families and their young children. I joined the field in the mid-1980s, just as research results on brain development and the importance of the first three years of life to a child's potential were hitting the press. It was exhilarating, though the general public seemed slow to tune in to the breaking news. But being in the trenches, I knew and could see the results of our efforts to help children and their families. Right before our eyes, families were strengthened and children launched, ready to succeed in school. We knew we were making a difference. We drank it in and felt good.

At the ten-year mark, I made the leap from the trenches to the agency's first fund-raising department (staff of one—me). There were upsides and downsides to that leap.

The upside was that I knew the agency backward and forward. I knew exactly how its work made a measurable difference, could site persuasive research-based evidence, and describe its importance with passion. The downside was that not everybody (make that almost nobody) had caught the news—that providing high-quality early learning and care to at-risk children improves their outcomes in school and in life.

In order to be successful in my new fund-raising job, I had to learn how to inform *and* inspire. I honed my written message; I developed a verbal presentation that described the potential of a donor's gift. I dared to share my enthusiasm and belief in the mission without restraint. It worked. Funders were inspired and opened their wallets.

Raising money made me a more generous donor. In learning how to inform and inspire funders, I learned a great deal about the potential of even small donations (i.e., those even *I* could afford) to help effective charities. The numbers astounded me:

$3 a year could help eliminate tuberculosis, the widest-
    spread disease around the world and responsible for
    more than 5,000 deaths every day.[2]

$20 provides *400 pounds of food to hungry children in
    the United States.*[3]

$50 pays a teacher's salary in Afghanistan *for a month*,
    allowing 30 children to get an education.[4]

Examples like these were everywhere, yet even I, steeped as I was in fund-raising and the nonprofit sector, had been unaware of the tremendous potential of my own small donations. Now I no longer thought that the only way to change the world was to do the work myself. I knew that there was no "doing" without the funds needed to pay for it.

Not only do our donations fund the doers' work, the results of that work ripple outward—ultimately far beyond the initial beneficiaries of the doers' efforts. Our gifts to effective charities create waves of positive change that dramatically increase the impact of our contributions. I'll explain how this "ripple effect giving" works and the kind of organizations that maximize the impact of these gifts in Chapter 3.

THE EMPTY BOWL EFFECT

The interconnectedness of today's global society brings to mind the phenomenon popularly known as the "butterfly effect," wherein the flap of a butterfly's wings in one part of the world leads to a tornado in another distant place. In these times, none of us or our communities, states, provinces, or countries is immune to the circumstances and events taking place around the world. I have a similar principle that I call the "empty bowl effect," which illustrates the far-ranging impact of one child's chronic hunger.

Imani's Story

Imani is a five-year-old girl living in a developing country who typically eats only one meal at the end of each day. At breakfast and lunch times, her bowl remains empty. Her one meal usually consists of a thin gruel made of whatever plant and vegetation can be grown or scavenged near her home. Milk or meat is a rarity.

As a result of her empty bowl, Imani spends most of every day hungry and is suffering the effects of malnourishment, including small stature, delayed intellectual development, and lowered resistance to disease. Because she is often ill, she frequently misses school. Eventually, she is removed from school altogether, as the family can no longer afford the fees required to send both her and her older brother, and she is needed to help the family produce and gather enough food to feed the family. Imani now spends her days helping to maintain the small plot of land farmed by her parents and scavenging for additional food as well as animal dung and wood to be used as cooking fuel.

Imani's brother eventually finishes primary school, then leaves the family village to try to find work in the nearest city. Her father soon joins him for the dry season, during which crops are impossible to grow and he is otherwise unemployed.

In the meantime, Imani and her mother remain in their village and continue to grow what they can and scavenge for available food sources. Imani marries and becomes pregnant, but her child is stillborn as a result of nutritional deficiencies during the pregnancy. Her second child survives, but her third dies at age four from malaria that his body might have successfully resisted had he been better fed and physically stronger. In total, Imani has five children with three surviving into adulthood.

Like her father, Imani's husband lives in the family village during the growing season but goes to the city for half of every year when crops cannot be grown. In the city, he contracts HIV from a sex worker and infects Imani, who passes the disease to their last child. Eventually, Imani and her husband die of AIDS and their three surviving children are orphaned. None of the children goes to school—instead, each scavenges and works on the family's small plot of land trying to eke out enough food to feed the family.

When civil war breaks out in their country, Imani's oldest son joins the citizen-led militia when it comes to the village seeking recruits. The son believes in the militia's mission to over-throw the corrupt government and redistribute the country's re-sources among the poor. Eventually, the government-backed military invades the village forcing Imani's remaining son and daughter to flee to a makeshift refugee camp in a neighboring country. People are dying of starvation on their treks to the refu-gee camps, and food sources are even scarcer in the camp than at home. Within the camp, opportunistic diseases are taking hold among the malnourished population, including cholera, menin-gitis, measles, and tuberculosis.

As thousands begin to flood the informal refugee camp, the United Nations and a multitude of nongovernmental organiza-tions (NGOs) mobilize their response. Millions of dollars and thousands of volunteers are needed to provide food, shelter, clean water, cooking supplies, latrines, and medical care to the dis-placed people. In addition, a multinational military presence will be necessary for years to help end the violence and maintain a future peace.

Imani's story is an amalgam of many similar stories across the developing world. Empty bowls cut a devastating swathe of suffering, disease, and death across a society and across genera-tions. Hunger breeds desperation, which breeds violence. Ulti-mately, empty bowls become the world's responsibility.

AFFORDABLE GIVING FILLS EMPTY BOWLS

Imagine a scenario in which Imani has enough nutritious food to eat each day. Her family acquires the tools necessary to irri-gate and fertilize their land and grow enough food to both con-sume and sell. Irrigation allows them to grow food year-round, keeping the male members of the family at home. Imani's husband works and makes a sustainable living within the village, doesn't spend half of the year in the city, and doesn't contract HIV. Imani's children are born healthy, protected from mosquito-borne malaria by bed nets, and the family can afford to send them all to school.

Because the adults are working and providing a decent standard of living for their families, they are too busy and lack motivation to foment a civil uprising or intergroup conflict. Instead of warring and fleeing to refugee camps that require aid from governments and NGOs around the world, they are building thriving communities that interact peacefully and participate in mutually beneficial cultural engagement and trade.

Your affordable donations can transform the lives of multitudes of Imanis. The key to unlocking enormous human potential around the world lies in your wallet, slim as it may be. Together, you and that wallet are going to do a world of good.

chapter 2

Four Big Secrets About Giving

"To give away money is an easy matter and in any man's power.
But to decide to whom to give it, and how large,
and when, and for what purpose and how, is neither in
every man's power nor an easy matter."

—ARISTOTLE[1]

BIG SECRET 1:
americans are extraordinary givers!

When you think of the world's "deep pockets," do you think of multinational corporations, Bill Gates, or maybe the federal government? I've got news for you: One of the world's deepest pockets, perhaps *the* deepest pocket of all, is the collective and *generous pockets* of American citizens. And, I'm not talking about wealthy citizens only; I'm talking about everyday individuals who have an enormous leverage that most know nothing about. That leverage is the billions of dollars you donate to charities every year. In 2007, your donations amounted to $229,000,000,000. That is not a mistake. The figure is, indeed, $229 billion.[2]

This $229 billion came strictly from living individuals. It does not reflect bequests, corporate giving, giving by foundations, or even small family foundations, which together, typically account for about 25 percent of total charitable giving each year. These donations came directly out of the wallets of millions of individuals, and the majority of those wallets were not overflowing with cash.

The magnitude of individual charity in America can be difficult to fully embrace. To help you put it into perspective:

- $229 billion is greater than the gross domestic products of 136 of 180 countries around the world.[3]
- $229 billion is over 21 times Wal-Mart's profits of $11.3 billion in fiscal year 2007.[4]
- $229 billion is 114.5 times the total giving by the Bill & Melinda Gates Foundation in 2007 ($2 billion).[5]

Americans tend to believe that only the wealthiest donors and large private and public institutions can solve the world's really big problems. This is not true. You do not have to be Bill Gates, Oprah, the Ford Foundation, or the federal government to save the world. In fact, none of them can save the world without *you*.

Consider this: In 2006, Warren Buffett pledged to donate an enormous portion of his personal wealth to the Bill & Melinda Gates Foundation. The donation will be made as an annual gift of shares of stock in Buffett's company, Berkshire Hathaway. In 2007, the Bill & Melinda Gates Foundation received shares worth $1.76 billion.[6]

It is impossible to know the total future amount of Buffett's donation, because it will be determined by the value of the stocks donated each year; however, at the time of his announcement, the present value of the stocks earmarked for donation over time to the Bill & Melinda Gates Foundation was estimated to be over $30 billion.[7]

Buffett's pledge was certainly prodigious, and it received a corresponding amount of media coverage. It may seem like your own charitable giving is inconsequential in comparison. My message to you: Not true! Total giving by individuals in 2007 ($229 billion donated by folks just like you) was *more than 130 times* Buffett's 2007 donation to the Bill & Melinda Gates Foundation. It was *more than 7 times* the total anticipated value of Buffett's gift. Collectively, it is everyday citizens who are the extraordinary philanthropists of our time.

BIG SECRET 2:
affordable donations DO make a difference!

Donors give for many different reasons: to address important societal needs, from a sense of moral obligation, to improve their social standing, to give back to society, or simply because someone asked them to. Many give simply because it feels good!

Yet, even as they're writing their checks, donors are often skeptical about whether their gifts will mean anything in the grand scheme of things. As your giving adviser, I assure you that *yes* your gifts do, indeed, make a difference.

Ten Bucks Beats Malaria

Let's say an individual makes a single donation of $10 to provide an insecticide-treated bed net to a family in need. Malita, a young girl in Malawi, sleeps under the net and therefore is less likely to contract malaria. This improves her developmental outcomes, as malaria could leave her with long-term disabilities and health problems such as neurological damage and anemia.

The bed net helps preserve Malita's health during early childhood, giving her a better chance of succeeding in school, and because Malita is well, she is likelier to attend school regularly. Children who attend and succeed in school are better positioned to become self-sufficient providers for their families when they are adults.

Because Malita is well, her parents are more productive in their work, thus allowing them to improve their family's economic security. Malita's entire community is stronger when children's parents can work productively and when fewer resources must be directed at caring for sick children, neurologically disabled adults, and poor families.

This is the potential outcome *of the gift of a $10 bed net.*

Given the statistics from the World Health Organization, the malarial epidemic seems absurdly uncontrollable:[8]

- "A child dies of malaria every 30 seconds."
- "More than one million people die of malaria every year, mostly infants, young children and pregnant women."
- "Symptoms of malaria include fever, headache, and vomiting, and usually appear between 10 and 15 days after the mosquito bite. If not treated, malaria can quickly become life-threatening by disrupting the blood supply to vital organs. In many parts of the world, the parasites have developed resistance to a number of malaria medicines."

Yet in 2006, Rick Reilly, then a senior writer for *Sports Illustrated*, wrote a transformational column describing a simple solution. In the column, Rick described a family trip to Tanzania where they had seen a group of children playing soccer using a wad of paper for their ball and rocks for goals. When the Reilly family returned home, they wanted to help those kids, so they sent soccer balls and real nets for goals. Later, Rick saw a television program about the malarial epidemic in Africa and realized that he could have better served those children by giving them insecticide-treated bed nets that would protect them from malaria-infested mosquitoes rather than nets for soccer goals. Rick asked his readers to send $10 to the United Nations Foundation to fund the total cost of producing and distributing one bed net. Within six months of the column's publication, more than 17,000 donors had given over $1.2 million.[9] The response was so dramatic that the ongoing "Nothing But Nets" campaign was born, which, by the end of 2008, had received enough contributions to distribute over two million nets in Africa.[10]

As Rick put it to his readers, "You're a coach, parent, player, gym teacher or even just a fan who likes watching balls fly into nets, send $20. You saved a life. Take the rest of the day off." Small effort, big reward.

Dimes Destroy Polio

Throughout the first half of the twentieth century, polio (also known as "infantile paralysis") was one of the most feared diseases in the developed world. At its worst, the disease caused paralysis and use of the dreaded iron lung to force air into and out of the lungs. In the United States alone, there were tens of thousands of infections each year with a peak of 57,628 cases in 1952—more than 21,000 of them resulting in paralysis.[11]

In 1938, President Franklin D. Roosevelt, a polio victim himself, established the National Foundation for Infantile Paralysis (NFIP). The NFIP hired Eddie Cantor, a star in radio and vaudeville, to lead a campaign to combat polio by asking his fans to send a single dime to President Roosevelt. Cantor called the campaign "the March of Dimes," referencing a popular newsreel called *The March of Time*.[12]

Soon, the White House was awash in dimes and was forced to hire extra clerks to help manage the waves of mail. In the first year, the effort raised $1.8 million, with $238,000 arriving *one dime at a time*. According to some White House workers, the difficulty of finding official mail among the millions of envelopes with dimes nearly halted daily operations within the government.

The campaign was wildly successful, and donations increased every year. Even during the war, dimes poured in with nearly $20 million raised by 1945. In total, *the campaign raised a total of $622 million by 1959*.

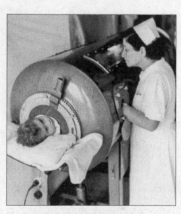

Photo courtesy of the World Health Organization

Those dimes helped fund research by Dr. Jonas Salk, who was able to produce an effective vaccine that reduced the number of infections from over 20,000 each year in the early 1950s to approximately 3,000 in 1960. By 1979, the disease was eradicated in the United States. An ocean of dimes had eliminated one of the century's worst nightmares.

BIG SECRET 3:
giving changes YOU as well as the world

Here's the thing: Helping others will make you happier and healthier. You will experience the same physiological response and emotional rewards (sometimes referred to as the "warm glow" effect) from charitable giving that you would get from sex, food, drugs, or receiving money.[13]

Dr. Jordan Grafman, of the Cognitive Neuroscience Section at the National Institute of Neurological Disorders and Stroke in Bethesda, Maryland, led a study that showed this by using MRI imaging to identify areas of the brain that are activated by monetary rewards alone and those activated by charitable giving. The researchers found that *giving was more rewarding than receiving money.*

According to Dr. Jorge Moll, a member of the research team, "Many people think they should not do anything for others unless it has a material benefit for themselves. But our brains show that you profit emotionally from doing so. Something in our brains shaped by evolution allows us to feel joy when we do good things. It is a biological force and we should not ignore it in promoting social welfare."[14]

Studies suggest that giving is hardwired into our genetic code and has a long evolutionary history that strengthens our prosocial behavior.[15] So, what we have here is a do-good, feel-good cycle that keeps us giving, keeps us connected, and *contributes to the preservation of our species.*

Contrary to what most of us believe, money is only weakly connected to our happiness, particularly once we feel our basic needs are met. Multiple studies show that within developed countries (i.e., those that are wealthy relative to the rest of the world) incomes have risen dramatically over the past several decades, yet happiness levels remain flat.[16] The truth appears to be that *what we do with the money we have is the key to our happiness.*

Elizabeth Dunn, a social psychologist at the University of British Columbia, confirmed this by showing that giving money away makes us happier than accumulating personal wealth.[17] Dunn believes that while giving once causes a temporary boost in feeling good, making it a lifestyle could have long-term positive effects for donors. Best of all, her study showed that one doesn't have to give large sums of money to benefit. Study participants benefited from *giving away as little as $5.*

To complete the circle of benefits giving provides to you: The mind-body connection kicks in when you give. Science has demonstrated that those who suffer poor mental health engage in unhealthy behaviors such as drug and alcohol use, smoking, poor eating habits, and lack of exercise.[18] Giving improves your mental well-being, making you more inclined to take better care of yourself and improve your physical health.

Giving changed me in a different way when I was just seven years old.

In honor of making my first Communion, my parents began sponsoring a little girl who lived in Cambodia. We put a picture of her on an end table in our family room. I looked at that picture so many times and so closely that I can still see it perfectly in my mind. She was my age, in first grade, wearing a white blouse that was part of her school uniform. I noticed the collar of her blouse was frayed and just a little bit dirty or stained, but it looked perfectly starched as though great care had gone into making that blouse as presentable as possible. She had a beautiful unsmiling face with dark eyes and black hair cut in a traditional bob. I tried to imagine what her life was like.

My family moved from Ohio to Michigan when I was in fifth grade, and I don't remember her picture being on an end table in that house. I don't remember her being part of our lives after that move.

What I've learned since is that the Khmer Rouge had taken siege of Cambodia and aid organizations were forced to leave. World Vision, which had a child sponsorship program in Cambodia at that time, was forced out in 1975. I wonder now what must have happened to that little girl. Had she become a refugee as so many Cambodians did?

My brother is married to a Cambodian woman whose family fled the Khmer Rouge on foot to a refugee camp in Thailand, but not before her father was killed and her uncle died of starvation, and not before she spent time in a child labor camp where she was separated from her family, worked in fields from dawn to dusk, and participated in "re-education"—a common practice of the Khmer Rouge, which believed that the notion of "family" was contrary to the good of the state. Was this the fate of the little girl in the picture? Or, had my family's sponsorship somehow helped spare her?

My parents sent me a powerful message when I was seven. We are fortunate. Others are much less fortunate. We can help make their lives better, so we should do what we can. That message and the little girl in that picture have influenced my entire life.

When my twin daughters were in first grade, I became one of their Girl Scout troop leaders. We talked to the girls about poverty, hunger, and homelessness. Things they'd certainly not seen much of in their own neighborhoods. Despite our meetings

being right after school when the girls were full of pent-up energy and more often than not simply wanted to run and skip and
chase each other around the gymnasium where we met, these
conversations about people living in poverty stopped them dead
in their tracks. They sat with rapt attention, asked insightful
and poignant questions, and were genuinely moved. They loved
making a difference by contributing to the food bank. One of
our favorite annual activities was putting together food baskets
for Thanksgiving dinners for those who otherwise wouldn't have
one. We'd fill baskets with all the foods the girls enjoyed at their
own Thanksgiving gatherings. The girls would consider the
practicalities of what they put in the baskets: What if the family
didn't have staple foods like milk to make mashed potatoes or
bread for turkey sandwiches the next day? What if they didn't
get time off from work to bake a pie from scratch?

When my children were very young, I wanted to protect
them from the harsh realities of the world. Then I remembered
the girl in the picture and how she made me a better person. I
wanted to empower my daughters to believe they could make a
difference, too. I've "empowered" them so much that they now
say things like "If you could, you'd give all our money to poor
people!" and "Mom, we GET IT already." Ah, adolescence.

BIG SECRET 4:
the millennium project

Even as you read this book, a massive undertaking called the
Millennium Project is working toward radically improving living
standards among the poorest people around the world. Member
countries of the United Nations' General Assembly ratified the

UN Millennium Declaration in September 2000. The Millennium Project arose from the Declaration, which sets forth a broad agenda intended to improve international relations and spread prosperity throughout the world.

Surprisingly, many Americans do not know about the Millennium Project and its eight specific goals for global development to be reached by 2015. In other parts of the world, people are much more aware and informed about the project and are supporting it through increases in their income taxes or user fees such as a $1 tax on airline tickets, which, to date, has been adopted by eight countries with an additional twenty countries intending to do the same.[19]

I think it's high time we got a little enlightened, so I've included the ambitious but achievable Millennium Development Goals and their associated targets here. Around the world, these are commonly known as "the MDGs." They are aimed at reducing the scourge of extreme poverty and improving prospects for those living in the poorest nations.[20]

Goal 1: eradicate extreme poverty and hunger
Targets:
- Reduce by half the proportion of people living on less than a dollar a day
- Reduce by half the proportion of people who suffer from hunger

Goal 2: achieve universal primary education
Target:
- Ensure that all boys and girls complete a full course of primary schooling

Goal 3: promote gender equality and empower women

Target:

- Eliminate gender disparity in primary and secondary education preferably by 2005, and at all levels by 2015

Goal 4: reduce child mortality

Target:

- Reduce by two-thirds the mortality rate among children under five

Goal 5: improve maternal health

Target:

- Reduce by three-quarters the maternal mortality ratio

Goal 6: combat HIV/AIDS, malaria, and other diseases

Targets:

- Halt and begin to reverse the spread of HIV/AIDS
- Halt and begin to reverse the incidence of malaria and other major diseases

Goal 7: ensure environmental sustainability

Targets:

- Integrate the principles of sustainable development into country policies and programs; reverse loss of environmental resources [a project's "sustainability" typically refers to its ability to be operated locally over the long term—after initial involvement from NGOs has ended. It also refers to the project's healthy fit with the local environment.]

- Reduce by half the proportion of people without sustainable access to safe drinking water
- Achieve significant improvement in lives of at least 100 million slum dwellers, by 2020

Goal 8: develop a global partnership for development

Targets:

- Develop further an open trading and financial system that is rule-based, predictable, and nondiscriminatory, includes a commitment to good governance, development, and poverty reduction—nationally and internationally
- Address the least developed countries' special needs. This includes tariff- and quota-free access for their exports; enhanced debt relief for heavily indebted poor countries; cancellation of official bilateral debt; and more generous official development assistance for countries committed to poverty reduction
- Address the special needs of landlocked and small island developing states
- Deal comprehensively with developing countries' debt problems through national and international measures to make debt sustainable in the long term
- In cooperation with the developing countries, develop decent and productive work for youth
- In cooperation with pharmaceutical companies, provide access to affordable essential drugs in developing countries

- In cooperation with the private sector, make available the benefits of new technologies—especially information and communications technologies

THE UNITED STATES AND
THE MILLENNIUM PROJECT

Many of us assume that the majority of aid to foreign countries comes from government sources. *In America, this is not true.* A study conducted by the Center for Global Prosperity at the Hudson Institute determined that, in 2005, private entities provided more humanitarian and economic aid to poor countries than did the American government. Foundations, corporations, individuals, and other private sources donated $33.5 billion while the federal government provided $27.6 billion.[21]

In 2006, Knowledge Networks (a polling, social science, and market research firm) and the Program on International Policy Attitudes (PIPA) conducted a survey of Americans' assumptions about U.S. spending on foreign humanitarian and economic aid. The study revealed our misconceptions about our government's generosity.

Study respondents were shown the federal government's budget for the allocation of discretionary funds (those not already committed to mandatory social programs such as Social Security) for fiscal year 2006. Below, you can see their reactions to the budget they had viewed:

When the respondents were asked to estimate what percentage of the entire federal budget is devoted to humanitarian and economic aid, **their median estimate was**

10%—even though they *had just seen for themselves* that it only constituted a small fraction (*actually, 1.6%*) of the discretionary budget shown.

Only 18% of respondents estimated that the amount was 3% or less. Furthermore, when respondents were asked what percentage of the overall budget *should be* devoted to humanitarian and economic aid, the median response was a remarkable 15%—substantially more than the median estimate of the actual amount, and completely inconsistent with the amounts proposed in the budget exercise. Only 12% of respondents said the amount should be 2% or less of the entire federal budget.[22] (Italics and bold added by the author.)

So, respondents *believed* that the federal government was spending over six times the amount it actually contributed to humanitarian and economic aid (10 percent versus 1.6 percent). Even more startlingly, *they felt the appropriate portion would be 15 percent of the entire federal budget*—or more than nine times the actual portion.

Many of the respondents were so convinced that the U.S. government provided more aid in this area that they believed it must be hidden in another part of the budget and not presented in the survey. Notably, in past surveys respondents reported believing that the United States generally devoted approximately 20 percent of its entire budget to foreign aid.

The truth is that, from 1996 to 2005, official development assistance ranged from a low of 0.58 percent to a high of 1.75 percent of total U.S. revenues.[23]

The point is that Americans are clearly poorly informed about how much their federal government is spending each year on humanitarian and economic aid to foreign countries, and when asked, they believe that a good deal more of the federal budget should be aimed at addressing needs overseas. (See Author's Notes for more information about the United Nations' 0.7 percent solution to ending extreme poverty around the world.)

Your affordable donations are necessary to achieving the Millennium Development Goals.

You'll see; *you* are going to help transform the future for less than it costs to fill up your gas tank.

~~~~~~~

chapter 3

Ripple Effect Giving

*"Remember there's no such thing as a small act of kindness.
Every act creates a ripple with no logical end."*

—SCOTT ADAMS[1]

Compared to the sea of problems related to poverty around the world, a single small gift may seem like a drop in the bucket; however, that drop creates a ripple, and many drops create many ripples. In this way, *everyday donors have the capacity to help end poverty*, much as the millions of dimes sent by individuals eradicated polio in the United States.

Still, it's easy to be overwhelmed by the magnitude and urgency of the problems related to poverty around the world, and thanks to the Internet and cable television, you're often bombarded by images of those who are in dire need. Likewise, you may be overwhelmed by the number and variety of charitable organizations working to alleviate these problems. You probably receive many requests for donations from organizations that you know very little about, often nothing more than the solicitation letter tells you. It's hard to know what to do with a request that, on the surface, looks like a good cause but doesn't provide the details necessary to convince you that the charity is actually making a difference in a cost-effective way. You don't want to feel like you're tossing money into a black hole, so you put the letter aside (usually permanently) or toss it in the trash with the other junk mail. You can't make a decision, so you don't. I don't blame you. I've set aside and tossed plenty of letters.

Donating to a charity can be likened to investing in a stock. You expect your stock to generate a positive return as measured by the dividends you receive. Your investment in a charity should also generate a return. The return on your charitable investment is measured by the organization's success in conducting its mission and producing positive outcomes. The organization's responsibility to you, the potential donor, is to describe its mission and quantify its outcomes in a clear and convincing way. This removes it from the black hole of uncertainty.

HOW TO GIVE WITH CONFIDENCE

I use the following four criteria to examine an organization's capacity to use my affordable donation to create ripples of positive change.

1. Creates substantial change in the lives of recipients. For instance, providing a goat to a family in India dramatically improves the family's physical and economic health by providing milk full of protein to consume and to sell. More income allows families to send children to school, and stronger, healthier children attend school more regularly.

The positive life changes created by receiving a goat are immediate, broad, and long lasting.

2. Creates long-term, demonstrated, positive outcomes that are measurable. The organization should have data that illustrate results and justify its approach. Along with manufacturing and distributing micro-irrigation pumps to some of the world's poorest areas, KickStart International is committed to carefully and thoroughly measuring the results of its efforts and can show potential donors *exactly how a $60 donation lifts an individual out of poverty for good.*

3. Generates high returns. Basically, every $1 of ripple effect giving generates many times $1 of good. That "good" is the mission of the organization that receives your donation, and it should be quantifiable by some means. For instance, if you donate $25 to an organization that increases a family's self-sufficiency, your gift should generate a return many times $25 through the savings realized by the community because that family no longer requires social services such as groceries from the local food bank. These resources are now free to be directed to another need. The return on your $25 gift will multiply over the months and years that a family and its future generations no longer require assistance from the community. If you take the long view, you'll see that the value of an affordable donation is much larger than the figure on the initial check.

4. Builds self-sufficiency. Many of the projects profiled in this book use affordable contributions to help the poorest people around the world access assets and services that allow *them* to improve their short- and long-term health, educational, and economic prospects.

The world's poorest people are highly driven and capable of improving their own lots when given the right tools. What poor people everywhere want most is the very same thing you and I desire—a job that pays well enough that we can acquire the things we want and need ourselves. Therefore, *the most effective giving creates access to jobs, tools, and assets that produce self-sufficiency*. Unlike handouts, which can be demeaning, demotivating, and ultimately unsustainable, ripple effect donations improve *opportunities* for families, communities, *and* future generations. This giving is really an investment in long-term societal well-being.

In some cases, however, I believe that short-term direct aid programs can be shown to have such important implications for future outcomes that they are equally worthy of your donations. For instance, ensuring that a young child has enough to eat, even if it must come through direct aid, vastly improves his or her ability to create a better future and ultimately become self-sufficient.

MONEY MATTERS AND COMMON SENSE

In addition to the criteria described previously, I scrutinized the charities included in *Give a Little* for two additional qualities: financial health and the common sense or "aha!" factor. You can use these tests to remove charities from the black hole and give with confidence.

There are several well-established and reliable charity watchdogs that evaluate various combinations of organizations' financial health, transparency, makeup of their governing boards, and adherence to applicable regulations. These groups include the American Institute of Philanthropy, which evaluates the financial health of large nonprofits in the United States, the Better Business Bureau's Wise Giving Alliance, which focuses on business practices such as governance and regulatory compliance, and Charity Navigator, which rates the financial health and stability of a large number of U.S.-based charities.

I used Charity Navigator to vet the financial health of the organizations profiled in *Give a Little*. In 2007, over 3,500,000 other donors used Charity Navigator to help them decide where to send their donations as well.[2] Charity Navigator uses a zero to four star rating system to grade each organization's financial efficiency and capacity.

Appendix B explains Charity Navigator's comprehensive system of evaluating charities' financial standing, offering you important insights into the qualities that comprise financial soundness among nonprofits. You can apply these criteria, or simply consult a service like Charity Navigator to ensure the viability of the organization you are interested in supporting.

My recommendation: Be an enlightened donor! Trust Charity Navigator's overall rating for the nonprofit you're considering.

If you are interested in a charity that meets the four criteria for ripple effect giving but hasn't been rated by Charity Navigator, you should apply the final *common sense criteria*. Here's what to consider:

- Do their methods seem logical?
- Does their approach seem likely to produce the desired results?
- Have they achieved their goals in the past?

You can apply the criteria by looking at an agency's Web site, reading its annual report, observing its program, and talking to staff, board members, or donors. If your research demonstrates that the agency meets all or most of the criteria described in this section, go ahead and make your ripple effect gift with confidence! Send your check, donate online, and revel in the joy of helping to transform despair into hope and prosperity.

chapter 4

Ending Extreme
and Cyclical Poverty

*"Poverty is like heat; you cannot see it, you can only feel it;
so to know poverty you have to go through it."*

—A POOR MAN, ADABOYA, GHANA[1]

*"Poverty is pain; it feels like a disease. It attacks a person not
only materially but also morally. It eats away at one's dignity
and drives one into total despair."*

—A POOR WOMAN, MOLDOVA[2]

Our mission is to make small donations that can help end the
pain of poverty. In 2004, the European Commission's Joint Report on Social Inclusion defined poverty this way:

Extreme or Absolute Poverty[3]
- Absolute or extreme poverty is when people **lack the basic
  necessities for survival.** For instance they may be starving,
  lack clean water, proper housing, sufficient clothing or
  medicines, and be struggling to stay alive. This is most
  common in developing countries, but some people [in other
  regions] still experience this type of extreme poverty.

Relative Poverty or "Being Poor"[4]

- People are said to be living in poverty if their income and resources are so inadequate as to preclude them from having a standard of living considered acceptable in the society in which they live.

  Because of their poverty they may experience **multiple disadvantages through unemployment, low income, poor housing, inadequate health care, and barriers to lifelong learning, culture, sport, and recreation**. They are often excluded and marginalized from participating in activities (economic, social, and cultural) that are the norm for other people and their access to fundamental rights may be restricted.

BEING "POOR" IN THE UNITED STATES

Undoubtedly, you've heard innumerable references to the problems of poverty and the challenges faced by "the poor" in America, but you may not know how we define being "poor" in our country. In 2008, an individual could earn no more than a *total gross income of $10,400* in order to be classified as living in poverty. The income limit for a *family of two* (typically a single mother with one child) was *less than $14,000*. A family of three could earn no more than $17,600, and the maximum allowable income for a family of four was $21,200.[5]

You might be shocked to see how poor an individual or family must really be in order to be classified as such by the federal government. Can you imagine living for a year *on $10,400*? In 1986, I earned approximately $14,000 as a college-educated adult teaching preschool. I wasn't able to sustain myself on that

2008 Health and Human Services Federal Poverty Guidelines

PERSONS IN FAMILY OR HOUSEHOLD	48 CONTIGUOUS STATES AND D.C.	ALASKA	HAWAII
1	$10,400	$13,000	$11,960
2	14,000	17,500	16,100
3	17,600	22,000	20,240
4	21,200	26,500	24,380
5	24,800	31,000	28,520
6	28,400	35,500	32,660
7	32,000	40,000	36,800
8	35,600	44,500	40,940
FOR EACH + PERSON, ADD	3,600	4,500	4,140

SOURCE: *Federal Register* 73, no. 15 (January 23, 2008): 3971–3972.

income, and my fiancé stepped in and paid many of my utility bills. I realize that I could have lived more cheaply than I did; for instance, I lived alone in a studio apartment instead of sharing an apartment with a roommate. I'm sure there are other ways I could have saved money. However, the bottom line is that I lived quite simply and frugally and ultimately could not survive on that salary *twenty years ago*. Can you possibly imagine supporting a family of four on a gross income of $21,200?

DID YOU KNOW?

In 2004, the poorest sixty million Americans
lived on less than $7 per day.[6]

WHY ENDS JUST DON'T MEET

It is true that very low-income families receive subsidized services such as food stamps and school lunches. They may have a portion of their health care costs covered by state or federal programs. Yet, even with every support available, there are innumerable expenses that come up for families that are not subsidized, including transportation costs; clothing; car and home repairs; co-payments for child care, health care, medications, and dental care; supplemental food costs (food stamps can be used only for very specific food items, and with food costs soaring, do not even cover the cost of staples); utility bills not fully covered by energy assistance programs; and school fees and supplies. These are only some of the most basic and necessary expenses and do not include items that would provide better opportunities for the parents or children such as a computer and Internet access, enrichment experiences like a summer drama class or trips to museums, or costs for higher education not covered by scholarships.

Another problem with the current federal poverty guidelines is that the maximum income levels are so low that it is difficult to qualify for any services if an individual or parent works full-time—even in a minimum wage job. For instance, in 2008, if you worked a full-time minimum wage job ($6.55 per hour at the time), you earned approximately $13,100 in a year ($6.55 × 40 hours per week × 50 weeks per year). That's far above the poverty line of $10,400, so lucky you, you're not poor!

Likewise, if two parents in a four-person family worked full-time in minimum wage jobs, they earned $26,200; also far above the poverty line of $21,200 making them "not poor" by federal poverty guideline standards and, therefore, ineligible for some subsidized services. Some federal and state programs increase the eligibility guidelines by allowing individuals and families to qualify with incomes of up to 125 percent or 150 percent of the federal guidelines. This is a helpful and necessary adjustment to the grossly outdated and inadequate federal poverty measure.

Nevertheless, the federal poverty guidelines create a high-risk population in our country known as "the working poor." These are individuals and families struggling desperately to survive on low incomes that are yet too high to qualify them for assistance. They are literally one car repair or doctor visit away from destitution. Remember, few minimum wage hourly jobs provide benefits such as health care or paid leave.

STOPPING THE CYCLE

Nearly one in every five children under the age of six lives in poverty in the United States, and the consequences are dire, including poorer health, lower levels of education, higher risk for teenage pregnancy, and higher rates of criminal behavior to name just a few.[7] The remaining chapters of this book will describe projects you can afford to support that *can stop the cycle of poverty in America.*

POVERTY IN A DEVELOPING COUNTRY

~~~~~~~~~~~~~~~~~~~~~~~~~~~~~~~~~~~~

DID YOU KNOW?

In 2008, 82 percent of the world's population
lived in developing countries.[8]

About half of all people live on less than $2 per day.[9]

~~~~~~~~~~~~~~~~~~~~~~~~~~~~~~~~~~~~

In developing countries, being poor means being "dirt poor."
It means literally living in the dirt—in crude shelters with dirt
floors, no plumbing, and little or inconsistent access to food or
potable (i.e., safe to drink) water. This is extreme poverty, and *for
as many as 50,000 people every day, it means too poor to live.*[10]

Economists and organizations focused on developing countries define "extreme poverty" as living on less than US$1 per
day at U.S. prices for housing, food, health care, etc. Sadly, in
2004 approximately one billion people, or about one in every five
around the world, lived in extreme poverty.[11] The extremely poor
struggle every day simply to survive, and many do not. As many
as 50,000 people die every day from causes related to extreme
poverty. They die for lack of adequate food and clean water, lack
of medications, and diseases that cannot be staved off by bodies
weakened by hunger.

Those living on between $1 and $2 per day are referred to as
the "moderate poor." In 2004, this included another 1.6 billion
people.[12] Moderately poor individuals are just barely surviving
from day to day. They have more of their basic needs met than
the extreme poor, but they are at high risk of falling back into

that category as a result of any number of possible setbacks. If a parent gets sick and can no longer tend crops or earn an income, the family becomes destitute.

What will amaze you is how little is required to help such families realize economic security and a far better standard of living. Let's look first at eliminating hunger.

part two

hunger

Filling Bowls with Small Gifts

"The first freedom of man, I contend, is the freedom to eat."

—ELEANOR ROOSEVELT[1]

"My children were hungry, so I told them that the rice was cooking until they fell asleep."

—A POOR MAN, ETHIOPIA[2]

Having enough to eat is the foundation of prosperity. In order to be healthy and strong enough to pursue the kinds of activities that can lift one out of poverty, including going to school and working productively, one requires continuous access to enough nutritious food. *For nearly one in every six people around the world*, this is not the case, and whether we realize it or not, their hunger affects us all.

HUNGER AT HOME

Like poverty, hunger has a language all its own. In the United States, approximately one in ten people suffers periods of "food insecurity," or times when he or she is uncertain about having, or is unable to obtain, enough nutritious food to eat.[4]

~~~~~~

DID YOU KNOW?

Worldwide, 24,000 people die each day from
hunger-related causes.[3]

~~~~~~

Food-insecure households often struggle most when an un-expected expense occurs (such as a car repair), between pay-checks, and at the end of the month when subsidies such as food stamps have run out and money is short. This is when households are forced to make horrifying decisions about whether to pay rent and bills, purchase medications, or buy food.

In November 2005, National Public Radio aired the story of the Hankins family from Smyth County, Virginia. Theirs is a common example of the struggle to feed a family when high-paying jobs and federal assistance are scarce.

Wreatha Hankins is a 37-year-old mom with three chil-dren and a working husband. She has resorted to extraor-dinary measures to make sure her family eats, including skipping meals herself, skipping medicine for epilepsy and chronic back pain, doing her own dental work, selling fam-ily heirlooms, and scouring Smyth County for the cheapest food available. She searches for food bargains at dollar stores, flea markets, roadside stands, and the nearly expired meat section at supermarkets.

"We're the working poor," Wreatha says. In fact, Robbie Hankins works full-time at a cement plant. Wreatha works part-time as a substitute teacher. Last year, the couple made

$22,000. That puts them just below the federal poverty threshold for a family of five. But it's too much for food stamps. The family does get a monthly, 125-pound box of groceries from a local food pantry. And the children get free lunches at school. Eating otherwise is sometimes a challenge. "It bothers me knowing that I don't know whether we're going to have food from one week to the next," says Robbie.[5]

HUNGER AT ITS WORST

In the poorest countries, hunger is defined by terms like "malnutrition," or lacking enough healthy food to "maintain natural bodily capacities such as growth, pregnancy, lactation, learning abilities, physical work and resisting and recovering from disease."[6] It includes horrible conditions like "stunting" in which a child is both underweight and short for his or her age due to hunger, or even "wasting," which is physical deterioration caused by starvation or disease and leads to death.[7]

What these clinical terms don't adequately describe is the pain and devastation caused by not being able to provide your child with enough to eat or the fact that malnourished people lead miserable, shortened lives marred by frequent and serious illness and deep poverty. They live and die in hopelessness.

When I leave for school in the mornings I don't have any breakfast. At noon there is no lunch, in the evening I get a little supper, and that is not enough. So when I see another child eating, I watch him, and if he doesn't give me something I think I'm going to die of hunger. —A ten-year-old child, Gabon, Africa, 1997[8]

Action Against Hunger (*Action Contre la Faim*, or ACF) works in developing countries around the world to prevent and treat malnutrition and starvation. Kelly Delaney, medical and nutrition coordinator in Kenya and South Sudan, described her horror when she first came face-to-face with hunger at its worst.

THIRTY DAYS CAN SAVE A LIFE:
reflections of a nutritionist

I came to Mandera, Kenya, on October 5, 2005. My first day on the job I was in our feeding center and in walks this mother carrying an 8-year-old girl that was half the size that she should be. I'd been a nurse at Sloan-Kettering Hospital taking care of patients with cancer. I thought I was ready to go and work in Kenya. But nothing could have prepared me for seeing this girl so close to death.

Her name was Habiba. Her mother and her sister had taken turns carrying Habiba and her newborn sister as they walked for three days from their remote village. A village with no

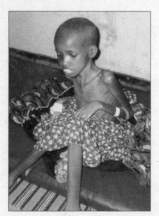

clean water let alone health care. The drought had already started in Kenya, so there was no water along the way. The family of four had shared one bottle of water and one bottle of milk for their meals for three days. And it was hot. So when

Habiba enters the Therapeutic Feeding Center. *Photo courtesy of ACF–Kenya.*

they arrived they were exhausted, dehydrated and pleading for help.

When Habiba arrived she was close to death. She could barely manage a blank stare when I looked in her eyes. She was suffering from malnutrition, tuberculosis, malaria, and anemia. I brought her a cup of our specialized formula called F75, it's a treatment that has the right balance of nutrients needed by a severely malnourished body. It slowly wakes up the person's stomach, liver, spleen, kidneys and other body systems and tells them that it's time to start working. Habiba had been deprived of food for so long that she no longer remembered what it was like to eat. Our staff and her family gently urged her to eat and she was fed every three hours for a week. At the end of the week Habiba could sit against the wall by herself and take the cup and drink it. And for the first time since I arrived, I saw Habiba's mother smile.

But Habiba still had a long way to go. In the second week we gave her a higher-calorie therapeutic milk. She began drinking more and playing with her baby sister. We then started treating her tuberculosis. In the third week she stood for the first time in over a year. I will never forget the morning when I walked into the feeding center and Habiba walked over to me and greeted me with a hug. I could not believe that this smiling little girl was the girl that was so close to death.

While Habiba was getting better, her mother was taught how to weave mats. She sold the mats and with the money she made, she purchased clothes for herself and her daughters. 40 days after arriving, a smiling healthy Habiba walked out of our center. I didn't believe it was possible, but I watched her walk out.

Habiba one month later. *Photo courtesy of ACF–Kenya.*

We followed Habiba for nine months to treat her tuberculosis and make sure that she did not become malnourished again. We also started water, sanitation, and hygiene programs in her community. Today as you can see, Habiba is a happy and healthy young girl. I saw 600 children come into our center near death and walk out healthy. If we can get a child into a feeding center, we can save their lives.

For the pastoral people of northern Kenya, like Habiba's family, living conditions are harsh. Water and food are scarce and unaffordable to many, leading to widespread acute malnutrition.

Incredibly, Action Against Hunger *can save a child like Habiba for just $50,* which provides nutrition and care for 30 days at an Action Against Hunger Therapeutic Feeding Center. In addition, Action Against Hunger has innovated successful programs that can stop and prevent the most widespread cases of malnutrition and starvation.[9]

PREVENTION OF MALNUTRITION THROUGH PLUMPY'DOZ

This new Action Against Hunger strategy deploys a Ready-to-Use Food (RUF) called Plumpy'doz, which is designed to supplement other food sources that provide some calories but are otherwise deficient in essential micronutrients.

"Strategic use of these foods can prevent children with moderate acute malnutrition from becoming severe acute cases," says Marie-Sophie Simon, Senior Nutrition Advisor for Action Against Hunger.

In one application of this strategy, a "blanket" distribution of RUFs is provided to all children under the age of three in a food-insecure area, before a full-blown crisis occurs. This approach proved successful in Niger, where a six-month-long RUF distribution resulted in a significant decline in mortality. Moreover, researchers found that malnourished children whose natural growth had been delayed had resumed a normal growth curve, and that they had built up a reserve of essential nutrients that would provide long-term protection from acute malnutrition and other diseases.

The same $50 donation could also provide *preventative treatment* to one child. In this case, a child consumes Plumpy'doz three times each day for six months. So, for *27¢ per day you could prevent a child with moderate malnutrition from suffering the severe, life-threatening hunger of Habiba.*

Action Against Hunger aims to save starving children, restore their health, and strengthen their families and communities *in order to prevent future episodes of hunger.* As children receive life-saving treatment, Action Against Hunger teaches women trades that earn them living wages, installs community water and sanitation systems, and provides health care that focuses on vaccinations and treating opportunistic diseases that are common where there is hunger.

You and I can save children like Habiba, and they can go on to lead fulfilling lives, particularly if they have access to the kinds of opportunities created by the programs in this book. Even better, we can make small donations to the programs in *Give a Little* and *prevent* the kind of suffering experienced by Habiba and millions like her.

~~~~~~~~~~~~~~~~~~~~~~~~

chapter 6

KickStart
kicking hunger out of kenya

*"As farming families do better, they start to put their kids in
school for longer periods. Almost every country that has become
wealthy started with a huge increase in farming productivity."*

—BILL GATES[1]

Kenya is one of the world's poorest nations. In 2005, its gross
national income was $540 per capita. One out of every eight
children dies before turning five years old. Life expectancy is a
short forty-nine years.[2] In 2003, 62 percent of Kenyans lived in
houses with mud, dung, or sand floors, and 69 percent had no
access to piped or public tap drinking water.[3]

At one time, Kenya was a food exporter. However, agriculture has suffered from drought, lack of irrigation, and shortages
of seed supplies. Kenyans now face chronic food deficits, and
periods of famine are frequent.[4] In 2003, one in every three Kenyans (31 percent) was malnourished.[5]

FARMING TO EAT

It may be difficult for Americans to fathom, but millions
of families worldwide live by subsistence farming. In Africa,

70 percent to 80 percent of the population is involved in agriculture.[6] These families are growing just enough food, and sometimes not enough food, to feed themselves. They lack the ability to accumulate assets such as cash, equipment, reliable water sources, fertilizer, and seeds that would improve their productivity and provide better nutrition and higher income.

Unfortunately, subsistence farming almost always traps families in a devastating cycle of poverty and hunger. Few subsistence farmers have a real chance of improving their or their children's lives. Typically, subsistence farmers have small plots of land that are only capable of producing enough food in a good year to sustain the family. Even if they had more land that would allow them to grow crops to sell for income, they often lack access to the markets in which to sell them. Desperation to produce enough food to feed their families leads to over-farming and depletion of the soil, which in turn decreases the productivity of the land over time. Subsistence farmers are often at the mercy of the weather—depending on rain alone for irrigation. During droughts, they go hungry. Without income for school fees, children stay home and grow into illiterate, subsistence-farming adults.

THE TOOLS TO END POVERTY

The idea behind KickStart is simple—*that the poorest people in the world are also among the most entrepreneurial.* They have to be as a matter of simple survival. KickStart harnesses that spirit to help people help themselves out of poverty. We create tools that people can use to start successful and profitable businesses.[7]

For Africa's poorest farmers, KickStart may be one of the most important and effective projects working to eliminate chronic hunger and poverty. KickStart empowers subsistence farmers in Africa to lift themselves out of poverty permanently.

Nick Moon and Martin Fisher, cofounders of KickStart, met while working for the British nonprofit agency ActionAid in the 1980s. The men discovered they had a common interest in developing effective and affordable tools and technologies that create income-generating opportunities for the poor. Nick and Martin also shared a philosophy that defined the enterprise they launched in 1991, originally named ApproTEC (for "appropriate technologies") and later renamed KickStart: *The best way to end chronic poverty is to provide the poor with access to the means of earning a sustainable income.* They knew from experience that people living in the poorest areas of Africa had the capability, time, and desire to achieve prosperity through their own efforts and did not want or need to rely on handouts. KickStart's products allow individuals and groups to operate profitable commercial microenterprises, permanently moving them from subsistence farming, hunger, and poverty to a middle-class standard of living.

FARMING IS MY BUSINESS

Two billion people . . . live and work on smallholder farms. Most are poor, struggling to survive on less than $2-a-day. Supporting them would not only contribute to world food security, but would make a significant dent in poverty.

—Lennart Båge, President, International Fund for Agricultural Development, 2008[8]

Increasingly, experts believe that the dual problems of poverty and food insecurity can be addressed by empowering subsistence farmers to develop microenterprises that can provide food and income. (See Author's Notes for source materials discussing smallholder farming and the Millennium Development Goals.) Unfortunately, in Kenya, farming is seen as a means of surviving and not as a profitable business. In order to address the stigma attached to farming and inspire residents of Kenya to imagine the possibilities of farming, KickStart launched a campaign titled "Farming Is My Business." Campaign materials depict a farmer standing in front of lush, productive crops—clearly enough to sell in the marketplace and earn an income. Kenyans are beginning to embrace the opportunities presented by successful farming.

THE TOOLS

KickStart's premier products, the ones that have most effectively created *thousands* of new businesses and middle-class citizens, are its micro-irrigation pumps. These wonder tools have helped the poorest farmers in Africa move from subsistence to profitable commercial farming.

Money-Making Micro-Irrigation Pumps

About 10 percent of Kenya's land is well suited to farming and used to grow crops.[9] Of this land, only about 1.5 percent to 2.0 percent is reliably irrigated by means other than rainfall.[10] In nonirrigated areas, farmers suffer the inconsistencies of rain and dry periods or the laborious efforts required to bring water to their fields from streams, ponds, or shallow wells *bucket by bucket* to irrigate their small plots of land. In many cases, farmers experience complete crop failures or are able to produce only enough food to eat for three-quarters of the year.

Fisher and Moon recognized that an affordable, durable, and effective water pump capable of maintaining a consistent water supply would provide an income-generating opportunity for these isolated and low productivity farms. In response, KickStart developed micro-irrigation pumps and now produces and distributes the following: the MoneyMaker Hip Pump, which is the least expensive (retailing for only US$33) and can irrigate up to three-quarters of an acre; and the Super MoneyMaker, which costs US$95, pulls water from up to twenty-three feet, and can irrigate two acres of land. KickStart is currently distributing the pumps in Kenya, Tanzania, and Mali.

With reliable irrigation, *farmers are quickly able to triple or quadruple their crop outputs and typically increase their income by up to ten times!* [11] The purchase price of the pumps is recovered within three to six months.[12]

Pumps Create Ripples

Ownership and use of a KickStart micro-irrigation pump improves the lives of the farmer's family, those the farmer employs (and their families), those who consume the farmer's products in the local community, and ultimately, the broader region where crops are exported.

Use of the pumps generates multiple benefits in the following ways:

- The pump dramatically increases the farmer's productivity (i.e., crop output)
- Higher productivity leads to crop surpluses, which takes the farmer from subsistence to commercial farming

- Commercial farming increases the farmer's income as well as any future employees' income
- Pump owners typically grow higher-value foods that garner a higher price in the marketplace, as opposed to low-value food staples
- Higher income allows the farmer (and any employees) to acquire better food, clothing, health care, housing, and schooling for the children
- Future prospects for the children's well-being and prosperity are improved
- Farmers typically use the pumps to grow high-nutrition foods rather than low-nutrition staples, which improves the diets of the farmer's family and those who purchase the surplus
- Many crops are sold locally, keeping the consumer's purchase price lower

In general, KickStart farmers are examples of how small-holder (small acreage) farming benefits entire communities and can be a legitimate and important part of the solution to high food costs and food insecurity in many parts of the world.

The Power of a Pump: How a $33 Investment Helped One Family Out of Poverty[13]

Felix Mururi is a landless Kenyan in his early thirties who is married with three children. His eldest children are twins who are seven years old and in the first grade at a local primary school. The youngest is three years old and hopes to join a nursery school. In order to make enough money to look after his family Felix left his rural home to look for a job in the city. He

found work serving food in an informal restaurant in the slums of Nairobi
where he managed to earn $40 per
month—but this was barely enough to
meet his family's most basic needs.

One day last August he saw a
KickStart Hip Pump being demonstrated in a local shop. It was selling
for $33, and he saw that it was both
affordable and easy to operate. He realized that with this pump he could

Photo courtesy of KickStart

make more money farming than he could make in the city. He
decided to go back to his home area and work to save the needed
funds.

He rented a small plot of land and he and his wife started
using a bucket to irrigate a few French beans from a shallow
well. After two months of hard work they harvested their first
crop and made enough money to buy a Hip Pump.

Since then they have rented five more small plots of land
with a total area of an acre. They are paying $53 per year to rent
the land and they have started to grow French beans, tomatoes,
baby corn, and green maize. They planted the land so that they
will have a mature crop to sell throughout the year, and their
lives have already changed drastically.

After two months they harvested the crops on two of the six
small plots and they made $580 profit. They are also renting out
the pump to a neighbor who pays them $0.65 per day. Felix says
"hii pump ni faida tupu" ("this pump is purely for profit") and the
family is making plans for its future. They plan to rent and irrigate another acre of land, and they hope to soon have enough

money to reach their dream of buying land and building a decent house. And as Felix's wife says "halafu tuendelee na tuendeleee kabisa" ("then we will continue to prosper").

KICKSTART AND YOU ENDING HUNGER AND POVERTY

At this point, you may be wondering, as I originally was, where the donor fits into this picture. KickStart subsidizes the cost of taking pumps from production to the rural farmers. Even at subsidized prices, farmers often save for many months to purchase a pump, which Fisher and Moon say is critically important to KickStart's success. Like many experts in third world development, their experience indicates that end users are more likely to properly and consistently use products or services intended to benefit the poor when they have paid, even sacrificed, in order to acquire them.

Small contributions help KickStart provide affordable products to their customers (pumps are priced such that the cost to the farmer is recouped within three to six months after purchase), continue to develop additional, innovative technologies that lift individuals out of poverty, and expand their work into other developing countries.

Eventually, increased sales of the pumps will reduce production and marketing costs enough that donor subsidies will no longer be needed. In the meantime, imagine turning poverty into productivity and hunger into history for an entire family.

KickStart meticulously tracks the outcomes realized by farmers who purchase their pumps and have determined that *a $60 donation will lift one individual out of poverty*. "Out of poverty" is defined as being able to meet all basic survival needs for nutritious food, decent shelter, clothing, basic medication, and health care; being able to send all children to primary school; and having enough money left over to save and invest in the future.

Ken Weimar, senior development officer for KickStart, says the pumps provide "economic freedom meaning perhaps for the first time, going to bed and knowing you will be able to feed your kids the next day without a struggle or sacrifice."

Think of $60 as the equivalent of $5 each month. If you're like me, you spend $5 many, many times every month on things you would not miss. Instead, you could create a wealth of good. Consider that, for the same $5, you could permanently change the future for a farmer, her family, their neighbors, their community, etc.

That's a pretty good use of $5.

A Donor's Story: Patrick Grace

I met the cofounder and CEO of KickStart, Martin Fisher, at a philanthropy conference in 2005. At the time, I knew virtually nothing about Africa, poverty alleviation, or economic development among people living on less than $1 per day. The thought of a family of five investing in themselves, buying an irrigation pump, multiplying their income by 10, and changing virtually all aspects of their lives was intriguing to say the least, but almost seemed too good to be true.

I went to Africa a few months later to learn more. After two weeks of travel in rural Africa, and many conversations about the myriad challenges on the African continent, I finally saw the KickStart system in action on farms outside of Nairobi. The lives of every family I met were totally transformed. Their stories were crystal clear and simple: Human energy, when combined with an effective product can change lives. I used the pump myself, feeling for a moment a part of the solution.

Sometimes simplicity is the hardest of all things to find. Helping many for a short time sometimes sounds better than helping a relative few to find their way out of poverty forever. Sometimes scalable [the ability to readily expand a project to reach as many potential beneficiaries as possible] sounds better than sustainable. KickStart has devised a system that balances all of these variables: It is simple, sustainable, allows its customers to escape poverty forever, and is scalable as the product is rolled out. That is why I love and support the company.

~~~~~~~~~~~~

chapter 7

Heifer International
how a cow can save a life

"These children don't need a cup, they need a cow."

—Dan West,
Founder, Heifer International[1]

I must credit Katherine Hoak with introducing me to Heifer International. One year, she made a donation to Heifer on behalf of our extended family. As a group, we donated a goat. She sent us a Heifer donation card that displayed an ark full of animals destined for poverty-stricken areas throughout the world and a description of Heifer's mission and methods. That donation and Heifer's description of its benefits to the recipient deeply influenced my ideas about charity. Of course, a cow instead of a cup! Brilliant! As Chinese philosopher Lao Tzu taught: Give a man a fish and you feed him for a day. Teach him how to fish and you feed him for a lifetime.

Heifer International is yet another example of how donations from private citizens just like you *can and do* radically improve lives around the world every day. Together, donors and Heifer International have ended hunger for millions of families in 140 countries.

DAN'S EPIPHANY

Dan West conceived Heifer International as he passed out rations of milk to refugees and orphans of the Spanish Civil War of 1936–1939. Dan was a relief worker with the Church of the Brethren and saw firsthand that limited rations of direct food aid would never sustain the desperate masses of people. He realized that they needed to be taught to fish (metaphorically speaking). Specifically, he believed that delivering heifers* to the rural poor would offer a reliable source of nutritious milk as well as income through the sale of surplus milk. He also realized that many more would be helped if each recipient of a heifer passed on its first female offspring to another needy family.

Originally called Heifers for Relief, the organization sent its first shipment of seventeen heifers to Puerto Rico in 1944. Following World War II, when nearly all means of farming (equipment, irrigation, livestock, etc.) had been destroyed across Europe and in Japan, Heifer scaled up its efforts and sent heifers all over Europe, and later, pigs and heifers to Japan.[2]

Thus was born one of the most effective and lauded hunger and poverty relief organizations in the world. Over the years, Heifers for Relief became Heifer International and refined and expanded its efforts to create economically and environmentally sustainable projects around the globe.

---

* A heifer is a female cow or bovine younger than thirty months old that has not yet given birth to a calf.

LLAMAS, AND HEIFERS, AND BEES—OH MY!

Like KickStart, Heifer International's programs make an *immediate, substantial, and measurable change in the lives of recipients.* Heifer's basic approach remains the same—providing an animal, typically to smallholder farmers in poor rural areas around the world, that improves the nutritional and economic status of the family. The receiving family must pass on the animal's offspring; in this way, the impact of Heifer's work ripples outward, ultimately raising the standard of living among neighbors and within entire villages and communities.

Since 1992, Jo Luck has presided over Dan's visionary organization as president and CEO of Heifer International. Here is how she described Heifer's impact to me:

> I have seen in the field time and again how the seemingly small gift of a goat, or rabbits, or a flock of chickens can bring hope to entire communities. The transformation that occurs in the lives of children, men and women continues to remind me that even the simplest—yet meaningful— actions are far-reaching whose impact never fades away. Because of passing on the gift, hope burns brighter as more and more people live their lives free of hunger and poverty.

The scope of Heifer International has changed dramatically since those first heifers were sent to Puerto Rico. For one thing, they no longer ship only heifers and pigs to poverty-stricken areas. They typically don't *ship* animals at all. It is far more economical and beneficial to the local economy to purchase and distribute indigenous animals already acclimated to the local area. Heifer International helps improve these animals, which are already resistant to local diseases, by breeding to increase their production capacity (e.g., more liters of milk per cow). The animals now being distributed include: heifers, oxen, sheep, water buffalo, goats, camels, llamas, alpacas, donkeys, pigs, bees, ducks, geese, chicks, guinea pigs, and rabbits.

Some of these animals, such as heifers, chicks, and goats, provide food sources such as milk, eggs, and meat. Animals such as water buffalo and donkeys are used as draft animals that can work in fields and haul products to markets (although water buffalo milk, which many believe produces the best mozzarella cheese, is also highly prized for consumption and sale). Llamas and sheep provide raw materials (i.e., wool) that can be sold or used for the production of clothing and other cloth items. All of the animals' manure fertilizes and increases crop output.

Every donated animal is uniquely suited to the environment in which it lives. Llamas and alpacas are common in Peru for several reasons: They are hardy and withstand the harsh climate well; they can easily navigate the rocky terrain; their soft hooves have a low impact on the delicate ecosystem, which does not reliably support agriculture; and their coats are ideal for fine garment production in isolated rural areas.

Goats are another hardy animal well suited to extreme climates and difficult terrain. For instance, they can feed on land unsuitable for farming by eating grass and leaves.[3] Goats have been provided to impoverished Polish families in Stoczek Łukowski, where they are developing a small-scale breeding and milk production industry in an area where poor soil prohibits farming.[4]

As an example of *the immediate impact of the gift of a single goat*, consider the following facts from The World's Healthiest Foods and Heifer International:[5]

- "Goat's milk is a good source of low-cost high-quality protein" and also provides calcium, phosphorous, riboflavin (vitamin B2), and potassium.[6]
- One dairy goat can supply a family with up to several quarts of nutritious milk a day—a ton of milk a year.
- Extra milk can be sold or used to make cheese, butter, or yogurt.
- Families use goat manure to fertilize gardens.
- And because goats often have two or three kids a year, Heifer recipients can start small dairies that pay for food, health care, and education for their families.

The cost of donating one goat is $120*; however, you can donate a "share" of a goat for $10. And remember, the returns on your donation will be evident now *and long into the future, as many more families and future generations will benefit from the passing on of the goat's offspring.*

MUCH MORE THAN ANIMALS

Part of what makes Heifer such an exciting and effective organization is its holistic approach. Although providing animals is the

---

* The cost of donating animals through Heifer International represents "the complete livestock gift of a high-quality animal, technical assistance and extensive training. Each purchase . . . represents a contribution to the entire mission of Heifer International. Donations will be used where needed most to help struggling people." (Heifer International)

hallmark of Heifer International, its total mission also includes protecting the environment, promoting gender equity, and providing training in animal management and business practices that create profitable entrepreneurs, such as Shi Guangzhi, who developed a successful silkworm microenterprise in the Sichuan Province of China.

Weaving a Hopeful Future,[7]
by Barbara Justus for Heifer International

On a chilly spring morning, Shi Guangzhi wakes around dawn to the papery sound of silkworms rustling through the fresh mulberry leaves she laid out the night before. The sound is comforting, an assurance that all is well with her precious livestock.

Guangzhi is a sericulturist, or silkworm farmer, in Sichuan Province, China. Her first priority of every day—before putting water on for tea or preparing her children's breakfast—is checking on her silkworms.

The silkworms noisily munch their way through layers of leaves in large wicker trays stacked in her kitchen. Guangzhi picks through them carefully and selects a few to inspect, rolling them gently between her forefinger and thumb. The silkworms' white velvety heads bob hungrily as she evaluates their progress on their journey toward remarkable metamorphoses.

These silkworms mean everything to Guangzhi. The beautiful iridescent fibers they spin have lifted her and hundreds of women like her out of poverty, with the help of Heifer International.

Since Guangzhi began working with Heifer just two years ago, she has quadrupled her family's annual income.

In Guangzhi's community in Lezhi County, the gift of silk-worms from Heifer has woven a hopeful future for hundreds of women and their families.

These women are quite isolated, their small homes perched amid rugged and remote mountains in western China. Yet they are part of a growing community group started in 1997 and known as "Heifer International's Lezhi Women's Silkworm Project."

The fact that an organized group of highly trained entre-preneurs exists in this remote, impoverished pocket of the world is remarkable. However, what's most amazing is that its members are primarily female—women who not long ago were considered second-class citizens with no education, no means to contribute to their families' incomes, and little decision-making rights within the family structure.

Now most women in this silkworm project provide more than 60 percent of their families' income.

Their quality of life has increased immeasurably, not only because of this rise in income, but also because of the elevated status brought on by their hard-won self-sufficiency.

They now have an equal say in how the family income is spent—on nourishing food, including protein-rich duck eggs for their children; on school fees and books; and on medical care that was once out of reach.

The Lezhi women have worked hard to become skilled seri-culturists.

The silkworms, so delicate and tiny upon hatching that they must be handled with a feather, increase their body weight 10,000 times under the women's meticulous care. The worms feed on leaves of the fast-growing mulberry trees that the women have planted in a way that also curbs soil erosion on their small plots of land.

When a farmer determines that a silkworm is ready to spin, she moves it to a pile of straw where it begins its miraculous spinning. The silk comes from two glands filled with a fluid called fibroin (like liquid silk) that the worm squeezes out, along with a thick paste called sericin that cements the two filaments together. The cemented double strand hardens and dries when it is exposed to air.

When the last drop of liquid silk is spent and the cocoon is complete, the women remove the cocoons from the straw. At that point, either they take the cocoons to a local silk cooperative to be processed or they do the processing themselves.

Each precious cocoon may yield more than a half mile of life-giving silk.

Now when the women of Lezhi County come together, their conversations don't dwell on the severe hardships of the past, but on their dreams for the future.

With their extra income, several women in the group have had wells dug near their homes, saving untold hours previously spent hauling water. Others have installed energy-efficient stoves in their kitchens—using less fuel while saving themselves and their children from the noxious fumes of open fires.

With additional training from Heifer, many have leveraged their extra income to expand their agricultural operations.

Guangzhi, for example, is now also raising 17 goats, which live under her precious mulberry trees, eating rye grasses she planted and leftover mulberry leaves not needed by the hungry silkworms. She collects the dead silkworm pupae, grinds them into meal, and

adds it to her goats' feed as an excellent protein supplement.

Nothing goes to waste in Guangzhi's integrated farming operation.

Ask Guangzhi or any other
Heifer project partner about the
most gratifying aspect of their
partnership with Heifer, and they'll
tell you it is their obligation—and
privilege—to pass on a comparable
gift to another family in need.

"Passing on the Gift."
Photo by Darcy Kiefel, copyright, Heifer International.

And this one small gift starts a
chain reaction that results in widespread self-sufficiency and
dignity within a community.

"SMALL INPUTS CAN LEAD TO BIG IMPACTS"

Speaking at Heifer International's Little Rock World Head-
quarters in 2006, Dr. Jeffrey Sachs, author of the best-selling *The
End of Poverty: Economic Possibilities for Our Time*, director of the
Earth Institute at Columbia University, former director of the UN
Millennium Project, and president and cofounder of the Millennium Promise Alliance, said Heifer has proved that "small inputs
can lead to big impacts." He called this "the Beatrice Theorem"
for the story of a child in Uganda who lived in desperate poverty
with her family and siblings until they received a goat from
Heifer International.

At nine years old, Beatrice Biira had never attended school in
her tiny village of Kisinga in the rolling hills of south central
Uganda, though she longed to do so and often peered through

the window of the crude one-room structure and watched the children study. With an annual income of only US$1,000, Beatrice's family couldn't afford to pay for the uniforms and books required for any of their six children to go to school, so instead, Beatrice worked with her parents tending to their small crops and helping to generate food for the family.

But Beatrice's mother, Evelyn Baluku, who was married at age twelve and today has eight children, wanted a better future for Beatrice and her siblings. Together with a committed group of women in her village, Evelyn applied to Heifer International for a herd of goats. In 1992, twelve arrived at the village, and Evelyn's family received a goat pregnant with twins.

Beatrice took on primary responsibility for caring for the family's goat, which she named "Mugisa," meaning "luck" in the language of Beatrice's village. Indeed, her family's fortunes were changed by the nutrition and income generated by the goat's milk, which among other things, allowed Beatrice to finally go to school. Beatrice's family was also able to construct a sturdier house and purchase medication and many other necessities that dramatically improved their standard of living.

One little goat, one mighty change in the trajectory of a child's life. And when you think about it, that goat changed the future not only for Beatrice's entire family, but for those who benefitted from the surplus milk that the family sold, and perhaps most importantly, from the offspring, which was passed on to other families in need. Those families then passed on their goats' first offspring, and on and on. The effects of that single gift to Beatrice's family in 1992 continue today.

Recently, Beatrice graduated from Connecticut College with a self-designed bachelor's degree in Inter-disciplinary Studies.[8]

Still, she clearly remembers being hungry as a child. She now plans to pass on Heifer's gift in her own way: by getting a master's degree in public service and returning to Africa to work for an aid organization, thus expanding Heifer's impact even further.

AGROECOLOGY AS ANOTHER ROUTE FROM POVERTY TO PROSPERITY

In addition to providing animals to create food and income sources, Heifer provides expertise and training in "agroecology," which aims to maintain healthy ecosystems while simultaneously supporting sustainable and successful agricultural productivity. Agroecology can transform languishing migrant groups into thriving communities.

Thailand Tribes Find Self-Reliance in Their Own Backyards[9]

For decades, the Akha tribes of northern Thailand relied on one method of survival: constant migration throughout the region necessitated by the slash-and-burn technique of farming. Then everything changed.

New government policies included tribe members' forced settlement. It didn't take long for them to find that the only farming method they'd known quickly depleted what little land they had. The notorious dry season only made things worse, and soon the youth of the villages were leaving home to find work that too often involved prostitution and led to drug addiction. Meanwhile, those left behind still had to eat.

Mrs. Nakha, an Akha tribal member, remembers that while migrating, their food and income ". . . came only from what we found in the forest." And although it was illegal, "We were forced to collect charcoal [for cooking] in the middle of the night. We didn't even use a flashlight to guide us, only lighted matches, so that we wouldn't get caught."

During the daylight hours, "We were idle and isolated ourselves from each other." Forming a village community seemed impossible.

In 1999, Heifer International's Thailand program began working with these families, teaching them how to plant kitchen gardens and care for the water buffalo, cattle, pigs, and poultry Heifer provided. The villagers learned how to use biogas for their fuel. Ten neighboring villages even banded together to plant almost 50,000 trees in a one-hundred-hectare area where water springs are located. Now this new forest absorbs rainwater and supplies it to the villages during the dry season.

"Today we can establish ourselves as a community," said Amui Wazu, another member of the Akha tribe. "And Heifer has introduced us to the kitchen gardens, which have been our savior. We have vegetables year-round!" "Since Heifer International [came], we are always busy with our animals and our kitchen gardens," Mrs. Nakha added. "We do not need to go elsewhere for our food, because everything for our survival is here."

A Donor's Story: Katherine Hoak

I learned of Heifer International initially from advertisements featuring Susan Sarandon, whose views I trust. After investigating, I learned of the responsible financing practiced by Heifer. I felt assured that whatever donation I made would result in some person or family somewhere benefitting in a manner which would result in their being able to finally thrive, and that there was a good chance their success would spread in their communities. Donating to Heifer feels to me like a person-to-person manner of making an important difference.

For several years now, I have purchased a goat, with shares representing many family members. It has been most rewarding to send each family member a card indicating a donation made on their behalf at the end-of-the-year holidays. Hearing back from a couple of them that it opened the door to them for their own contributions is beyond what I expected. Now my extended family is spreading the word about Heifer to their friends, families, and communities.

Heifer has proven to have integrity and to make an important difference. How wonderful that is in what seems to me an increasingly cynical world.

chapter 8

Feeding America

small donations battle
hunger in the united states

*"Hungry people cannot be good at learning or
producing anything, except perhaps violence."*

—PEARL BAILEY[1]

Hunger means suffering for anyone who experiences it. Children, however, are hardest hit by its damaging effects. Inadequate nutrition in childhood can alter a child's lifetime trajectory through school and life.

While chronic hunger is a problem primarily in developing countries, "food *in*security" strikes anywhere poverty lurks, including within the rich industrialized nations of the world. The U.S. Food and Agriculture Organization defines "food *security*" as "a situation that exists when all people, at all times, have physical, social and economic access to sufficient, safe and nutritious food to meet their dietary needs and food preferences for an active and healthy life."[2]

In 2007, 11 percent of U.S. households, or *36 million people*, experienced at least one period of food insecurity when they were uncertain they would have, or were unable to obtain, enough nutritious food to eat.[3] Of these 36 million people, 23.8

million were adults, representing 10.6 percent of all adult Americans. Worse yet, 12.4 million were children, meaning in 2007, 16.9 percent of all children or *about one in every six children in the United States didn't always have enough healthy food to eat.*[4]

Very likely, there are hungry children and adults in your own community. I know there are in mine. In the very same school my children attend—my children having access to more than enough nutritious and not-so-nutritious food at all times—there are children who save their government-provided lunches to bring home and share with siblings for dinner.

The Center on Hunger and Policy at Brandeis University examined and summarized the results of numerous studies on childhood hunger and food insecurity in the United States.

Youngsters from food insecure and hungry homes have poorer overall health status: they are sick more often, much more likely to have ear infections, have higher rates of iron deficiency anemia, and are hospitalized more frequently. In short, going hungry makes kids sick. As a result, they miss more days of school and are less prepared to learn when they are able to attend, making the relationship between hunger, health and learning of far greater importance than we previously realized. Further exacerbating this interactive impairment of young bodies and minds are the emotional and behavioral impacts that accompany food insecurity and hunger. At-risk children are more likely to have poorer mental health, be withdrawn or socially disruptive, and suffer greater rates of behavioral disorders.[5]

Food insecurity and hunger among children leaves them poorly prepared to be self-sufficient, contributing, adult members of their communities.

The good news is that small donations can provide enough nutritious food for children so that the *entire trajectory of their early development is altered and improved.*

TWO PROGRAMS THAT FILL BOWLS

Feeding America (formerly America's Second Harvest) supplies food and other support to a network of local food banks around the country. It also operates two especially effective programs, Kids Cafe and BackPacks, focused on feeding vulnerable children so they can succeed in school and realize their potential.

Kids Cafes

In 1993, ConAgra Foods, Inc., partnered with Feeding America to create Kids Cafe, which now has over 1,600 locations around the country. Kids Cafe programs provide meals to children after school, on weekends, and other times when school is closed in order to fill the gaps left by the federal government's food programs for children.

Kids Cafe programs operate in places where children often gather, such as Boys and Girls Clubs and after-school programs. According to Feeding America, aside from federal food programs, "Kids Cafe is the most expansive child-feeding program in the nation."[6] In fiscal year 2006, Kids Cafe programs served at least *82,828 individual children* and more than *6.8 million meals and 4.5 million snacks.*[7]

Typically, Feeding America provides the local Kids Cafe sponsoring agency with start-up funds to equip a kitchen, and in some cases, short-term operating grants. Ultimately, each Kids Cafe is to become self-sustaining with ongoing support from its sponsoring agency. In Chicago, forty-three Kids Cafe programs are administered by the Greater Chicago Food Depository.

Chicago's Corazon Community Services "Fuerza Youth Program" serves youth ages fourteen to twenty-one during non-school hours—after school, on school holidays, weekends, and during the summer. In Spanish, "fuerza" means "strength, power, energy, and might." The Fuerza Youth Program strives to inspire these qualities in each young person they serve.

The program helps youth develop and maintain positive lifestyles. Students participate in quality out-of-school experiences that provide opportunities to improve their academic and life skills, outlets for creativity, varied recreational activities, and mentoring. Fuerza wants its students to emerge as leaders; more confident of their abilities, encouraged by newfound talents, and ready to pursue future opportunities, including college, a career, and fulfillment of their dreams.

Through its partnership with the Greater Chicago Food Depository, the Fuerza Youth Program is able to operate a Kids Cafe program. All the meals served in the Kids Cafe are prepared by the Community Kitchens of the Greater Chicago Food Depository and delivered to the Corazon Center. There is no doubt that the Kids Cafe is an essential part of the program and an invaluable service to the families whose children attend.

For the Martinez family, Kids Cafe means the difference between full bellies and almost daily hunger. Mrs. Martinez heads a family of six children ranging in age from five to seventeen. Mr. Martinez abandoned the family shortly after the youngest child was born. To sustain the family while still caring for her younger children, Mrs. Martinez works several part-time jobs.

The two oldest Martinez daughters, Maria (sixteen) and Sandra (fourteen), participate in Fuerza's Youth Program. The girls revealed their household's food scarcity one evening when they were the last students at the center before closing. They were helping clean up when they asked about the leftover food. A staff member asked them if they wanted to take it home. The girls hesitated a little before answering yes. She then asked about their favorite foods and their mother's best dishes. Their answer was troubling. They said they didn't have favorites and were happy to eat anything that was available.

The girls said their family was always short on food, and even though they went to places like food banks, there was never enough. Trying to save food at home for the younger children, the sisters sometimes went an entire day eating only a snack that someone shared with them at school. It wasn't until the Martinez sisters started coming to the Fuerza Youth Program that they ate full meals, typically a nutritious snack and hot dinner every day after school.

With two fewer dinners to serve each weeknight, Mrs. Martinez is much better able to provide full meals to the rest of the family. In that way a single hot meal helps feed an entire family.

BackPacks

In a June 2006 *Wall Street Journal* article about Feeding America's BackPacks Program, Kim Matthews, the youth services coordinator for the Chapel Hill, Texas, school district, shared the following observation about the need in their community. "On Friday at lunch, I see a kind of panic in some children that I didn't see before. They eat as much as they can, then on Monday at breakfast, they not only eat the food on their tray, but the food on the trays of the five kids next to them."[8]

Feeding America's BackPacks Program is based on a project originated in 1995 in Little Rock, Arkansas, where a school nurse noticed recurring episodes of stomachaches and dizziness caused by hunger rather than illness.[9] In the same school, the counselor noted children's inability to pay attention, lack of effort, and disruptive behavior in classrooms—all behaviors consistent with hunger. The Arkansas Rice Depot, a local food bank, began filling backpacks with child-friendly, nutritious foods that provided breakfasts, lunches, and dinners to prevent weekend hunger. The backpack concept spread throughout Arkansas and was ultimately taken to scale by Feeding America. Today, over 110 Feeding America Members operate BackPacks programs in thirty-nine states and Washington, D.C.

Here are some facts about the Feeding America BackPacks Program:[10]

- Food is child-friendly, nonperishable, easily consumed, and vitamin fortified.
- Backpacks are discreetly distributed to children on the last day before the weekend or holiday vacation.
- In addition to providing nutritious food to school children in need, some BackPacks programs provide

Volunteers pack food for a Kids
Cafe. *Photo Courtesy of Feeding America.*

extra food for younger
siblings at home, and
others operate during the
summer months when
children are out of school
and have limited access to
free or reduced-price
meals.

- Nationally, members send as many as 35,000 separate backpacks home on Fridays.
- The Backpacks Program is the fastest growing National Program within the Feeding America network. Within the last year, the program has experienced close to 100 percent growth.

The *Wall Street Journal* article, titled "For Hungry Kids, 'Backpack Clubs' Try to Fill a Gap," told the stories of children and families who relied on the backpacks to supplement their meager food budgets.[11] One family was spending only $50 per week on food for their entire family of five. According to a 2005 report by the USDA, the median food-secure American household spends *$40 per person* on food each week.[12] This family was spending *$10 per person per week*. As you can imagine, it is a terrific relief for a family like this when their children come home on Friday afternoons with their backpacks.

Backpacks don't always feed just the school child. According to the *Wall Street Journal* article, "While some backpack-carriers say they jealously guard their food—one boy says he hides it under his bed—others say they share it with their families. At Annie Sims Elementary School in Mt. Pleasant, Texas, a

10-year-old named Leonard said he shared his milk with his grandmother, his crackers with an aunt, and his Apple Jacks cereal with his older sister. Leonard asked the school counselor for an extra jar of peanut butter for his mother."[13]

FEED A CHILD, CHANGE A LIFE

Contributions to Feeding America generate enormous returns with *every $1 providing sixteen meals*.

Small donations are also more than welcome at local food banks. According to Bob Dolgan, director of communications at the Greater Chicago Food Depository, "Fighting hunger in Chicago is truly a community effort. The majority of our donors give us $25 or less. Many of the people who donate to the Food Depository are stretching their budgets so that we can provide food for the hungry."

A $50 donation could feed an otherwise hungry child over 133 weekends or 800 meals. Few other charitable investments promise as many short- and long-term benefits as keeping a child's belly full of nutritious food.

A Donor's Story: Sonya Woods Anderson

I have not always been aware of the significant problem of hunger here in our United States of America. Even now I have difficulty comprehending the magnitude of that problem. Millions of people in our country face hunger daily. These people include families, children, and the elderly. Ours is a country of abundance. We are not a third-world country. How can this be happening?

I am very impressed by what Feeding America is able to accomplish in an area in which there is so much need. I am also very impressed by their efficiency in utilizing the dollars that are contributed. It is important to me to know that my contributions go primarily toward their programs. In addition to the donations I have made since 1995, I have recently included an endowment to Feeding America in my estate plan. Thus, my support can continue when I no longer need those resources. It is a way of giving back for the abundance that I have experienced in my own life.

FULL BOWLS EQUAL FULL POTENTIAL

In Chapter 1, I described the empty bowl effect on a young girl named Imani. Throughout her life, hunger dictated virtually every important aspect of her living conditions, opportunities, and fate. Empty bowls act like erasers wiping out health, potential, and opportunities for individuals and entire communities.

On the other hand, when you regularly fill those bowls with nutritious food, children and families grow stronger, and eventually, given the opportunity, become healthy and self-sufficient. KickStart and Heifer International are providing the poorest people around the world the tools to create their own food sources. Food becomes a source of ongoing income for the recipients and ultimately provides them a chance to climb out of poverty through their own power and ingenuity.

Providing direct food aid to children in the United States through projects like Feeding America's Kids Cafe and Back-Packs Program is a different kind of empowerment. Although many would not consider this a lasting solution to child poverty, to the child who receives enough nutritious food to allow her to realize her developmental and academic potential, this is the manna that preserves all of her future possibilities.

Giving, even very small giving, can mean a lot in the short term. It provides relief in response to an immediate crisis and will permanently alter lives for the better.

part three

~~~~~~~~~~~~~~~~~

health

chapter 9

~~~~~~~~~~

The Cycle of Poverty
and Poor Health

*"Inequity is becoming less and less affordable not
only for poor people but for the global community as
a whole. The world can no longer turn a blind eye to
the cost of diseases that poverty generates."*

— MAMPHELA RAMPHELE,
MANAGING DIRECTOR, WORLD BANK[1]

*"Take the death of this small boy this morning,
for example. The boy died of measles. We all know
he could have been cured at the hospital. But the
parents had no money and so the boy died a slow and
painful death, not of measles, but out of poverty."*

— MAN FROM GHANA, 1995[2]

Throughout the world, poverty and poor health are inescapably
intertwined. Living in poverty dramatically increases one's risk
of becoming sick, and for those living on the edge, becoming
sick often delivers the final push into poverty or destitution. For
poor people in the United States and around the world, this is a
devastating cycle, but we must also remember that this atrocious
cycle ripples, just like the benefits of your donations. Poverty and

its health-related consequences affect you and me every day. Don't doubt it for a minute.

Here's how it works: Remember little Malita from Malawi who received the bed net? Let's imagine she hadn't and contracted malaria instead. Now she is ill and cannot attend school. She falls behind. A family member must stay home to care for her, thus diminishing the family's income. The anguish of helplessly watching their daughter suffer immobilizes her parents, and their productivity plummets. Malita's siblings stop going to school to help with the chores that her parents can no longer manage. In short, Malita's illness brings the entire family to its knees.

Many other children in Malita's village are similarly ill. Nearly every family is struck by the end of the rainy season, and nearly every family suffers during that period. Food stores are scarce. Some will not make it through the dry season. Children will be orphaned. Some will end up in cities, living on the streets, selling sex to survive. Many will contract HIV/AIDS. Because so many are sick, unable to work, and needing health care, the economy of the entire nation is impacted. Opportunities for economic growth such as tourism are lost. Even within the country, those living in cities lose their natural immunity to malaria and cannot safely travel to remote areas, thus restricting the spread of ideas, information, and technology.

The stress, hopelessness, and resentment of their undignified and unhealthy lives breed civil unrest. A multinational crisis ensues as refugees flee the developing turmoil. The rest of the world must react.

The scenario I've described is told in countless stories and statistics gathered by groups like the Global Fund to Fight

AIDS, Tuberculosis and Malaria,[3] the World Health Organization,[4] and the United Nations,[5] whose studies demonstrate the intermingled effects of poverty, malaria, and civil unrest on the African continent.

Poverty and its coconspirators, hunger and disease, are shaping all of our lives every single day.

POVERTY TO POOR HEALTH:
a slippery slope

With enough to eat, the poor have a fighting chance of warding off or beating diseases. Unfortunately, in addition to hunger, there are many other risk factors of living in poverty that lead to poor health, including:

- Lack of access to health care or medications
- Living in unhealthy and unsanitary environments
- Being exposed to diseases associated with dense populations
- Lack of access to clean drinking water
- Lack of education about healthy practices
- Experiencing chronic stress
- Practicing unsafe sex
- Having more hazardous and physically demanding jobs
- Exposure to indoor and outdoor pollution, among many others

Caught in a vicious downward spiral, poor people who get sick also have a harder time getting well and going back to work. According to the United Nations Population Fund, the poor "have less access to health care, and the services they do have are low in quality and do not respond to their needs. They get less respect and time from doctors and nurses. They are less likely to recover completely from illness, and die earlier. In addition, they are likely to fall even deeper into poverty as a result of working time lost to ill health and the cost of health care."[6]

In other words, being poor makes you sick, and being sick can make you poor.

AMERICAN-STYLE HEALTH HAZARD:
poverty and asthma

Every job has its downsides—certain tasks that are unpleasant, that you avoid, that you'd love to take off your job description. In all my years of adult employment, there is one task that I dreaded more than any other.

The child care program where I worked for ten years served low-income families with children under age three. Truly, the only children enrolled in our program were those between six weeks and three years. You probably know that very young kids get sick—a lot. That's where the worst part of my job kicked in. When a child got sick at the center, I had to call his or her mother (almost all of the low-income families were headed by single moms) at work and tell her that she had to come and pick up her child.

Often, mom would begin to panic, suddenly forced into the mental gymnastics of simultaneously figuring out how to tell her boss she had to leave work; considering what her boss's reaction was likely to be; wondering if she would need to take the child to the doctor; thinking of who she might be able to arm twist into caring for her child so she could come back for the remainder of the workday; and worrying that she might *not* be able to come back to work that day *or* the next. God forbid the child had something that an antibiotic couldn't treat in a quick day or two; she might miss the rest of the week.

I realize that plenty of working parents have lived this scenario. I lived it many times. I have twins who had a knack for getting sick sequentially, thus creating twice as many days that my husband or I missed work. Yet, we were lucky. We both had jobs that provided benefits including paid leave to care for sick children and health insurance, so we never had to decide whether or not we could afford a trip to the doctor's office or the co-pay for the antibiotic.

The moms I called worked in hourly jobs without benefits. When they stayed home from work, they didn't get paid. When they didn't get paid, they had a hard time affording the co-pay for the doctor's visit or the medications.

I once called a mom to tell her that her child was sick, and she asked me to hold while she went to talk to her boss about needing to leave. I was surprised when her boss picked up the phone to talk to me, but I was shocked by what he had to say: "Do you realize that you are putting this woman's job in jeopardy by telling her she needs to leave work?" No, I'm not kidding.

Moms whose children had chronic conditions like recurrent ear infections or asthma suffered the most. Many did lose jobs for missing work. These moms didn't have a chance of getting ahead financially while their children's health was poor. Fortunately, children generally grow out of ear infections around age three. Not so for asthma. Asthma, if uncontrolled, is a chronic condition that lasts into adulthood, keeping children out of school and mothers out of work.

In Chapter 10, I'll describe the far-reaching effects of childhood asthma as well as innovative programs that help poor families control their children's asthma. The benefits to the children are enormous and ripple forward throughout their lives. In addition, for their families, better management of asthma means fewer missed days at work, better chances for promotions, and better-paying jobs and a shot at realizing financial security. All this can be realized with your help.

POVERTY IS DEADLY IN DEVELOPING COUNTRIES

> *"The body is sometimes poor people's only asset and is a major source of insecurity."*
>
> —Deepa Narayan, World Bank Poverty Group[7]

In 1999, Deepa Narayan, of the World Bank's Poverty Group, initiated and led a project titled "Voices of the Poor," which resulted in three books, each examining the major challenges faced by those living in poverty combined with direct quotes describing their experiences. In total, 60,000 poor people in fifty countries contributed to the series. Here is just one description from the series:

They had no spare money on them, but this was not a special problem as it was one shared by many. They had something to feel happy about, having been among the few to fully pay their . . . school fees for two out of their five school-age children. Difficulties started in March, when their five-year-old daughter, Grace, had a serious bout of malaria. Given lack of money, their first recourse was with local herbs. Unfortunately, the little girl's condition did not improve. The family borrowed some money and bought a few tablets of chloroquine and aspirin from the local shop. After some improvement, the girl's health sharply deteriorated two weeks later. By the beginning of May, Grace had become very weak. Her parents then sold some chickens for Shs. 2,500 (approximately $2 US dollars in 1998) and, with the help of neighbors, took her to Ngora Hospital where she was immediately admitted. She was seriously anemic and required urgent blood transfusion. However, the family was asked to pay Shs. 5,000 ($4 US dollars in 1998) that they did not have. They went back home to try and look for money. It was too late. She died on 8 May and was buried the following day. (Uganda 1998)[8]

The health status of those living in developing countries is grim. Very grim.

- Average life expectancy among the fifty least developed countries around the world is fifty-five years.[9]
- Fifteen percent of children die before age five.[10] *That's 1 in every 6.5 children.*
- The following list represents six of the top ten causes of death in developing countries in 2002. Together, these *mostly preventable and treatable conditions* caused 37.5 percent of all deaths. By contrast, the only one of these conditions to make the top ten list in high income countries like the United States was lower respiratory infections, and only 4.3 percent of all deaths were caused by these infections:[11]

- Lower respiratory infection—10 percent of deaths
- HIV/AIDS—7.5 percent of deaths
- Perinatal conditions—6.4 percent of deaths
- Diarrheal disease—5.4 percent of deaths
- Tuberculosis—4.4 percent of deaths
- Malaria—3.8 percent of deaths

If you live in a developing country, you are likely to live a short and miserably unhealthy life. Chances are quite good that you will die of a condition that is almost entirely preventable and/or treatable.

Fortunately, there are many effective programs you can support that will improve the health of the extremely poor. In fact, I'm going to describe the work of two organizations that together address four of the six preventable causes of millions of deaths in the developing world—the Global Fund to Fight AIDS, Tuberculosis and Malaria and PATH: a Catalyst for Global Health. You *can* join the fight against these epidemics.

chapter 10

Asthma Care on Wheels

"The burden of asthma is not borne equally
throughout this country."

—PARTNERS ASTHMA CENTER[1]

In the United States, asthma is an epidemic in poor communities. It puts low-income families in double jeopardy: It robs children of their future potential by causing them to miss school and places their families in economic peril by keeping parents home from work.

Managing a child's asthma is a tremendous challenge for any family, particularly those with fewer resources such as paid leave from work, insurance, and transportation.

ASTHMA'S PATH TO POVERTY

Jonathan was an eight-year-old patient of Dr. Joseph Carrillo at the South End Community Health Center. According to Dr. Carrillo, Jonathan was diagnosed with asthma when he was two years old. Jonathan's mom was a working single mother juggling two jobs and the family had no health insurance. In first and second grade, Jonathan's asthma caused him to miss 40 days of school and forced many trips to the hospital emergency room. Jonathan's mom missed so much time from work to take care of him that she lost one of her jobs and subsequently fell behind in making utility and rent payments. She also fell into debt due to thousands of dollars in medical expenses.[2]

Throughout the world, those living in poverty or on its edges fear the unexpected costs of an illness or injury. *Chronic* illness spells almost certain economic doom. In the United States (and in impoverished urban areas around the world), one of the most devastating chronic diseases among poor families is asthma.

~~~~~~

DID YOU KNOW?

On average, three children in a classroom of thirty are likely to have asthma.[3]

Asthma is the number one cause of school absenteeism, and in 2003, children with asthma missed an estimated 12.8 million days of school.[4]

In 2005, there were approximately 679,000 emergency room visits due to asthma among those under fifteen.[5]

It is estimated that children with asthma spend nearly eight million days per year restricted to bed.[6]

A disproportionate number of poor children have asthma, which exacerbates the obstacles they already face to succeeding in school.

~~~~~~

Asthma is both a cause *and* effect of poverty:

- Low-income people living in urban environments are disproportionately affected by asthma for a number of reasons including higher rates of exposure to indoor and outdoor pollutants.[7]
- This group experiences more emergency department visits, hospitalizations, and deaths due to asthma than the general population.[8]
- Low-income families are less likely to have health coverage that adequately supports asthma management.
  - A survey conducted in 2005 found that 43 percent of people with asthma in the family did not have enough money to pay for health care in the past year.[9]
  - Forty-four percent of asthma households skipped treatment, cut pills, or didn't fill prescriptions because of costs.[10]

If your family hasn't experienced asthma, you may think of it, as I once did, as a relatively benign disease. Think again. Working with low-income families and children schooled me in the harsh realities of dreading cold air, heat and humidity, "ozone alert" days, any significant change in the weather, allergy seasons, colds, flu, or a stranger's perfume or hair spray. For a temperamental toddler, even a tantrum can trigger an asthma episode. It is a chronic emotional, financial, and physical drain on any family. If you don't have good health care coverage or a job with paid leave, the stress can be overwhelming.

Asthma takes a heavy toll on children and families who are already at risk for poor health and economic circumstances. For many vulnerable families, it is the push that sends them into the generational cycle of poverty. There is a way out: Asthma can be controlled with proper diagnosis, appropriate asthma care, and management activities.[11]

Remember Jonathan, who missed forty days of school and whose mother went into debt getting him treatment for his asthma? His doctor referred Jonathan and his mother to an asthma education program that helped the family acquire Medicaid and develop an asthma management plan to keep at home and school. As a result, "Jonathan missed only one day of 3rd grade and did not make any asthma-related visits to the hospital or emergency room."[12]

Programs in a number of U.S. cities are offering asthma diagnosis and treatment in urban areas that work.

ASTHMA AND ALLERGY FOUNDATION OF AMERICA

The Asthma and Allergy Foundation of America's (AAFA's) mission is "to improve the quality of life for people with asthma and allergies and their caregivers, through education, advocacy and research."[13] AAFA provides practical information, community-based services, support, and referrals through a national network of chapters and educational support groups. AAFA also sponsors research toward better treatments and a cure for asthma and allergic diseases. Research has shown that AAFA's programs improve parental knowledge, increase symptom-free days, and reduce rates of emergency room visits and hospitalizations.

Treatment to Go

Over the last decade, several AAFA chapters have put asthma screening, education, and treatment on wheels, bringing services directly to those who need it most. Phoenix, Baltimore, Mobile, Alabama, and southern California have "Breathmobiles," and Chicago has three "Asthma Vans." In each program, organizations operating the mobile programs partner with inner city schools to identify children with asthmatic symptoms, screen them for asthma, create treatment plans if necessary, and arrange for follow-up care provided in mobile asthma care vans.

For families without paid leave, good health insurance, or transportation, the vans are an enormous blessing. Services are provided at no cost to low-income families; the vans visit schools regularly, so families can make appointments in advance that don't conflict with their work schedules; and getting to the van is only as difficult as getting to school—families don't have to travel long distances to get the care their children need. In addition, mobile asthma care does not require a referral from a primary care physician or a co-pay.

Programs in Baltimore and Chicago demonstrate the dramatic impacts of mobile asthma care for at-risk children.

Baltimore Battles Back

A survey by the Baltimore City Health Department shows that asthma is an acute public health crisis in Baltimore City with city schools reporting prevalence rates up to 20 percent, more than twice the national average.[14] Hospitalizations and emergency room visits for Baltimore children are two to three times the national average.[15] In 2002, the University of Maryland Hospital for Children decided to take action to keep kids out of emergency rooms and in their classrooms by launching the Breathmobile.

BETTER BREATHING IN BALTIMORE

When Joanne's two grandchildren came to live with her, seven-year-old Bobby seemed to be sick all the time with severe congestion, sinus infections, and constant coughing. He'd seen his doctor before moving in with his grandmother, but the repeated bouts of illness just didn't end. Fortunately, Joanne heard about the Breathmobile at Bobby's school and made an appointment for him to be evaluated there for asthma. The Breathmobile staff recognized Bobby's asthma immediately, and Joanne is convinced that "If not for the Breathmobile, it may never have been diagnosed." Shortly thereafter, Bobby's four-year-old sister was also diagnosed.

In addition to her relief that her grandkids have been properly diagnosed, Joanne says that the Breathmobile offers her convenience and support that are crucial to her and other working families. The Breathmobile arrives at school on the same Tuesday every month; there are no treks to and long waits at a doctor's office and no delays in getting an appointment. Joanne can schedule an appointment in advance or simply walk in with the kids. Prescriptions are given for medications or sample medications for those without insurance, and the Breathmobile ensures that every patient gets the medications and devices they need. Joanne believes that a lot of children wouldn't get their medications regularly otherwise.

The kids and parents are comfortable with the staff and not ashamed to ask questions. "When the children were first diagnosed, I knew nothing about asthma and they helped me understand what I need to do." They also educate the kids so they can take responsibility for their own treatment. "Once we started going to the Breathmobile, we felt so much better. We don't panic now because they train you in what to do. If you stay on the regimen they give you, most kids keep their asthma under control." Another benefit is that the Breathmobile educates the teachers who might not have known the symptoms of asthma and sent kids home from school thinking they had colds—forcing kids to miss school and parents to leave work. Now they can refer the children and their families to the Breathmobile.

Joanne says that she would never give up her visits to the Breathmobile and recommends it to everyone. "When I told my pediatrician that we were being seen by the Breathmobile, she said 'you are going to the perfect place.'"[16]

Baltimore's Breathmobile is operated by the University of Maryland's Hospital for Children under the direction of Dr. Mary Bollinger. In 2008, the Breathmobile served thirty-two sites in Baltimore City and seventeen schools in Prince Georges County, Maryland. School nurses, parents, or primary care providers refer children to the Breathmobile who exhibit signs or symptoms of asthma. Once referred, children receive the following services:

- Comprehensive asthma-focused history and physical
- Lung function testing
- Allergen skin testing
- Extensive asthma education (child, caregiver, and school health personnel)
- Prescriptions for medications or samples if needed, asthma care devices, and action plans

- Communication with primary care providers
- Case management

For those patients without insurance, Breathmobile supplies medication, services, and devices free of charge. Breathmobile staff then helps families apply for Maryland statewide health insurance.

In addition to children's treatment and asthma education for parents and educators, Breathmobile runs a successful after-school Asthma Club where kids go to learn what asthma is, how their medications help them, and how and when to take their medications. Asthma Club empowers the kids who become "peer educators" to help inform others, including their caregivers, about asthma and what to do.

Traveling Care in Chicago

"The mission of Mobile C.A.R.E. Foundation is to provide free and comprehensive asthma care and education to children and their families in Chicago's underserved communities via 3 mobile medical units, the Asthma Vans." Mobile C.A.R.E. currently sends its vans to sixty-two schools and Head Start programs throughout the city of Chicago.

Mobile C.A.R.E. conducts asthma screenings in Chicago schools and preschools by having families complete a five-question survey that determines their children's potential for an asthma diagnosis. Every survey is reviewed, and a Mobile C.A.R.E. staff member contacts families whose children appear to be at risk to offer a diagnostic appointment. Children diagnosed with asthma by Mobile C.A.R.E. are then enrolled in its program to provide ongoing treatment and education to help them and their families manage their children's asthma.

Mobile C.A.R.E. shares information with children's primary care physicians, and when appropriate, transfers patients' asthma care back to their physicians. Pediatricians appreciate Mobile C.A.R.E.'s focus on controlling children's asthma as it allows them to manage the overall health and well-being of their patients. Mobile C.A.R.E. also helps young adults transition from its services to a primary care physician for adults when they finish high school.

In 2008, Mobile C.A.R.E. provided the following services, free of charge, to approximately 1,500 children at sixty-two sites in Chicago:

- Specialized medical diagnosis and treatment, utilizing lung function and allergy skin testing
- Medications, equipment, and supplies
- Individualized family education sessions provided by bilingual personnel
- Take-home educational materials
- Training for local health care providers

How Mobile Asthma Care Creates Ripples
Both the Breathmobile in Maryland and Mobile C.A.R.E. in Chicago carefully and thoroughly track outcomes for the at-risk children and families they serve, and both programs have demonstrated important positive results.

- In Baltimore, trips to the emergency room for symptom flare-ups decreased by 60 percent.[17]
- In Chicago, asthma-related hospitalizations decreased by 20 percent.[18]

- The number of school days missed in Chicago declined by 40 percent,[19] and in Baltimore, children missed 1,674 fewer days of school.[20]

Both programs also decreased the number of days parents missed work due to their children's asthma, and families reported critical, but less tangible, improvements in their quality of life such as fewer restrictions on children's ability to participate in physical activities and an increase in their understanding of and ability to effectively manage their children's asthma. Baltimore's Breathmobile staff even found that children whose asthma symptoms are under control are more alert and less likely to fall asleep during the day at school because they sleep better at night.

According to Breathmobile's data, *$5 is saved for every dollar spent on providing mobile asthma care.* The Mobile C.A.R.E. Foundation calculates a total savings of $1,200 to $1,700 per child served. These economic benefits are realized by the entire community in lower emergency room and hospitalization costs, increased ability for parents to work and earn an income, and decreased costs of providing remedial education services to children who struggle academically because they miss many days of school.

In Baltimore and Chicago, over 6,000 children with asthma now face much brighter futures because mobile asthma care improved their health, and, therefore, their chances of succeeding in school and in life. These cities benefit in the long run by needing fewer social services for adults who didn't achieve their potential because they were just too sick as children.

Chicago's Mobile C.A.R.E. and Baltimore's Breathmobile are supported in part by donations from individuals. Your contributions to these programs will make a real and lasting difference in the lives of thousands of children with asthma, their siblings, their parents, and their schools and communities.

chapter 11

The Big Three
the global fund to fight aids, tuberculosis, and malaria

*"We often need small organizations to innovate
and create new models of delivery and large
international organizations to take those to scale."*

— JEFFREY SACHS[1]

On March 8, 2006, I was driving my daughters to school and listening to a story on National Public Radio about tuberculosis (TB) in the twenty-first century. I was shocked to learn that one-third of the world's population is infected with TB.[2] The host and several guests discussed the challenges of treating TB, including reaching those in remote areas of developing countries, battling drug-resistant strains of TB, and ensuring that sufferers completed the rigorous six-month treatment regimen necessary to cure their disease.

Jeffrey Sachs, director of Columbia University's Earth Institute and one of the architects of the Global Fund to Fight AIDS, Tuberculosis and Malaria, spoke briefly. What Dr. Sachs said changed the direction of my life and inspired this book.

Dr. Sachs said that the total cost to fund the treatment and prevention of TB over the next ten years was $30 billion per year. Then he broke that figure down:

To put that in perspective, that is three dollars per year from each of us. That's all we're talking about, a cup of coffee once per year from a Starbucks. You do that over a decade. That's $30 billion. That shows how affordable is this fight against this massive killer.[3]

That was $3 from each person living in the world's wealthiest nations—about one billion of us. I was stunned by the notion of such a tiny sacrifice doing so much good. I wasn't sure I had heard Dr. Sachs correctly. I researched the Global Fund to Fight AIDS, Tuberculosis and Malaria and saw that $3 was, indeed, the magic number, and I began to think about ripples.

THE DIMENSIONS OF THE BIG THREE

Together, the triple threat of tuberculosis, HIV/AIDS, and malaria claims more than six million lives each year.

Imagine losing the entire populations of Chicago, Phoenix, and Philadelphia *every year* or the equivalent of five September 11s *every day*.

As you know, poverty makes people more susceptible to disease, but here's another twist: Having any one of these "big three" makes you more susceptible to the other two. And around and around we go.

~~~~~~

DID YOU KNOW?

"In the early 1900s, TB, then called 'consumption,' killed 1 out of every 7 people living in the United States and Europe."[4]

~~~~~~

The following are a few key facts about each.

HIV/AIDS

- Around forty million people worldwide are infected with HIV, 95 percent of whom live in developing countries.[5] In 2004, 3.1 million people died of AIDS.[6]
- AIDS is the leading cause of death in Africa and the fourth-leading cause of death worldwide.[7]
- More than thirteen million children under the age of fifteen have been orphaned by HIV/AIDS, and this number is projected to double by 2010.[8]

Tuberculosis

- One-third of the world's population, or two billion individuals, currently carries the bacteria, *Mycobacterium tuberculosis*, which causes tuberculosis and most often attacks the lungs. It spreads from person to person through airborne droplets in crowded conditions and prolonged exposure to an actively sick individual.[9]
- Nine out of ten people infected with the TB bacteria *will not* become actively sick: Their immune systems will hold the bacteria at bay, preventing it from multiplying or spreading to other parts of the body. They will have "latent TB" and are not infectious.
- One in ten will become actively sick and will spread the disease to another ten to fifteen people.[10]
- The vast majority of TB deaths occur in developing countries, with more than half of all deaths occurring in Asia.[11] TB kills approximately two million people each year.[12]

- The average TB patient loses three to four months of work time as a result of TB. Lost earnings can total up to 30 percent of annual household income.[13] Some families lose 100 percent of their income.

Malaria

- Forty-one percent of the world's population lives in areas where malaria is transmitted (parts of Africa, Asia, the Middle East, Central and South America, Hispaniola, and Oceania).[14]
- Each year over one million people die of malaria—most of them young children in sub-Saharan Africa.[15]
- Persons may receive hundreds of infectious mosquito bites a year, becoming perpetually weakened by the parasite. Over a quarter of a very poor family's income can be absorbed in the cost of malaria treatment, and each bout of malaria causes its victim to forego, on average, twelve days of productive output.[16]

ANOTHER KEY FACT:
hope is affordable!

Despite these formidable statistics, *everyday donors can make a significant contribution to the prevention and cure of these diseases.* There are innumerable NGOs, government bodies, and other private and public entities working toward this goal, *but they will not succeed without help from YOU!*

THE GLOBAL FUND TO FIGHT AIDS, TUBERCULOSIS AND MALARIA

The Global Fund to Fight AIDS, Tuberculosis and Malaria was created to dramatically increase resources to fight three of the world's most devastating diseases, and to direct those resources to areas of greatest need.   —The Global Fund to Fight AIDS, Tuberculosis and Malaria[17]

If you're like many Americans, you've heard of the Global Fund but aren't certain what it does. Allow me to explain.

The Global Fund was conceived in 2000 by a consortium of NGOs; world leaders in development, economics, and public health; worldwide institutions including the G8, United Nations, World Health Organization; and scores of other public and private entities alarmed by the devastating HIV/AIDS, tuberculosis, and malaria pandemics. The Global Fund was created to be a single global trust that could raise, manage, and direct large amounts of funding and other resources in the effort to control and eventually reverse these three threats to worldwide health.

Unlike other organizations profiled in *Give a Little*, the Global Fund does not directly operate programs. It funds local programs already operating effectively in areas of urgent need.

The Global Fund employs a rigorous application process and requires careful monitoring of project outcomes. It vets the organizations that ultimately implement the programs, some of which are local, small in scale, and remote (and nearly impossible to discover by everyday donors) like the Suryodaya Women's

Empowerment Group in Nepal where a small group of determined women are helping to prevent and treat HIV/AIDS.

AIDS Widows Band Together for Support[18]

In the remote hilly areas of far western Nepal, the most unlikely of Global Fund partners are turning the world upside down. Kamala Malla is the founding member and president of a group of people living with HIV/AIDS. Even though she is a "high caste" woman, her husband's legacy has caused her to belong to a group that is discriminated against—she is living with AIDS.

Kamala Malla's husband passed away five years ago. During the first seven years of their marriage, her husband worked in India. Four years into the marriage her husband became sick. He told her to go to Dhangadi to get herself checked [for HIV/AIDS] and tell their neighbors that she was going to get checked for tuberculosis. When her husband died, she and her son were as good as ostracized by her community. They would not allow her to wash her clothes in the river. Her son was not welcome at the school. This did not mean that Kamala was planning to become a recluse. She had other plans.

Kamala has started the Suryodaya Women's Empowerment Group to provide care and support among each other and to others.

They make home visits, help with personal hygiene, massage the numb parts of the body with oil, and look after the needs of severe cases.

Kamala Malla cares for a man living with HIV/AIDS in his home. *Photo courtesy of the Global Fund to Fight AIDS, Tuberculosis and Malaria.*

Out of their twenty-five members, sixteen are widows and the remaining nine all have husbands with AIDS. These members are also sent regularly for CD4 counts, to test the level of HIV in their systems. The nearest facility is in Dhangadi, in the neighboring district, some five hours by bus. All members are on antiretroviral drugs (ARVs) and a nutritional support program.

Of the many services that the Suryodaya group offers, Kamala is particularly proud of the fact that they now are able to keep track of any person returning to the community from India, get their medical records, take them for AIDS counseling and testing and ensure they attend the follow-up process, according to the results.

Kamala recalls that a man had returned from India and was very ill. He immediately asked for Kamala. She remembers the man being tall and strong when he left for India. The same man was now unable to walk. The man has now been receiving ARVs for five months.

The Suryodaya members wish that CD4 counts could be done in Dipayal rather than having to send people all the way to Dhangadi. They have coordinated with an organization in Dhangadi for food and accommodation for those who cannot afford anything at all.

They would like to see the health officials at the Health Posts trained so that they do not have to go far for ARVs. Kamala says, "If such facilities were available nearby, we would even use a stick to drag ourselves for the medication."

According to the World Health Organization, Pakistan had the eighth highest incidence of tuberculosis in the world in 2006 with over 291,000 new cases of TB reported that year.[19] The Global Fund to Fight AIDS, Tuberculosis and Malaria has partnered with the Pakistani National TB Control Program and Greenstar Social Marketing (along with additional nonprofits and government entities) to fight tuberculosis in Pakistan.

Greenstar TB Program[20]

Abdul Ghaffar, 20, lost his father as a young boy and is the sole provider for his family, running a pan shop in Lasi Muhalla, Kalakot, Lyari. In January 2007, he began coughing constantly with sputum, experiencing regular bouts of fever during the nights with rigors and losing weight at an alarming rate.

Ghaffar visited multiple doctors to find the source of his illness, but only received treatment for his symptoms. After two months, his condition had deteriorated to the point that he was unable to walk or eat. His family became increasingly worried that his health would not improve.

Then one day his family received a pamphlet on the signs and symptoms of tuberculosis (TB) produced as a component of Greenstar's TB Good Life Project. As a result of the information provided in the pamphlet, Ghaffar's family was able to link his symptoms to those associated with TB. They immediately contacted Greenstar's community health officer (CHO), Amir Balouch.

The TB Good Life Project's slogans, "TB treatment at your doorstep" and "TB treatment only a phone call away," held true to its claim. CHO Amir Balouch made a house visit to Ghaffar to assess his condition. After recognizing the signs and symptoms of TB in Ghaffar, Amir called Dr. Abid Jalaluddin Shaikh of

Greenstar, for his professional opinion and recommendations on the next steps to take.

Since Ghaffar was bedridden and thus unable to make the trip to the nearby provider, Amir took a sample of his sputum and sent it immediately for microscopy at a nearby laboratory. Two days later, Amir collected the results from the laboratory and delivered the results to Ghaffar. Ghaffar had tested positive for TB.

"I was shocked to learn that I had TB and couldn't imagine returning to a normal life again," said Ghaffar. After undergoing counseling, Ghaffar was registered for TB treatment with Greenstar-trained provider, Dr. Daulat Lohano. He began his treatment in April 2007.

Ghaffar's treatment was monitored by CHO Amir to ensure compliance. His condition began to improve dramatically. The coughing and fevers had been controlled and he started gaining weight. After five months of treatment, Ghaffar returned back to his regular routine, opening his shop again to earn money for his family.

After eight months of treatment, in December 2007, Ghaffar was declared cured of tuberculosis, owing to his commitment to follow his treatment and the commitment of his family and the Greenstar team.

The Global Fund has worked with international NGO, Partners for Development, in Cambodia to create a network of health advisers in local villages who provide education to community members and referrals for services that reduce the incidence and/or mortality of HIV/AIDS, TB, and malaria.

One Mother's Loss Leads to Hope for Others

Kim Yeng is [a young mother] living in Cambodia. She was forced to leave school after the third grade because her parents could no longer afford to pay for her education. She had to help her parents by doing housework, farm chores, and taking care of her siblings.

Yeng married her husband at age 20, and the couple soon started a family. [T]he eldest child died at the age of 4 after several bouts of high fever. Yeng recalls, "The nurse said our child had 'krun sonthom' (cerebral malaria) and said we had waited too long to take her to the hospital. I was so careless with my kids. My child would have survived if we had given her better care."[21]

Kim channeled her grief by becoming a Village Health Volunteer (VHV) trained to improve overall health in her community by acting as a liaison between the public health system and local residents. In her role as VHV, Kim distributes information about a range of health matters affecting her village including malnutrition, sanitation, dengue fever, HIV/AIDS, diarrhea, and the prevention and identification of malaria—information that could have saved her own child's life.[22]

Yeng has earned the trust and respect of fellow villagers as a result of her work as a VHV, which was granted to her by the Provincial Health Department. Yeng is proud of her role and says, "I was elected as a Village Health Volunteer. I received strong encouragement from the PFD staff and wanted to learn everything I could about my new tasks. I have learned the importance of good health and what parents and the community need to do every day in order to improve the health of our families."[23]

A grant from the Global Fund to Fight AIDS, Tuberculosis and Malaria supports Kim's work to help prevent others from experiencing her family's tragic loss. *One affordable donation, one motivated mother, many lives saved.*

Here are some of the Global Fund's impressive worldwide results as of mid-2009:[24]

HIV/AIDS[25]
- More than 2 million people receiving antiretroviral treatment
- 62 million HIV testing and counseling sessions
- 3.2 million orphans provided with medical services, education, and community care

Tuberculosis[26]
- Detection and treatment of **4.6 million** cases of infectious tuberculosis

Malaria[27]
- Distribution of **70 million bed nets** to protect families from transmission of malaria
- Delivery of **60 million** malaria drug treatments

FUNDING THE FIGHT AGAINST THE BIG THREE

The Global Fund expands the scope of existing projects or initiates new ones in poor regions that need them. It relies on a network of volunteer experts to assess area needs. Then, from its large pool of donated funds, the Global Fund makes grants to the most promising projects.

Before it can make grants to projects, however, *the Global Fund must first fill that pool of funds.* I'm going to show exactly how *you* can afford to help the Global Fund take on the big three.

The Global Fund, working with other key organizations, has determined that worldwide costs of treating and preventing the big three range from $28 billion in 2008 to $31.2 billion in 2010. Pretty daunting figures, right?

Before we go on, however, keep in mind that American individuals gave a total of $229 billion to charities in 2007. That's *over seven times the total worldwide funds needed to be raised in 2010.*

The worldwide costs to treat and prevent the big three are not borne by the Global Fund alone. Other private and public sources fund projects as well. This leaves the following amounts

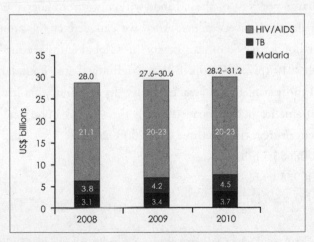

Global resource needs for the three diseases as estimated in March 2007.[28]

required by the Global Fund to meet its share of the fight against the big three.

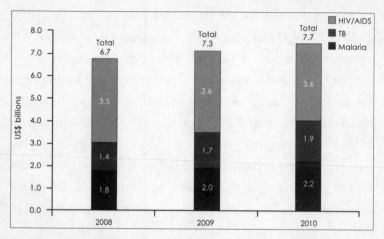

Resource needs for the Global Fund in US $ billions as estimated in March 2007.[29]

Large portions of these funds will come from contributions from national governments. Also, we can deduct the amounts other donors have committed to the Global Fund's efforts for 2008–2010 (primarily the Bill & Melinda Gates Foundation's $100 million pledge for each year).[30] In the end, this leaves a much smaller bucket needed to fill the Global Fund's pool to prevent or treat the big three over 2008–2010.

2008: $3.7 billion
2009: $4.9 billion
2010: $5.6 billion

Okay, now we're talking about *a tiny fraction of the $229 billion Americans gave in 2007.*

1.6 percent of $229 billion for 2008

2.1 percent for 2009

2.4 percent for 2010

This seems doable.

If every taxpaying household in the United States made an average contribution of $32.50 per year over the three-year period, the Global Fund could meet *the worldwide need* for treatment and prevention of the big three.

But the funds don't need to be donated by Americans alone. They'll be raised around the world, probably from additional public and private entities within other wealthy nations. If each of the billion people living in the world's wealthy nations donated *just $4.50 each year* (the average donation needed for 2008–2010), the world would be well on its way to controlling and eventually eradicating the big three. Just $4.50 once each year to help the Global Fund meet its goals, and you will help to prevent *over six million unnecessary deaths each year* from malaria, TB, and AIDS.

It can be done. Polio no longer terrorizes America's families. Millions of dimes did it.

By investing in the Global Fund, you can help finance a crusade on a massive scale. Your affordable check will join millions of other small donations creating a massive wave of action that will CHANGE THE WORLD.

~~~~~~~~~~~~

chapter 12

PATH
kits for clean deliveries

"Working for the survival and well-being of mothers is an economic, as well as a moral, social and human rights imperative. The well-being of children depends in large part on their mothers, and maternal survival has ripple effects that go beyond the family to bolster the economic vitality of whole communities."

—UNFPA, 2002[1]

"If a woman has a difficult delivery, a traditional cloth is tied between two sticks and we carry her for seven kilometres to the health centre. You know how long it takes to walk like that?"

—Togo, 1996, in "Dying for Change"[2]

Contagious diseases are not the only health threat in the developing world. *One of the most dangerous threats is simply being born.* Approximately one in twenty babies dies within a month of birth in sub-Saharan Africa.

IN THE WAKE OF MATERNAL DEATH OR INJURY

Infant and maternal mortality take a terrible toll on developing countries. What may seem like one family's tragedy contributes to the impoverished status of an entire nation.

When a poor woman needs care for complications during pregnancy or childbirth, she and her family face costs such as transportation, medications, admission fees to health care centers, and lost productivity and wages.[3] Some simply cannot afford these costs, and the lives of the mothers and infants are compromised. Others borrow money in order to obtain health care and are left under mounds of debt.

While 500,000 women die each year due to perinatal-related causes, another fifteen to twenty million experience acute or chronic debilitating injury or disability after giving birth.[4] Many of these women become less able to work in paid jobs or at home. Some disabilities, such as obstetric fistulae (a rupture of tissue that occurs during prolonged labor, leaving a woman incontinent and leaking urine and/or feces) cause women to be shunned by their families and communities. Often there is no source of health care or social supports for these women who are forced to beg to survive.

According to the World Health Organization, when a poor mother in a poor country dies, surviving children are three to ten times more likely to die within two years than children who live with both parents. They are also less likely to go to school or receive health care.[5] Some will have to enter the labor force, which "results in illness, injury and poor hygiene for the children."[6] Overall, "society is left with a higher number of one-parent households and an increased number of orphans, which may lead to deterioration or loss of social cohesion . . . and may foster depression and other psychological problems within households. Ultimately, these consequences have a repercussion on society in a number of ways, such as higher crime rates."[7] Studies also suggest higher instances of prostitution and drug use.[8]

~~~~~~

DID YOU KNOW?

Every year throughout the world:[9]

Over four million babies die within the first four weeks
of life.

Three million of these deaths occur within the first week
of life.

Ninety-eight percent of these deaths take place in the
developing world.

Twenty-six percent of newborn infants who die do so as a
result of infections that occur around birth.

More than three million babies are stillborn. One in
three of these deaths occurs during delivery, is largely
preventable, and is closely linked to the place of and care
provided during delivery.

~~~~~~

PATH: A CATALYST FOR GLOBAL HEALTH

PATH is an award-winning and inspiring nonprofit that innovates health-related technologies and systems that improve the well-being of the most vulnerable people around the world. PATH collaborates with individual donors (like you!), large private funders, NGOs, and governments to bring novel solutions to the most serious health challenges in the developing world. In particular, their work focuses on the following issues in more than seventy countries:[10]

- Safer childbirth and healthy children
- Solutions for emerging and epidemic diseases, like AIDS, tuberculosis, and malaria
- Health technologies designed for areas with few resources, by the people who will use them
- Health equity for women within the world's most vulnerable—and influential—populations
- The basic protection of vaccines for women and children around the world

PATH's activities can be grouped into three broad efforts: creating health technologies that are effective and appropriate for use in poor areas; strengthening existing distribution systems, so technologies can reach the poorest areas; and disseminating information and challenging local customs that contribute to poor health and disease.

An excellent example of its work is PATH's development of a sticky dot that affixes to vials and measures the viability of polio vaccine, which is highly heat sensitive, and therefore, easily destroyed while being transported to remote areas. Each sticker costs between 4.5¢ and 5.5¢ to produce and saves the international community millions of dollars each year by allowing open vials of vaccine to be used more than one day and preventing the use of nonviable vaccine, which could lead to hundreds of thousands of additional cases of polio and its crippling effects and deaths. In Author's Notes you can read more about this simple but ingenious technology now indispensable throughout the world.

PATH applied this same ingenuity when it developed a simple kit that significantly reduces the danger of giving birth or being born.

~~~~~~

DID YOU KNOW?

In 2005, about 536,000 women died of causes related to pregnancy or childbirth.[11]

Nearly all of these deaths occurred in developing countries, and most were preventable.[12]

"The adult lifetime risk of maternal death (the probability that a 15-year-old female will die eventually from a pregnancy or birth-related cause) is highest in Africa at *1 in 26*." By contrast, the lowest among developed countries occurs in Ireland, where a woman's lifetime risk is *1 in 48,000*.[13]

Among the least developed countries, only 38 percent of births were attended by a skilled health care provider in 2006.[14]

Infection is the second leading cause of maternal deaths.[15]

~~~~~~

PATH's Simple Solution to Saving Mothers and Babies

Clean delivery practices can result in reduction of neonatal mortality or morbidity by 58 percent to 78 percent and of incidence of neonatal tetanus by 55 percent to 99 percent.[16]

When clean delivery kits were used, women were 69 percent less likely to develop genital tract infections, and newborns were 92 percent less likely to develop cord infections.[17]

In 1992, PATH worked with Save the Children, UNICEF, and the United Nations Population Fund (UNFPA) to research, develop, and test a prototype of a single-use clean delivery kit designed particularly for use in remote areas. The kit would help prevent infections that cause so many deaths among mothers and newborns.

The World Health Organization had identified six principles for clean deliveries (the "Six Cleans") that could dramatically reduce the incidence of infection during deliveries: (1) clean hands, (2) clean perineum, (3) nothing unclean introduced into the vagina, (4) clean delivery surface, (5) clean cord-cutting instrument, and (6) clean cord care.[18] PATH turned these principles into five simple but essential tools to create a clean birth environment.[19]

- A piece of soap for cleaning the birth attendant's hands and the mother's perineum

- A plastic sheet about one square meter for use as a clean delivery surface
- Clean string for tying the umbilical cord (usually two pieces)
- A clean razor blade for cutting the cord
- Pictorial instructions that explain how to use each item in the kit

Photo courtesy of PATH

The kit was designed to be culturally appropriate and self-sustaining such that small commercial enterprises could ultimately assume production and distribution directly to users or to NGOs that would employ them through their work. Thus, the clean home delivery kit technology benefits local entrepreneurs in addition to users.

PATH conducted studies of the effectiveness of the clean home delivery kits in both Nepal and Tanzania. In both studies, the kits proved to significantly reduce the incidence of infection to mothers and newborns.[20]

Today, PATH does not construct or directly distribute the kits; however, it provides technical support to local organizations that want to create clean delivery kit programs around the world like Maternal & Child Health Product described next.

WOMEN'S MICROENTERPRISE PRODUCES AND SELLS KITS

In 1994, former employees of Save the Children who were involved in the creation and study of the clean home delivery kits in Nepal established Maternal & Child Health Product Pvt. Ltd. These local women produce and sell the kits affordably to local communities and NGOs. PATH provided technical assistance that helped the founders establish their business. Since that time, Maternal & Child Health Product (MCHP) has produced over 1.3 million kits.

In 2008, MCHP's cost to produce the kits was 27¢. They sold them for 28¢. Not exactly a cash cow for MCHP.

MCHP produces several other low-cost tools to help improve reproductive health in Nepal. To a small degree, profits from these projects help subsidize the low profit margin of the kits. *MCHP is a profit-making entity* that provides an income to its owners and employees; however, *their profits are modest and wages are livable but low.*

Contributions to MCHP can help ensure its ability to continue to produce and sell affordable clean home delivery kits. In this case, *you would not be making a deductible charitable donation*; instead, *you would be investing in a microenterprise* whose business is saving the lives of mothers and babies.

Think about it: An investment of $5 underwrites the production of eighteen kits, so $5 could save as many as *eighteen mothers and eighteen babies.* Safe births mean healthy mothers and babies who incur no hospital costs (and family debt) to care for infections or injuries. Healthy mothers are more productive at home and have healthier children who are more likely to go to school. Healthier and more educated children are better equipped to be self-sufficient adults. The ripple effect expands the value of your $5 investment exponentially!

INDIVIDUALS KEEP PATH PUSHING THE ENVELOPE

> The journey from an innovative idea to a program with worldwide impact is long. PATH is distinguished by our determination to carry good ideas from the first spark to sustainable, widespread impact. We rely on individual donors at every step along the way.[21]

PATH has worked with some of the largest funding bodies in the world to help study, develop, and distribute the technologies that are saving so many lives each year, for instance, USAID, the Bill & Melinda Gates Foundation, and international governments. But PATH couldn't even access these funds *without support from everyday donors like you and me.*

Many grants from the largest funders require organizations to raise "matching funds" in order to demonstrate the organization's commitment to the project and their access to resources. In these cases, small pools of funds from individuals allow organizations like PATH to leverage large pools of funds from the big guys. For example, PATH used $2,000 in funding from individuals to leverage nearly $300,000 in grants from the UNFPA and the Thai Health Promotion Foundation to provide new health services to vulnerable low-income teens in Thailand.[22]

PATH's Catalyst Fund comprises less than 4 percent of its total budget and is comprised of gifts from individuals. Yet, this 4 percent allows PATH to pursue large grants, innovate flexibly without the restrictions of large funders, and expand technologies and models it creates after grants for innovation expire.

In other words, *you* are the catalyst for global health.

A Donor's Story: Aeron Noe and Jacob Grotta

Aeron Noe and Jacob Grotta don't consider philanthropy a choice or a luxury. They see it as a social obligation.

The San Francisco Bay Area couple grew up in families with strong senses of civic duty, from global activism to local grass-roots causes. "We were both raised with the primary value that if you have more than you need, you give back," says Aeron, a full-time mother and freelance writer.

"We're hardly rich people in the *American* world," adds Jacob, chief operating officer for Moody's Wall Street Analytics. "But we're very rich in the *world* world. It just seems like it's a very natural thing to do."

Now the couple is doing their part to make a difference in communities throughout the world—and instill that same principle of giving in their own children, a three-year-old daughter and one-year-old son.

Aeron and Jacob made their first gift to PATH at the end of 2006, inspired by both the organization's financial responsibility and its impact on the health and well-being of other families like theirs. Health, says Aeron, is "a fundamental starting point for improving everything else in the world. If people don't have health, they're not likely to make any changes for the better in their own communities."

Having children has helped Aeron and Jacob put themselves in the shoes of other parents—and value even more the effect their contribution to PATH can have on the world.

"I hope that it's giving families like ours, that are growing up in communities without resources that we have access to, some kind of level playing field," Aeron says. "The thought that my children might need health care and I can't provide it for them is devastating. And no one should be in that position."

part four

education

chapter 13

Education and Poverty

The World Bank estimates that achieving universal primary education could cost approximately $11 billion a year—half of what Americans spent on ice cream in 2006.[1]

Like hunger and poor health, lack of education has the same reciprocal relationship to poverty: One begets the other. Low levels of education lead to poverty much as being born poor decreases one's opportunity to get an education. And I assure you, the effects of poor education run right across families, villages, nations, and the world.

Many countries do not provide a free primary school education. Even among those that offer free tuition, there are fees for books, school uniforms, transportation, etc. In sub-Saharan Africa, school fees can consume one-fourth of a family's income.[2] As a result, throughout the world, *75 million children* of primary school age do not go to school, and another *774 million adults are illiterate—that's nearly one in every six adults around the world.*[3]

Low levels of education are associated with many negative outcomes. Consider just the following three:
- Poorer nutrition and health
- Lower incomes and higher rates of unemployment
- Younger age at marriage and first birth

These three alone create the perfect storm for creating endless cycles of poverty here and around the world—wherever children and adults lack an education.

As you might expect, school attendance is lowest in the world's poorest countries. For instance, in 2005, only 34 percent of girls and 48 percent of boys completed primary school in Ethiopia.[4]

> *I go to collect water four times a day, in a 20-litre clay jar. It's hard work!... I've never been to school as I have to help my mother with her washing work so we can earn enough money...*
> *If I could alter my life, I would really like to go to school and have more clothes.*   —Elma Kassa, a thirteen-year-old girl
>   from Addis Ababa, Ethiopia[5]

When so few children attend school, many adults are certain to be illiterate. The World Bank describes literacy as "the percentage of people ages 15 and above who can, with understanding, read and write a short, simple statement on their everyday life."[6]

In Ethiopia in 2005, only 36 percent of the adult population was literate.[7] Low levels of education and illiteracy create barriers to critical information such as:

- Improved health and sanitation practices, dangers and symptoms of local diseases, directions for taking medication
- Improved agricultural methods that increase productivity
- Reproductive health practices such as family planning and prevention of STD transmission

- Child nutrition and health: Remember Kim Yeng in Cambodia who was unaware of the danger of malaria to her four-year-old daughter?
- Economic opportunities such as small business development

EDUCATION CAN END CYCLICAL POVERTY

Once a family is fed and reasonably healthy, acquiring an education can provide a lasting boost to a better standard of living. Educated parents have higher paying, more stable jobs. Educated mothers have healthier, vaccinated children with fewer instances of preventable diseases, malnutrition, and mortality. Educated mothers also have fewer children, so the family's resources of time, food, funds for education, health care, etc., are greater for each family member.

Healthier, stronger children go to school more regularly, and families living beyond subsistence are less likely to pull their children out of school in order to help provide for the family. Children who attend school regularly are more likely to succeed academically and have better odds of continuing to secondary school and beyond. Better-educated children and adults create a better-equipped workforce, which strengthens communities and the nation.

Finally, children who are in school and adults who are stably employed are busy improving their lives. They are unlikely to foment unrest and violence. Peaceful nations are more prosperous than those experiencing civil strife.

UNICEF operates programs that provide educational opportunities to the most underserved children around the world. Awatif's story describes the hope offered by an education.

Making Dreams Come True[8]

Awatif Morsy will never forget the day she heard that a new school would be opened in her village. "Someone came to the house asking for the names of the children who were not attending class," she recalls. "My mother gave them my name. I was so thrilled."

Like most eight-year-olds in Beni Shara'an Village in Egypt, Awatif's life until that day was divided between back-breaking work in the nearby wheat fields and confinement at home. To girls like her, the new school—a single classroom on the ground floor of a converted house—was a dream come true.

"We would go and watch the facilitators decorating the room. Everything was bright and colorful. There were games and pictures, things I had never seen before." Not everyone in the village was so enthusiastic, at least initially. Some farmers complained that the school would deprive them of the cheap labor the children provided. Even Awatif's own stepfather was unconvinced. "What does a girl need to study for?" he would ask.

Happily, that was not the view of Farouk Abdel Naim, the elderly merchant who was persuaded to donate the premises for the school to use. "I have come to believe that a girl's education is more important even than a boy's," says Mr. Abdel Naim. "A man can always make something out of his circumstances but a girl cannot. She needs to be educated in order to get on in life."

Eight years on, it's hard to find anyone in Beni Shara'an who does not share that opinion. The school—now expanded into three classrooms—is today seen as a wise investment from which the community is reaping tangible rewards.

Take the example of shopkeeper Ahmed Abdel Jaber. Himself illiterate (cannot read or write), he sent his daughter, Rawia, to the school as soon as it opened. "Until Rawia went to school, my store accounts were in a complete mess," he recalls. "But before long, she was taking care of all the books for me, as well as helping her elder sister to read and write."

In a village where illiteracy is an inescapable fact of life, there's no shortage of stories about how a daughter's education is making important differences to the quality of people's lives and businesses. How the instructions on a doctor's prescription or the writing on a sack of fertilizer suddenly seemed clear. And— more important still—how the example set by the children encouraged many older people to begin taking literacy classes themselves.

Awatif is now a student at the local secondary school, and is looking ahead to university, and beyond. "Many of the people here in Beni Shara'an want me to become a doctor," she says. "I myself want to be a teacher, so that I can pass on some of what I've learned to other children." That's already happening. Awatif has become a role model for other girls in the village. Eleven-year-old Faten is one: "I read all Awatif's stories," she says. "One day, I want to be just like her."

Much like filling an empty bowl, educating a single child can lift many lives. You can help provide that lift with an affordable donation to one of the programs described in the following chapters.

chapter 14

Developments in Literacy
getting girls to school

BHAGARATHI'S STORY

My mother married at an early age and had nine children. Only six are still alive. I stayed in school through the ninth grade so I am literate.

I could not study further because I was married at age 18, but I went to classes offered by Save the Children where I learned about how to take care of my family's health. I learned about the importance of cleanliness, nutrition and family planning. I have one son who is 10 months old. When I was pregnant, I went to

the hospital for a check-up every month. Now I am using contraceptives because I need to wait two years before my next baby. My husband and I want only one more child, either a son or a daughter. I am very satisfied with my present situation. I feel proud

Bhagirathi, age twenty, from Nepal.
Photo courtesy of Save the Children.

of myself, unlike some of my friends. I have discovered I am smart, capable and knowledgeable.

If my mother had had an opportunity to study, she never would have had an early marriage and given birth to nine children. Her life would have been entirely different like mine.[4] (Bold added by the author.)

~~~~~~

DID YOU KNOW?

Forty-six percent of girls in the world's poorest countries have no access to primary education.[1]

Worldwide, one in five adults cannot read or write: two-thirds of these are women.[2]

Universal primary education would prevent 700,000 cases of HIV each year—about 30 percent of all new infections in this age group.[3]

~~~~~~

Let's admit it: When we see impoverished families in developing countries with many children, we often wonder why on earth they keep having children when they clearly can't care for them all. There's an answer to that question, and it might surprise you.

An abundance of research shows that birth rates are strongly correlated with education levels among women and girls. This correlation is especially evident within the world's poorest countries. The following table, representing twenty of the world's

	NUMBER OF CHILDREN BORN BY EDUCATION LEVEL				
	NO EDUCATION	PRIMARY	PERCENT REDUCTION	SECONDARY OR HIGHER	PERCENT REDUCTION
Ethiopia 2005	6.1	5.1	16%	2	67%
Burkina Faso 2003	6.3	4.5	29%	2.5	60%
Haiti 2005/06	5.9	4.3	27%	2.4	59%
Mozambique 2003	6.3	5.3	16%	2.9	54%
Senegal 2005	6	4.8	20%	2.9	52%
Madagascar 2003/2004	6.5	5.7	12%	3.4	48%
Guinea 2005	6.2	5.1	18%	3.3	47%
Mali 2006	7	6.3	10%	3.8	46%
Liberia 2007	6	5.9	2%	3.3	45%

Lesotho 2004	5.2	4	23%	2.9	44%
Malawi 2004	6.8	6.2	9%	3.8	44%
Eritrea 2002	5.5	4.2	24%	3.1	44%
Nepal 2006	3.9	2.8	28%	2.2	44%
Uganda 2007	7.7	7.2	6%	4.4	43%
Benin 2006	6.4	5.2	19%	3.7	42%
Cambodia 2005	4.3	3.5	19%	2.6	40%
Rwanda 2005	6.9	6.1	12%	4.3	38%
Niger 2006	7.2	7	3%	4.8	33%
Chad 2004	6.3	7.4	-17%	4.2	33%
Bangladesh 2004	3.6	3.1	14%	2.5	31%

SOURCE: MEASURE DHS STATcompiler, http://www.measuredhs.com (accessed September 2008).

poorest countries, illustrates what happens to the number of children a woman bears when she acquires more education. You can see that fertility rates (i.e., the number of children born) drop between 31 percent and 67 percent when a girl finishes secondary school.

In a nutshell, girls and women with higher levels of education have and exercise more options for their lives. They get married later and are more informed and capable of controlling their fertility.

Unfortunately, in many poor nations, the education of girls is a low priority, often seen as a financial burden and loss of necessary labor in the home. In these countries, girls and women are valued for their ability to keep the home, produce food, care for children and other family members, and work in menial jobs to earn additional income for the family. Educated girls make less desirable wives as they are seen as being untrained in traditional responsibilities and likely to want a more educated husband, neither of these being compatible with village life. Often, it is dangerous for girls to go to school in rural areas; their low status puts them at risk of physical and sexual abuse and even kidnapping while traveling to and from school.

Sadly, those living in the poorest areas where women and girls are grossly undervalued don't realize that by keeping their girls out of school, they are keeping themselves locked in generational cycles of desperate poverty. Uneducated girls cannot earn a significant income; therefore their options are limited. They must marry at a young age, cannot practice family planning (both for lack of knowledge and lack of power), and have more children than they want or can effectively attend to. Thus, the children fail to achieve educational or economic success, and the cycle of poverty continues.

EDUCATE A GIRL, CHANGE THE WORLD

In 1992, Lawrence Summers, then vice president of development economics and chief economist at the World Bank, spoke at its annual meeting. The title of his presentation was "Investing in All the People: Educating Women in Developing Countries." Summers, formerly a professor of political economy and later president of Harvard University, Secretary of the Treasury from 1999–2001, and director of the National Economic Council under President Barack Obama, had determined that a large body of evidence demonstrated conclusively that *"investment in girls' education may well be the highest return investment available in the developing world."*[5] Summers described the social benefits of educating girls and women in his presentation.[6]

First, educating women reduces child mortality. The evidence that mothers channel more of their income to expenditures on children than their husbands do is overwhelming. Education also increases the willingness to seek medical care and improves sanitation practices. Small wonder that the children of more educated women are much more likely to grow up healthy.

Second, educating women reduces fertility. Educated women want to have fewer children and are better able to attain their desired level of fertility. In regions where female education levels are higher, fertility levels are lower; a pattern that continues to hold when a wide variety of country characteristics are held constant. Econometric studies within individual countries find that an extra year of female schooling reduces female fertility by approximately 5 to 10 percent.

Third, educating women reduces maternal mortality. A final group of beneficiaries of investments in female education is women themselves. Maternal mortality rates are ten times as high in South Asia as in East Asia. By increasing knowledge about health care practices and reducing the average number of pregnancies, female education significantly reduces the risk of maternal mortality. Based only on the impact on the number of births, and not including what are surely significant impacts on the risks associated with any given birth, one can calculate that an additional year of schooling for 1,000 women will prevent two maternal deaths.

Fourth, educating women helps prevent the spread of AIDS. Educated women are more likely to enter into stable marriages and look out for their reproductive health, and much less likely to become prostitutes. Each of these factors is crucial in stopping the spread of AIDS.

Fifth, educating women has important environment benefits. This year's "World Development Report" concluded that investment in female education is one of the highest return investments in environmental protection that developing countries can undertake. Educating women contributes to reduced fertility. By raising the opportunity cost of women's time, it discourages them from clearing forests, and it increases their ability to manage natural resources efficiently.

Summers then compared the financial cost of providing a single additional year of schooling to 1,000 girls in India and Kenya to the "cost to produce similar health and fertility benefits using standard medical and family planning interventions."[7] He determined that the cost to educate 1,000 girls in India (in the early 1990s) was $32,000, and $58,000 to educate 1,000 girls in Kenya. The resulting savings to the communities were significant. The reduction in costs related to infant and maternal mortality plus savings resulting from fewer pregnancies came to $109,300 in India and $136,600 in Kenya.

These savings do not include the additional social benefits realized by better educated girls in adulthood including reduced risk of contracting HIV, improved environmental practices, and better lives for future children (particularly daughters). Including these outcomes, savings (calculated to express the present value of these benefits to come in the future) rose by $52,000 in India and $66,000 in Kenya. Together, savings totaled $161,300 in India and $202,600 in Kenya. That's a 500 percent return on the investment in India and a 350 percent return for Kenya.

Since the time of Summers' work, both Kenya and India have greatly improved school enrollment, but each continues to have significant numbers of children in the poorest and most remote areas who are not attending school. The savings in Summers' investigation were realized by a *single additional year of schooling for just 1,000 girls in each country*. Imagine the potential for universal education throughout the world's impoverished countries.

DEVELOPMENTS IN LITERACY:
lighting the path to prosperity in pakistan

Developments in Literacy (DIL) is dedicated to providing quality education to disadvantaged children, especially

girls, by establishing and operating schools in the underde-
veloped regions of Pakistan, with a strong focus on gender
equality and community participation.[8]

Fiza Shah, DIL's founder and CEO, was acutely aware, even as
a child, of the disparities between rich and poor families in
Pakistan. She also realized that she was very fortunate. Her
family was financially secure, and education was the most important priority for the children—both the boys *and* the girls.
Fiza was able to attend high-quality private schools where she
excelled. By contrast, the children of the family's servants attended government-sponsored schools and could barely read or
write.

When she was eighteen, Fiza left Pakistan and began her
adult life. She raised her own family in the United States, and
as her children became more independent, Fiza realized that
she wanted to make a contribution to her country of origin. She
felt that she had, in a sense, taken a resource from Pakistan by
getting her education there and then leaving. Now she wanted
to give something back. She gathered like-minded friends
and went to work on behalf of poor women and girls in Pakistan, who she believes are among the most forgotten around the
world.

In 1997, Fiza launched DIL and took on the task of trying to
improve the state of education in Pakistan, primarily in the un-
derdeveloped rural areas. DIL grew quickly over the years, and
today it manages and/or operates 150 schools in all four provinces of Pakistan and educates nearly 15,000 students.

DIL'S VISION

> No child in Pakistan, no matter how poor or underprivileged, should be denied access to quality education. All children should have equal opportunity to reach their full potential and contribute toward the socio-economic betterment of their communities.[9]

Pakistan's gross domestic income of $2,570 per capita ranks it 155th out of 207 countries worldwide—reasonably far from the bottom, yet Pakistan has one of the world's worst literacy rates among girls and women.[10] In 2005, just 35 percent of women overall could read (as few as .05 percent in some rural areas)[11], lower even than the average 50 percent of women who could read within the world's twenty poorest countries.[12]

Here, a student in a DIL school explains why she feels it is necessary for girls to be educated.

Reema, Class Four, Rural Rawalpindi

> I live in an area where it is not considered necessary for girls to be educated; therefore, they are not provided with the right opportunities. In Pakistan, there are very few schools for girls in comparison with boys. Often parents do not allow their daughters to go to school, as they need them to do housework and take care of their siblings. It is important for girls to attend school so that they can play an equally important role in the progress of a society. Boys and girls have equal rights, and every child has the right to be educated so that they can lead a happy and prosperous life.

Education is the only thing that can change a person's life for the better.

Education gives girls self-confidence, which allows them to take an equal part in any walk of life.

HOW THEY DO IT

DIL establishes, adopts, and manages primary and secondary schools for underprivileged children in all four provinces of Pakistan. It manages 150 schools in total, which means it provides funds and has final authority over what happens at each school. DIL partners with local NGOs, which operate most of its schools on a daily basis.

DIL directly operates twenty-seven schools where its own staff conducts monitoring, provides administrative support, and works with the communities. These schools are in Islamabad, where DIL's main office is located, and in Orangi near its regional office in Karachi.

DIL's approach focuses on:

Local Partnerships
DIL establishes and operates schools in close partnership with regional NGOs and local communities. This has proven to be a highly successful medium for providing education to students in the most remote regions of Pakistan.

Child-Centered Education
DIL employs teaching methods representing the most current research on successful classroom practices. This approach is an alternative to the traditional system of repetitive memorization and has been shown to improve student achievement.

Child-centered education emphasizes creativity as well as social and critical thinking skills.

Curriculum Development

DIL enhances the standard government curriculum to prepare students for future success. DIL's curriculum is based on best practices used throughout the world and better equips students to succeed in the global marketplace.

Teacher Development

DIL recently opened the Teacher Development Center in Islamabad to provide ongoing in-service training as well as pre-service training for its teachers. The center, which caters to the needs of the rural teachers, designs, plans, and conducts training sessions based on student-centered teaching methods.

Access to Technology

DIL is in the process of implementing a plan to outfit its schools with computer labs so students will have greater access to technology. DIL is also developing educational software specifically designed to supplement DIL's curriculum.

Monitoring and Evaluation

DIL's key to success is a robust monitoring framework and complete financial transparency.

OVERCOMING OBSTACLES

Fiza and Annie Field, DIL's program manager, described the primary challenges to educating girls in Pakistan. DIL is working to push these barriers aside.

CHALLENGE: Lack of Parental Education

"This has been a challenge for our work in many of the rural areas of Pakistan. It has been difficult convincing the parents that educating their daughters is worthwhile and beneficial for them and their children. Often the parents do not want to send their daughters to school because of the high opportunity cost incurred to the family having her out of the home. The parents also come from a background and culture where girls have historically not been included in formal schooling, and we are faced with the challenge of

Mothers learning to read and write. *Photo courtesy of Developments in Literacy.*

trying to change their thinking. We have approached this obstacle in our work by working with local NGOs in the regions and developing relationships with the communities. It is only after an initial level of trust has been established that we can open a school and have the parents feel comfortable sending their daughters."

ANSWER: Teachers Empower Mothers in Janwari Goth

The Janwari Goth School is located in a remote village of Khairpur. It is a poor area where very few of the people are educated. Last year, the school was facing several major issues: Student enrollment was low, students were late to class, and their cleanliness did not meet school standards. Many of the teachers were worried that if the conditions did not improve, the school would be shut down for failing to meet the standards set by DIL.

That's when the teachers decided to take matters into their own hands. Farzana Sial, the school's head teacher, along with the other three teachers, gathered mothers for a meeting to discuss the problems plaguing the school. They wanted to get the mothers' buy-in on making the necessary changes to keep the school open. What they discovered, however, led them in a different direction.

When they asked the mothers to sign in for the meeting, they realized that none of the mothers could write. The mothers shared how embarrassing it was to use thumbprints because they weren't able to sign their own names. Seizing the opportunity, Sial offered to teach the mothers how to sign their names—with the condition that they made sure that their daughters came to school on time. "Nothing comes for free," she told them, "and, I am delighted to report that punctuality is no longer an issue at our school."

However, Sial did not stop there. "We then offered adult literacy classes twice a week for one hour after school to the mothers on the condition that they send their girls to school neat and clean and properly fed." The mothers attend class regularly and complete all their work assignments. Not only are they learning rapidly but are now making sure that their daughters get enough time to finish their homework. "I think we have achieved a lot through this endeavor and we will persevere." Sial's goal is to educate every member of the village. Sial and the teachers of Janwari Goth are indeed following DIL's mode of educating children and empowering communities.

CHALLENGE: Lack of Available Girls' Schools

"In many of the remote regions of Pakistan there are only schools available for boys. In many communities the boys and girls do not attend school together, and if there is only one school available it is designated as a school for boys. This circumstance has led to the involuntary exclusion of many girls. Even if the child (and her parents) had every intention of going to school, the lack of an available school meant that she could not. DIL has gone into many areas just for this reason, establishing girls' schools and even offering transportation for students who live far away from the school. We realize that in many areas accessing a school is still a very common problem."

ANSWER: Sisters Determined to Excel at School

Shamshad, an eldest child, has always willingly done extra household chores. She just didn't want to give her mother an excuse to pull her out of school. When Shamshad passed class three at the government-run primary school some distance from her village, her family members put a stop to her education. Unfortunately, the only school close by was a boys' school. A few years passed and her younger sister found herself in the same predicament. Around that time the DIL schools operated in partnership with Indus Resource Center started to offer transportation to students living within a certain distance. Shamshad and her sister pleaded with their mother to allow them to enroll, especially because this was a school for girls only; much to their delight, their mother agreed.

So Shamshad and her sister began their schooling once again. Both sisters work hard, always excel in their exams, and continue to help their mother with housework. Shamshad has passed class eight this year and is getting ready to enroll in high school. She is determined to open a school in her village, specifically for girls who do not have access to education. She hopes that by opening a quality school, she will be able to help other girls overcome the obstacles she faced in getting an education.

CHALLENGE: Low Enrollment Rates

"For many girls, education is only allowed in the primary grade levels. After that, many families keep their daughters home. Therefore, there is a high dropout rate as the children get to higher levels. DIL has worked hard with the families in the communities to ensure that the daughters are allowed to continue to go to school. **DIL's overall dropout rate in 2007 was only 2.4% compared to national dropout rate of 45%.**"

ANSWER: Getting Girls to Middle School

In Baluchistan, a rugged province in western Pakistan bordering Iran, the success of DIL's middle schools has been particularly striking, and the government is showing interest in replicating this model. They have also shown a willingness to take over the schools when DIL is ready to hand them over. This would make these schools sustainable and ensure lifetime support. DIL wants to make certain that the schools are well established, so that if they are handed over to the government at the end of the project period, they have a solid foundation and the quality of education does not fall. DIL would also continue its monitoring of these schools for a few years. The success of this project has been due to the close cooperation with the communities and the ability to address their challenges. For example, providing transportation for the students and the teachers helped enrollment and attendance, as the community members explained that it was difficult, in fact impossible, for their daughters to be seen walking to school on a daily basis.

DIL is committed to helping students get to middle schools. Previously the majority of girls would complete their primary schooling and then just sit at home. The boys found it easier to continue as they were allowed to travel distances and more schools for boys were available. Now the girls too are being provided the opportunity to pursue their dreams.

One of DIL's most important accomplishments has been convincing parents to allow their daughters to stay in school beyond the primary grades. According to DIL's 2006 Annual Report, "Slowly but surely, attitudes are changing and the new order is becoming acceptable. Seeing the earning power of females, parents are less keen to get them married, since the girls are no longer a burden but a financial asset." This represents a tremendous shift in beliefs and behaviors in many parts of Pakistan.

Here is a final story representing the determination required of so many girls and women in Pakistan to get an education. It is told by a DIL teacher.

Zuriat's Story

Since I started my primary education I have faced opposition from my relatives and community. When I turned 9 years old, I was very interested in studying further. My father refused to allow me to continue my schooling. He agreed to consent on one condition—I continue helping him look after the livestock till noon everyday. Permission to continue with my education was met with great opposition from our neighbors and community. So, after completing class five, I had to leave the school. For the next two years I remained very upset especially since I was exposed to programs on the radio and TV talking about the advantages of education. My interest and desire for education grew over this time, and I took to reading a book called *lengh munjha looh*, which was about a girl who struggles to achieve her goal in life.

She too faced many difficulties but eventually succeeded. The story motivated me into believing that death would be a better alternative to a dehumanized life. I told my father that I would commit suicide if he didn't allow me to study further. My father realized how keen I was and granted me permission to continue my schooling. This completely enraged my community. People made fun of us, and I was occasionally teased on my way to school. They tried everything possible to make it difficult for my family and finally ostracized us, cutting off all relations. Some powerful people of the community even came to my father and threatened him. They told him educating girls was against our culture and makes young girls choose who they want to marry. When all this didn't work they finally suggested poisoning me so that I would die rather than go to school. I had decided that if the community wanted to kill me, they could go ahead. I was not going to give up education, for death is better than an illiterate life.

During all that time I felt that everyone hated me, which hurt me a lot. I used to tell myself that our God and Prophet said that receiving education was an obligation on every Muslim man and woman. I wondered what kind of religion these people followed. Time passed and when I was in class eight, a post of LHW (Lady Health Worker) was announced. My father advised me to apply for the position and I was selected. I continued to study while I worked. It was during that time that the behavior of my community changed. They realized that by acquiring education, girls could contribute to the income of the family. They realized that without training, one could not even inject a syringe into a patient, as I was able to do.

In 2000, I started to teach in a school that was opened with the support of DIL. The same people who objected to my receiving an education are now sending their girls to be taught by me. Through my hard work I have succeeded in not only getting where I wanted to be but also in changing the attitudes and beliefs of my community. Now everyone respects me and it makes me happy that I am able to educate their children despite how they felt about me previously. As a schoolteacher I am confident that I can educate these girls and train them to be strong so that they too are able to resist social and cultural pressures and fulfill their dreams.[13]

HELP A PAKISTANI GIRL ON THE ROAD TO EDUCATION AND BEYOND

DIL's direct costs to educate a girl for one year are $80. That's less than *$1.54 per week* for you or me. The research has been done—Lawrence Summers showed us the economic value of educating a girl for a single year. These are tangible benefits that ripple. They ripple outward—into the community and beyond—and they ripple forward—through a girl's lifetime and even her children's. Just $80, the same amount you could spend on a couple of dinners out or a new pair of shoes, could completely change a girl's life.

~~~~~~~~~~~~~~~~~~~~~~~~~~~~~~

chapter 15

Safe Passage
education lifts children out of the city dump

"It struck me how little it takes to make a difference."

—Hanley Denning[1]

Guatemala isn't poor enough to be counted as one of the world's least developed countries. Far from it. The average gross national income (GNI) per capita among the least developed countries (as defined by the United Nations) was $1,182 in 2007.[2] Guatemala's GNI in 2007 was $4,440.[3] Definitely poor, but not far from the median GNI for all countries of $5,900.

Still, some of the world's poorest people can be found in Guatemala, and it has one of the highest levels of *extreme poverty* in Latin America. It has the highest level of malnutrition and is ranked lowest in Central America on the Human Development Index of United Nations Development Programme, which measures life expectancy and education.[4] This country's poorest people live on the fringes of society, tucked away, ignored by most of those around them. Some of these are the devastatingly poor children and families living in and around the Guatemala City Dump. Here, approximately 2,500 people spend each day digging through the garbage searching for food and other items that can be recycled, sold, or eaten to sustain their families.[5]

"EL ANGEL DEL BASURERO"
(ANGEL OF THE GARBAGE DUMP)

Hanley Denning's passion was helping children at risk, and during the last decade of her short life, she managed to help several hundred of the world's most destitute children—those living within the confines of the Guatemala City Dump and its adjacent slums. Hanley's path to the dump wound from Maine, where she was born, raised, and attended Bowdoin College, to Boston's Wheelock College, where she earned a master's degree in early childhood education, to a Head Start classroom in North Carolina, where many of the students she taught spoke Spanish. Hanley wanted to improve her ability to communicate with her students, and at the age of twenty-six, she left the United States intending to spend a year or so in Guatemala, serving the poor and improving her Spanish skills, but Hanley never made it back to that Head Start classroom. Her path ended at the fetid mounds of trash heaped in Guatemala's capital, Guatemala City.

One year became two as Hanley volunteered with *Nuestros Ahijados*, or "God's Child," an organization serving poor children and families on the outskirts of Antigua. Just as she was preparing to return to the United States in 1999, she accompanied a friend to see the slums of Guatemala City and the conditions of the urban poor in Guatemala. There, she encountered poverty and deprivation like she'd never seen: people living in and around the Guatemala City Dump, the largest landfill in

Central America, occupying a forty-acre ravine and containing one-third of the country's accumulated garbage.

Picking through the trash to collect recyclable materials they could sell for about 50 quetzals, or $6 per day, the *guajeros*, or garbage pickers as they're known in Guatemala City, were living in shelters built from tin, plastic, and wood found at the dump. They had no access to sanitation and were eating and wearing what they could salvage. Children were filthy and sick and mostly unsupervised in the dangerous landfill where adults and children were regularly run over by bulldozers and garbage trucks or buried and lost under sliding or collapsing mountains of refuse. The stench alone was unbelievable yet several thousand people called this home. Many came from generations of *guajeros* and had lived at the dump their entire lives.

Hanley was so moved by the living conditions and the plight of the children living in garbage that she sold her possessions, took her savings from the bank, and opened the first Safe Passage program, a drop-in center housed in a small church on the edge of the dump that provided a simple lunch and refuge to twenty children whose parents worked at the dump. The children didn't attend school as their families couldn't afford the fees for uniforms, books, and tuition, and many of them worked alongside their parents to supplement the family's income. Hanley was shocked by the children's living conditions yet came to understand that the *guajeros* were hard-working proud people who provided a critical service to their country by salvaging one million pounds of materials for recycling each day.

Still, Hanley wanted to give the children an opportunity they'd never had: to be safe, to learn, to be attended to, to be children. She recruited children as they walked to the dump with their parents, and over time, more and more children began attending and coming to Safe Passage regularly. Within the first several months, Hanley had raised enough money to get forty of the children enrolled in public school—many as old as ten and eleven beginning first grade. Public school in Guatemala meets for half the day, so the children returned to Hanley's program after school for educational reinforcement, lunch, and supervision until their parents returned from the dump.

By its second year, Safe Passage was no longer a drop-in program; children were required to attend school. Hanley convinced illiterate parents, otherwise ignored by their own city and nation, that their children could realize a better future through education. Over the next seven years, Safe Passage grew and expanded to include early childhood progams; health care; arts and vocational training programs; weekend clubs for children and mothers; and English, computer, and adult literacy classes. A beautiful new building was constructed to accommodate the many children, parents, and employees coming to Safe Passage each day. By 2007, Safe Passage was a thriving hub of opportunity for the residents of the dump and its surrounding slums.

In eight short years, Hanley's unstoppable determination had created something magical from a mountain of waste. She was known to residents as *El Angel del Basurero* (Angel of the Garbage Dump). Tragically, Hanley died in a car accident traveling from Guatemala City to Antigua in January 2007. She was only thirty-six years old.

Though Hanley's life was short, she created a ripple that endures and expands. Safe Passage now provides comprehensive services to over 500 children every year.

HANLEY'S HOPE

Luis Alfredo Batz was born on February 19, 1988. In 1999, Luis, his mother, and two sisters were working at the dump when Hanley invited the children to a small church with about twenty other children. At first, only Luis's sisters went

Luis Batz. *Photo courtesy of Safe Passage.*

to Hanley's program, because Luis was committed to working to help his mother sustain his family. Finally, after many invitations, Luis began attending, too.

At that time, the children received bread and cold beans; Luis smiles as he remembers that the juice was only water with sugar, but the children accepted these tokens happily. He remembers that at the end of the day, Hanley always shared her ideas with them; all of the things that she expected to come true some day.

Luis wondered if the program was going to survive. He saw that 20 children had grown to 100! When he was told that a new building was under construction for the children, he was very excited. His excitement doubled when the new building opened.

According to Luis, "The happiest moment of my life was when I came to Safe Passage. As its name says, I feel safe here."

Soon, Luis will be in high school. He has been an outstanding student. He has begun working at Safe Passage by helping in the kitchen. In addition, he is quite an amazing singer and actor. His English skills are advancing as well.

Luis's dream is to go to college and become a doctor or psychologist, because he likes helping other people, especially by telling his story. He says that he'll never forget Hanley's words: "Never stop struggling."

With tears in his eyes, Luis says that Hanley is his guardian angel and that she was like a mother to him. He thinks that everything he does is a gift, and he wants to go far in this life. He wants to do this for his family and the people who love him.

Today, Safe Passage continues to fight the perfect storm of poverty created by generational cycles of hunger, poor health, and lack of education faced by the children and families living in and around the Guatemala City Dump.

NUTRITIONAL SUPPORT

Safe Passage offers meals and snacks to children who attend its programs so they can concentrate and learn at school. For some, this is the only meal of their day. Through regular attendance at school and the educational reinforcement program, children at Safe Passage can also earn monthly bags of groceries full of food staples for their families.

HEALTH CARE

Children who are healthy attend school more regularly. Unfortunately, pollution and toxins generated at the dump create multiple health hazards. Common ailments among the children include recurrent respiratory and skin infections and stomach/intestinal disease. Adults who have worked at the dump for a long time risk methane toxicity and even cancer. Safe Passage operates a local health clinic that provides care for the children attending its programs as well as their direct family members.

EDUCATION

Many times, the children at Safe Passage are the first members of their family to attend school. As a result, "they often need the extra encouragement, guidance, and support to continue their studies." Safe Passage provides this to every child through tutoring and help with homework from its own Guatemalan teaching staff and volunteers from around the world. The half-day Educational Reinforcement program also provides enrichment activities that build the children's knowledge and skills.[6] In a relatively new effort to help them succeed in school, Safe Passage now provides an early education to preschool-age children from 8 a.m. to 4 p.m. The children participate in fun learning activities and receive a meal, two snacks, milk, and a vitamin.

All the children at Safe Passage participate in English language instruction, which expands their employment opportunities as adults. Finally, the parents of children at Safe Passage also have access to educational opportunities including instruction in basic reading and math literacy.

VOCATIONAL TRAINING

In order to ensure that every child can achieve self-sufficiency as an adult, Safe Passage offers vocational training programs including computer skills, English, and baking/cooking. Safe Passage also operates Posada Lazos Fuertes Guest Inn and Hotel

Training Program, a microenterprise that both generates operating revenue for the agency and provides training in the service industry to older youth.

WEAVING IT ALL TOGETHER

Families living on the very edge of destitution often need a safety net for times when circumstances cause them to slip through the cracks. Intensive, individualized support from social workers provides the final thread in the web of support created by Safe Passage. The social work team monitors the well-being and success of every child enrolled in its programs. It works with the twelve public schools that enroll Safe Passage students and aids children's performance in school by securing academic support services as needed and facilitating communication between parents and schools. Through case management, social workers strengthen families by helping with medical and legal issues and intervening in cases of neglect and physical or substance abuse.

When dysfunction or uncontrollable circumstances push a family over the edge, children's health and education suffer. Safe Passage social workers help these families pull their lives back together.

HOW YOUR CONTRIBUTIONS CAN HELP

- $10 will provide sixty children with Saturday programs including dancing, special excursions, theatre, music, sports, and art—offering them a safe place and fun activities when school is out of session.

- $25 will provide purified drinking water to the children, staff, and volunteers at Safe Passage for two weeks.
- $30 will provide a uniform for one child attending primary school in the Safe Passage program for the school year.
- $50 a month will sponsor a child by covering the educational expenses to attend public school, and provide him or her with medical attention, social development services, and nutritious meals.
- $100 will provide health care for 60 two- and three-year-olds at Safe Passage's nursery school program for one month.
- $150 will help build the scholarship fund for teens to continue vocational training programs and/or a specialized academic path to receive a recognized diploma ensuring them a successful future.
- $200 will provide a hot, nutritious lunch for all 500 children in the Safe Passage program for one day.
- $350 will provide the salary for one of Safe Passage's teachers for one month.

A Donor's Story: Jacob Carter

My most vivid memory of Safe Passage is when the children used to line up outside of the library and we would go over the rules. "Quien quiere compartir una regla de la biblioteca?!"

Since I left Guatemala in July 2006 I have visited twice. I participated in the one-year memorial service for Hanley and ran in the 5K in Portland. And of course, I've probably told about a thousand people about Safe Passage and how much I believe in its mission.

My experiences at Safe Passage have taught me many lessons. People are people everywhere, and we are where we are because of the circumstances that we grew up in. These days I am much more aware of, and thankful for, the privileges that I have in my life and that I experienced growing up: to never underestimate the power that each one of us has as an agent of change; to believe in the potential in every one of us, but especially our children in Guatemala, and the ability to overcome seemingly insurmountable obstacles; that everyone has something to give; that the cycle of poverty can indeed be broken by educating our youngsters and giving them the tools to make a better life for their families and future generations of Guatemalans.

I am now working for a student exchange organization called Youth for Understanding. We facilitate international exchange for high school students. I work as a Volunteer Manager, and my experiences at Safe Passage gave me the skills to be effective in the job that I am doing now.

I am living in Cambridge, Massachusetts, and am hoping to unite Safe Passage supporters in the greater Boston area to help raise awareness, and funds, for Camino Seguro.

chapter 16

Ounce of Prevention Fund
get 'em while they're young!

*"Research is clear that poverty is the single greatest
threat to children's wellbeing."*

—National Center for Children in Poverty[1]

Over the course of a decade, I had the opportunity to watch
theory and research affirmed five days a week in classrooms, on
playgrounds, and at lunch tables. The tiny cohorts in this "laboratory" that was our child care and early learning program learned
how to walk, talk, and take turns. They looked at books and
"read" the stories to themselves. They learned how to use a spoon
and put on their own shoes. They dazzled us with their two-
word sentences and ability to follow two-step commands. They
laughed, they cried, they tested their teachers to their wits' ends.
They turned three, they left us, and they thrived.

These children were "at risk." They came primarily from
single-parent, low-income homes, and accordingly, were at risk
of delayed development, failing in school, and a host of other
problems, including poor physical and mental health, poor social
skills, teen pregnancy, low levels of education, and unemployment. They ranged in age from six weeks to three years. Each of

them entered our program as a perfect, receptive vessel, just waiting to be offered every opportunity to explore and learn.

The children had a job, and they devoted themselves to it. Their work was to play. We provided the materials and a supportive environment; they did the rest. It was delicious to watch these tiny people blossom. They certainly didn't look like future failures. They looked like healthy, happy children with the whole world ahead of them.

For many children at risk in the United States, the picture isn't so rosy. Today, *nearly one in five children under age six lives in poverty*. Not just in low-income households, where income reaches up to twice the poverty level, but *in poverty*. In 2008, that meant a two-person household with an income of *$14,000 or less*.

Right here, in our own backyard, 20 percent of children live *in poverty*.

In Chapter 4, you saw the federal poverty guidelines, which are used to define "being poor" in the United States. Individuals and families with incomes below the guidelines live in poverty. Yet research shows that households require incomes of at least two times the federal guidelines in order to meet basic needs.[2] For example, in 2008, a family of two with an income of $14,000 or less was considered poor, yet studies show they actually needed at least $28,000 for a reasonable standard of living. Households or families with earnings in the range between poverty and twice the poverty guidelines are considered *low-income*.

Shockingly, *39 percent of all children in the United States, or nearly two in five, lived in low-income or poverty-level households in 2007. That is, they lived in households earning too little to meet their basic needs.*

Research by neuroscientists and child development experts over the past decade has established that very young children's early experiences permanently affect their brains. Early experiences help determine their IQ and potential for learning, their reactions to stress, their propensity for anger and aggression, their ability to have healthy relationships with others, and even their risk for disease.[3] Children from low-income households can reach kindergarten already lagging far behind their more fortunate peers, and once children reach kindergarten, delays in these areas are difficult and expensive to remedy.[4]

Yet like other issues in this book, the facts may be daunting, but there is a pathway out. Fortunately, there are programs that fortify children at risk so they can beat the odds and realize their full developmental potential before kindergarten even begins.

THE DOLLARS AND SENSE OF EARLY LEARNING

In 2003, Art Rolnick, senior vice president and director of research for the Minneapolis Federal Reserve Bank, released a paper titled, "Early Childhood Development: Economic Development with a High Public Return." Rolnick showed that public and private investment in early learning programs produce some of the highest returns compared to all other types of economic development projects. In the paper, he stated "The return on investment from early childhood development is extraordinary, resulting in better working public schools, more educated workers and less crime."[5]

Rolnick found that children who participate in early childhood learning programs are:[6]

- Much less likely to be retained in the first grade
- Much less likely to need special education
- Much more likely to be literate by the third grade
- Much more likely to complete high school
- Much more likely to get a good job and raise a family
- Much less likely to commit a crime

Nobel Prize–winning economist James J. Heckman of the University of Chicago reviewed the longitudinal results of the Perry Preschool Project, which provided preschool to three- and four-year-olds from 1962 to 1967. Participants were interviewed at age forty to determine their long-term outcomes. According to Heckman, the "report substantially bolsters the case for early interventions in disadvantaged populations. More than thirty-five years after they received an enriched preschool program, the Perry Preschool participants achieved much greater success in social and economic life than their counterparts who are randomly denied treatment."[7]

Additional research, most notably the Abecedarian Project conducted at the University of North Carolina by Craig Ramey, has demonstrated strong benefits to providing high-quality, full-time child care *beginning in infancy* to children from poor families.

SPEND A LITTLE, GET A LOT

Here it is. *One of the best bangs for your charitable buck in this book.* If you want to make a tremendous investment in reducing poverty for the 40 percent of children born into low-income households in the U.S., write a check to a high-quality early learning program. You'd have to get an interest rate of more than 16 percent to do more with that buck by letting it sit in a bank account. On the other hand, you can expect a 16 to 1 return on that buck *and improve our society for your children and their children* and beyond by donating it to an early learning program.

A CITY AT RISK

In 2006, the Chicago Public School system enrolled 401,738 students with *86 percent coming from low-income households.*[8] Nearly nine out of ten students attending public schools in Chicago that year were at risk of failing, and unfortunately, many did. The average dropout rate among Chicago's high schools in 2006 was 45 percent.

CHICAGO'S CHAMPION FOR CHILDREN

Fortunately, Chicago had a visionary businessman and philanthropist concerned about high school dropout rates and developing a well-prepared workforce. Irving B. Harris had an extremely successful career in business, founding the Toni Home Permanent Company with his brother and then selling it in 1948. He was later the chairman of Pittway Corporation and the Liberty Acorn Mutual Fund. An avid reader and student of life, Harris researched what was known about the roots of school failure, which led him to a profound and unwavering belief in the potential of early learning.

Harris paired his convictions with his wallet and helped found numerous projects that demonstrated the power of early education and changed public perception and policy, including

Head Start, the Erikson Institute for Advanced Study in Child Development, the Harris-Provence Child Development Unit at the Yale Child Study Center, the Harris Graduate School of Public Policy Studies at the University of Chicago, and in 1982, the Ounce of Prevention Fund.

"THE OUNCE"

In Chicago, Illinois, the Ounce of Prevention Fund (commonly known as "the Ounce") prepares the area's poorest children to succeed in school by targeting the entire prenatal through pre-school period of development. The Ounce also operates programs for at-risk mothers that help them experience healthy pregnancies, adjust to the challenges of parenthood, and become effective parents and advocates for their children's education. Building on years of developing and improving programs for at-risk children, the Ounce also trains early childhood professionals, helps build effective statewide early education systems, advocates for increased investment in quality early education in Illinois and nationally, and provides technical assistance to early childhood advocates in other states.

The Ounce's programming for children begins before birth through the services of "doulas"—women who are trained to provide guidance and support—to expectant and new mothers. Children as young as six weeks attend the Ounce's Early Head Start programs and then it's on to preschool. By the time an Ounce of Prevention Fund child starts kindergarten, he or she has experienced enriched learning environments, healthy meals, regular visits to the doctor and dentist, screenings for early learning delays, intervention for problems as needed, has parents who are better able to meet the challenges of parenthood, and has had plenty of time to work—that is to play, play, and play! Children are offered materials and experiences that challenge and stimulate every area of development, including language, intellectual, social, emotional, and physical skills and lead to early success in school.

Two Months into the School Year, and Five-Year-Old Kyle Is Struggling[9]

While others in his kindergarten classroom are able to chime in as their teacher leads them in an alphabet game, none of the letters seem to be "clicking" for Kyle. He will proudly tell you he can count to ten, but his disappointment is palpable when he isn't able to correctly recognize a "6" or "4" from among the other numbers. He's frustrated and unfortunately can't find the words to express how he feels. So he shows his frustration the only way he knows—by acting out, or lashing out at other students. Or sometimes he just withdraws completely. At least by misbehaving, he can get someone to focus on him for a while—and since he's often overlooked amidst his stressful home environment, it is attention he desperately craves.

Kyle's escalating frustration is matched by that of his teacher, who knows she just can't give him—or similar children—the attention and support needed to make up their academic deficits. Already, she's afraid she's looking at another case in which the education system—and ultimately another child—fails.

She also knows it didn't have to be that way. Another of her students, Nicole, on paper looks just like Kyle. The difference is that Nicole arrived at kindergarten having been immersed for five years in a high-quality, evidence-based, early education program uniquely geared toward at-risk children. Nicole's entry into public education has been positive and affirming, and she is clearly thriving. Early learning prepared her to succeed.

Each year, the Ounce helps nearly 11,000 children achieve their potential.

Irving Harris once said, "The first few months of life are not a rehearsal. This is the real show."[10] The Ounce provides a comprehensive range of services beginning prenatally that maximize its assault on the disadvantages of being born poor. Your donation to the Ounce will start a ripple that begins in the womb.

The Ounce of Prevention Fund is a public-private partnership that uses private dollars to develop and evaluate innovative programs and public dollars to bring those programs to scale. In Illinois, the Ounce works to break the cycle of poverty with its broad range of home- and center-based services:

Doulas—trained community professionals who guide young, inexperienced parents-to-be through the prenatal, birthing, and postnatal stages

Long-term home visitors—trained professionals who go into families' homes to support young mothers and fathers as they build strong relationships with their babies, return to school and work, create homes that facilitate early learning, and set goals for the future

Family and peer support groups—program staff who provide parent education, pre- and postnatal counseling, and facilitate peer support

Infant mental health—consultants who intervene to promote healthy parent-child attachment and to help decrease the impact of trauma a parent and/or child may have experienced

High-quality, center-based early education for children from birth to age five using Head Start (for ages three to five), Early Head Start (for birth to three-year-olds), and other public funding

Each year the Ounce trains over 600 home visitors and doulas who in turn serve over 7,000 children and families across Illinois. The Ounce partners with community-based agencies in Chicago and throughout Illinois to deliver high-quality Head Start and home-visiting programs.

In 2000, the Ounce opened the Educare Center, a school for infants, toddlers, and preschoolers that combines Early Head Start and Head Start programs and other research-based strategies to provide high-quality early learning experiences to approximately 150 low-income children in one of Chicago's poorest neighborhoods. At Educare, the Ounce puts best practices into action, and program and research staff work together closely to test innovations that ensure that every child receives individualized care and attention that promotes his or her optimal development. In

Reading begins early at Educare. *Courtesy of the Ounce of Prevention Fund.*

partnership with the philanthropic community, the Ounce has replicated its Educare model in programs in seven other states through its Bounce Learning Network of Educare Centers.

Angela and her son Rashawn participated in the Ounce's Educare program, and it changed the course of both of their lives.

I enrolled Rashawn at Educare when he was about three years old. I was working on and off part-time. I never had a problem with working but I didn't have a formal education. That factor lowered my ability to land a good paying job with benefits.

Originally Rashawn was enrolled in a school downtown, but when I expressed concern for the safety of one of the children, I was told to get out and never come back. As I drove down the street with tears in my eyes and Rashawn in the car, I noticed some pastel colored buildings, and I was curious about them. They seemed odd, almost out of place. So I stopped in and inquired about it. I was so taken by the beauty of the place and the comfortable calm feeling from the staff, I immediately applied for enrollment. He was accepted. His first teacher was Ms. Ruby.

I was inspired by the type of education Rashawn was receiving. The teaching staff was professional but you could talk to them and not feel like you were being investigated. Rashawn was a foster child at the time. We were constantly in conflict with his mother. I was in a dilemma due to housing and safety issues. He stayed in the system until he was six years old. I adopted him. During that difficult time, the staff at Educare counseled and mentored both Rashawn and me.

They encouraged me to go back to school. Reluctantly, I returned to college and received my associate's degree. I was hooked.

I kept going until I earned a bachelor's. I made the Dean's Honor Roll and then earned a masters degree. I am currently working as a literacy instructor.

In addition to going back to school, I became a parent that was involved with Educare. I recruited parents and families. I took it upon myself to help the Educare center out in any way I could. Whenever they needed a parent to help out I was there. I worked on several committees, became vice president of the parent committee, earned Volunteer of the Year, Most Hours Volunteered, Most Creative Volunteer, and more. Later, I was asked to join the Ounce's board of directors to help share the message and my story about Educare and the Ounce.

Today, Rashawn is in middle school and doing awesome in school and at home. He has an excellent attitude toward learning. He has always maintained an above-average standing in class; in fact, he is in the top 10 percent of all sixth grade students in the Chicago public school system.

Through its many programs, the Ounce
- reaches at least 11,000 children and families in programs across Illinois
- educates more than 3,000 program, community, and opinion leaders about key issues and policies in early childhood development
- trains as many as 700 early childhood practitioners through a statewide training institute
- advocates for more than $400 million in state funding and $2 billion in federal funding for early childhood services

- partners with a dozen states to build their innovative programs and sound public policies for at-risk children from birth to age five.[11]

A majority of the Ounce's funds come from government sources (69 percent), and these are directed to support specific programs and activities. Only 8 percent of the Ounce's funds are "unrestricted" and can be used at the organization's discretion. These funds come primarily from individuals and allow the innovation and evaluation of programs that improve the lives of children and families every day. Another real example of how small donations can fuel important change.

part five

~~~~~~~~~~~~~~~~~~

infrastructure, tools,
AND *technology*

chapter 17

Bridges, Bikes, and Buckets (of Clean Water)!

*"We think the earth is generous; but what is the incentive
to produce more than the family needs if there are no
access roads to a market?"*

—GUATEMALA 1997[1]

Merriam-Webster's Collegiate Dictionary, Eleventh Edition, defines *infrastructure* as "the underlying foundation or basic framework; the system of public works of a country, state, or region; the resources required for an activity." Prosperous societies require infrastructure.

Infrastructure provides access—to roads and bridges that lead to schools, to health care, to markets for buying and selling. The poorest areas around the world are also those that are most remote and isolated from the resources we use and take for granted every day.

The massive gap in infrastructure between developing and rich nations forces the poor to expend enormous amounts of time and energy simply to survive. Imagine spending hours every morning carrying a barrel and walking miles to the only reliable source of clean drinking water in the village. Imagine walking back carrying a full barrel of water on your back or your head.

©2007 Paul Jeffrey/ACT-Caritas,
courtesy of Photoshare

Imagine a three-hour walk to and from the nearest clinic to get modern medicine for your sick child—rather than hopping in your car for a quick trip to Wal-Mart or Walgreens.

Imagine not knowing how to give that medication to your suffering child because you never attended the nearest school, half a day's walk away, so you cannot read the label.

Imagine your children walking two hours to and from school each day. Imagine wondering if they will have to wade across a three-foot rushing stream to get home today because it rained heavily in the afternoon, and water now runs over their path.

Imagine saying good-bye to your husband as he leaves for the two-week expedition that is required to haul a harvested crop to market.

Imagine watching helplessly as your wife slowly dies in bed, possibly from malaria or AIDS or from a simple infected wound that went untreated and infected her bloodstream. Imagine having no medicine, no doctor, no hospital, no comfort within reach.

These are daily realities for the extreme poor without proper infrastructure.

The data that follow illustrate the infrastructure gap that exists between Ethiopia, Zambia, Cambodia, and the United States.[2] They show that those living in areas that lack roads, transportation, electricity, and clean water, live shorter, sicker, less educated, and less prosperous lives. (The data are from 2005 unless otherwise noted.)

	ETHIOPIA	ZAMBIA	CAMBODIA	UNITED STATES
Population, total	75,173,000	11,478,317	13,955,507	296,507,000
Surface area (sq. km)	1,104,300	752,610	181,040	9,632,030
Total network of roads (km) (thousands)	39,000 km	91,000 km[b]	38,000 km[c]	6,544,000 km
Percent of roads that are paved in 2004	15	22	6	65
Passenger cars per 1,000	1	2	na	461
Electric power consumption (kWh per capita)	34	721	53	13,648
Percent of population using improved water source in 2004	22	58	40	100
Life expectancy at birth	52	41	58	78
Mortality rate, under five (per 1,000)	127	182	87	8
Estimated total deaths caused by diarrhea in 2003	99,750	15,960	9,240	300
Percent of population that is literate	36[d]	68[a]	74[d]	100
GNI per capita, PPP (current international $)	$630	$1,090	$1,380	$41,680

[a] Number from 1999.
[b] Number from 2001.
[c] Number from 2002.
[d] Number from 2004.

MEDICAL EMERGENCY IN
THE MIDDLE OF NOWHERE

Little Banchamlak is six years old, and she has accidentally knocked over a pot of scalding water, which burns her severely on her entire arm and upper chest. If Banchamlak were Bianca, and instead of living in the remote Mauksane village in Gonder, Ethiopia, she lived in Detroit or Houston or Boston, she would be rushed to a children's hospital immediately and provided intensive care for her burns until she was fully recovered. Instead, the moment that Banchamlak knocks over the pot of boiling water begins a days-long journey—not to a hospital, but to her aunt's village, as her family has no money to get medical treatment, and anyway, there is no hospital within a two-day walk. Perhaps the aunt will be able to provide some help. So severely burned Banchamlak and her father begin their trek, which takes two days to walk, then two days by bus, then another day walking.

But to make that trek Banchamlak needs to be transported across a broken bridge—by rope. Men line up on either side of the 240-foot-long bridge, which spans the Blue Nile 50 feet below, and hold a rope across the gap—20 feet of missing bridge that separates them. People, animals, and parcels are tethered to the rope and pulled across the divide by the men. With her burns, Banchamlak cannot be tethered directly, so she is placed in a large sack, which is tied to the rope and pulled across. After the terrifying crossing, there are still days of travel to reach her aunt's village.

Unfortunately, Banchamlak's aunt is unable to do much for her burns, so the little girl makes the reverse trek home. Over time, scar tissue pulls her chest and upper arm together while her lower arm is locked in a 90-degree angle. She is unable to extend her arm at all. Now Banchamlak will be a burden to her family and her village where women conduct a great deal of physical labor in and out of their homes. In her current state, in her remote village in Ethiopia, Banchamlak is considered severely handicapped. Her lifelong prospects have been made bleaker than they were at her birth.

This is a true story, but with a much happier ending than one might expect. Lack of infrastructure, combined with grinding poverty, turned Banchamlak's burn into a potentially lifelong grave disability. Fortunately for Banchamlak, a group of determined Westerners were headed her way to fix that broken bridge. Along the way, they also managed to fix Banchamlak's broken body. We'll get to that in Chapter 19.

In places where infrastructure is scarce, innovative nonprofits are helping poor communities create or access needed tools and technologies. The following chapters describe three such programs that are massively transforming infrastructure with help from donors like you.

~~~~~~~~~~~~~~~~~~~~~~~~

chapter 18

Bridges to Prosperity
changing lives one bridge at a time

"We take bridges for granted. Yet, in the rural poor areas of the world, bridges are considered miracles."

—BRIDGES TO PROSPERITY[1]

In September 2004, National Public Radio aired a story about senior citizens retiring to countries in Central America in order to stretch their retirement nest eggs. The reporter interviewed a woman who had moved with her husband to Nicaragua's Pacific coast, where she said, "Our Social Security is much more than enough to live quite well here." The reporter described the retirees' $100,000 two-bedroom bungalow situated near a clubhouse, pool, and the ocean.

The woman then described the luxuries she and her husband could afford in their adopted country that would be far out of reach in the United States. Her comments were staggering and unforgettable: "Good heavens, you can get a maid for less than $3 a day really. I mean, it's marvelous. We have one three times a week. She didn't come today because, evidently, we had a rain the night before. *They could not swim through the river. During the dry season, they can just practically walk across. During the wet season, they actually swim across.*"

Later in the interview, the retiree mentioned that her housing development funds a local health clinic; still, I've never forgotten the image conjured by her description of her maid swimming across the river, potentially risking her life as the river is sometimes too dangerous to cross, to a job paying less than $3 per day. I've never stopped thinking about building a bridge across that river.

In international dollars, or at "purchasing price parity," which equalizes the currencies of different nations in order to provide a true picture of the relative strength of world economies and levels of poverty, Nicaragua's gross national income per capita was $2,510 in 2007.[2] That means the average Nicaraguan lived on what $2,510 could purchase in goods and services here in the United States that year. Imagine *living for a year in the United States on $2,510*. This is desperate poverty.

Fifteen months after I heard the story about retirees in Nicaragua, I was listening to *Worldview*, a program concerning global affairs that airs on my local public radio station. That day, the show's host, Jerome McDonnell, was interviewing Ken Frantz about his organization, Bridges to Prosperity, and its construction of footbridges in remote areas of developing countries.

At some point during the interview, as Ken was describing the many ways a footbridge transforms the prospects for local residents, I had the proverbial lightbulb moment. I distinctly remember thinking, "Of course, a footbridge!"

It occurred to me at that moment that there must be innumerable such projects, technologies, services, etc., that inspire that "aha!" that comes when simple logic meets ingenuity, when a big problem meets its match in a single determined and creative mind. I started investigating. I found irrigation pumps, backpacks full of food, low-energy lightbulbs, llamas, and asthma vans. I determined that these projects relied on everyday donors like me.

It turns out that Ken Frantz, the founder of Bridges to Prosperity, had a similar moment.

BRIDGING THE INFRASTRUCTURE GAP

In March 2001, Ken Frantz was killing time in a waiting room of a Ford dealership while one of the trucks belonging to his construction company was being serviced. He picked up a December 2000 copy of *National Geographic*, and opened it to a picture that brought Ken's life as he'd known it to a halt, and his life's mission into laser focus.

Photo courtesy of Bridges to Prosperity

The photo, taken by Nevada Wier while rafting on the Blue Nile on assignment for *National Geographic* with author Virginia Morrell, showed a man being pulled by rope across a massive stone bridge missing its midsection. It captured the sheer guts and determination that people living in the world's most remote areas display on any given day just to survive.

"I looked at the photo once, twice, three times," Ken recalls, "and it came to me: What I want to do is repair that bridge." With more than thirty years of experience in construction and development along with his own business, Ken knew he had the resources to do it.

In another twist of fate, Ken's brother, Forrest, had also seen the photo and had the same inspiration. Within a month of seeing the photo, Ken had formed Bridges to Prosperity and found a new calling: to build or repair bridges for the poor around the world. Three months after opening that copy of *National Geographic*, Ken and Forrest, along with Ken's nephew Brett Hargrave, were in Amhara in the north central region of Ethiopia conducting an initial assessment of the requirements to repair the Sebara Dildiy, or "broken bridge" in the local language of Amharic.

Rotary member Stephanie Heinatz traveled to Ethiopia and wrote an account of life surrounding the Sebara Dildiy for the August 2008 issue of *The Rotarian*, the monthly journal of Rotary International.[3] She described a typical crossing of the treacherous divide.

Life here, where most families barely survive on less than US$1 a day, revolves around the market. A good day could bring in enough money to allow a child to go to school. But most children stay home to shepherd animals and chase monkeys away from small vegetable plots. Homes are mud huts with dirt floors.

Barefoot and tired from a 20-mile trek, the young Ethiopian farmer nimbly descends a line of steep cliffs and jagged black rocks leading to the Blue Nile's edge. When he finally reaches the base of a bridge nestled deep inside a gorge, he lets out an exhausted sigh. He sets down his heavy basket of fresh bananas, bound for sale at the market, and waits.

The Sebara Dildiy looms before him. Only one person can cross the Blue Nile's broken bridge at a time, making long waits common. Eight men—four on each side of the missing span—tend a yellow rope stretched across the opening. After 20 minutes, the banana merchant slips a loop around his torso. Carefully, he eases himself off the edge of the bridge and for several minutes hangs danger-ously, 50 feet above the fast-moving river, as the men pull him across inch by inch. About 50 people cross safely on this day. Falling from the rope—as one man did not long before—means almost certain death. The merchant gathers his goods, which are pulled across the river after him, and begins hiking the last 26 miles to the market on the other side of the bridge.

Goats and donkeys are taken across upside down, their hooves tethered to the rope. Larger animals, such as cows and oxen, cannot be transported across with the rope. According to Bridges to Prosperity, at the time of this crossing the men who operated the rope collected and shared a charge of 26¢ (or 3 Ethiopian Birr) per man to cross, a huge portion of the traveler's daily wages, which at approximately $1.75 per day must support his entire family.

In his personal journal, Ken described a tiny village near the broken bridge:

Maksane village (area called Maksanet): On the top of a small hill that rises about 100 feet above the surrounding terrain. No electricity, no telephone, no running water (people walk 2+km to find water in wet season; probably 5 km in dry season), no vehicles. . . . just donkeys. No post office, no nothing . . . only grass hut homes. I would guess size of village and surrounding area at 800 people, but this could be on low side. No one in Maksane has an address to receive mail. There are no roads, but possible to get to by 4 wheel drive from Iste. Just wide trail that is impassable during wet season. No community building. There seems to be a small field for children to play football of sorts. There is also broken grinding wheel powered by one cylinder diesel that is community owned . . . but it has been broken for years. Corn and other grains requiring grinding must be sent to Arota by donkey.

The village lacked infrastructure of any kind, imprisoning its residents in centuries of poverty.

HOPE ARRIVES: SUNDAY, FEBRUARY 10, 2002

"11 months have gone by since I first saw the *National Geographic* photo of the broken bridge. After 10 months of preparation, I am headed to fix what I said I would fix, the 360 year old Broken Bridge on the Blue Nile."[4]

Less than a year after picking up that copy of *National Geographic*, having acquired the financing, materials, and technology needed for the project, Ken was overseeing construction of a steel truss to span the bridge's gap. The task required 25,000 pounds of steel, cement, and equipment, which were trekked 26 miles to the building site on the backs of donkeys. With the help of hundreds of volunteers from local villages, the bridge was in place and in business just ten days later.

Following the completion of the bridge repair, Ken made the following comments at a gathering to celebrate. The Nile River is called the Abai River in the Amhara region of Ethiopia. It separates two districts within Amhara named Gonder and Gojjam.

We meet here today to retire an old and very tired rope. A rope that has done its best to do the impossible. Was the impossible the thousands and thousands of people the rope carried to safety on the opposite shore? No it was not. Was the impossible the thousands and thousands of kilos of teff, animal hides, and coffee carried across? No it was not. The rope did much more than that . . . it kept hope *alive that someday the bridge would be fixed. I know this to be true, you see, for it was the rope that caused the famous photo to be taken and put in the world's largest magazine, and . . . it was I that saw the picture of the rope and the* hope *it represented . . . and it was the rope and the people on either end that stirred my heart to act . . . and that is why my friends that we came here to help.*

We came to retire this great rope of hope.

The Sebara Dildiy has been broken for too long. For too long have the people of the two great provinces of Gojjam and Gonder been separated. For too long have families been separated. For too long has the trading between the villages on either side suffered. For too long has crossing the Abai evoked fear among those forced to cross by the rope. And . . . for too long has hope and promise been kept waiting. So let us celebrate, for we shall wait no longer!

Ken was incredibly moved by the dignity and graciousness of the villagers. Here, he writes of their expressions of gratitude.

During the celebration, individual people continue to bring me gifts of eggs . . . yes eggs. Think of the poorest person you can imagine, one with children suffering from malnutrition, a small hut, a 2 acre farm they till by hand, and torn clothes. These people are bringing me eggs. All thank me, and then give me one egg at a time. I don't casually send off the gift to others. I help with each egg. By the end of the day, I am given more than 120 eggs.

More than 450,000 people live in the area surrounding the Sebara Dildiy bridge repaired by Bridges to Prosperity. Ken estimates the bridge provides *50 to 100 crossings per hour.*

BRIDGES—TO HEALTH, WORK, EDUCATION . . . PROSPERITY

Bridges create access—to schools, health care, markets, and other services such as post offices and government administration offices. More than that, bridges allow the most isolated people to obtain the advantages of modernity—despite living much as their ancestors did in their rural villages.

Bridges to Prosperity's mission is to "empower poor African, Asian, and South American rural communities through footbridge building, thereby advancing personal responsibility, community public works, economic prosperity, and access to schools, clinics, jobs, and markets." It estimates footbridges are needed in fifty developing countries and that bridges would improve prospects for one billion people.

Two elements are keys to Bridges to Prosperity's ability to operate a very lean enterprise while creating tremendous impact. First, Bridges to Prosperity does not construct footbridges for villagers; it teaches them to build and maintain their own bridges, and some of these newly inducted engineers go on to share their knowledge and skills throughout the country. Second, board members and volunteers with a shared passion for empowering others donate their time, energy, expertise, and personal financial commitments.

Bridges to Prosperity employs only three staff: two are located in countries with active bridge-building projects, and a director of operations works in the United States. A twenty-member board of directors and volunteers conduct the rest of the organization's activities—dozens of individuals bringing a vast array of skills to the projects. Many are engineers, Rotarians, and folks in the construction business.

Bridges to Prosperity staff and volunteers construct demonstration bridges that provide training to future builders. Those who are trained as "lead engineers" go on to other regions to initiate bridge-building projects and train additional engineers, thereby growing the number of bridges constructed exponentially and creating a wide variety of future economic opportunities for local residents including supplying and hauling materials and providing labor.

In order to maximize its impact, the organization spends two years in a country providing training and building partnerships with public and private entities that increase the country's internal capacity to build, maintain, and repair bridges once

Bridges to Prosperity moves to another country. By the time they leave, the organization has created a vast pool of stakeholders and future bridge builders.

A Donor's Story: Scott Cook, Founder and Chairman, Intuit, Inc; Board of Directors of eBay, Procter & Gamble, and the Asia Foundation

We became donors because of Bridges to Prosperity founder, Ken Frantz, and his groundbreaking approach that delivers high bang per philanthropic buck. He has created a unique delivery system that works. It does so by having no overhead or administrative expenses and by having the lion's share of work performed by volunteers. What is truly novel is how he turns those he trains into for-profit franchises in order to scale and aid the millions in need . . . this is groundbreaking and is a model for future aid and development strategies.

Funding comes from individual donations, Rotary Clubs, the Rotary Foundation, and corporate sponsorship, such as the well-known New York engineering firm Parsons Brinckerhoff (PB). Bridges to Prosperity does an outstanding job of leveraging its small annual budget ($188,426 in total revenues for 2006) to obtain additional funding to build bridges. Its two-year budget to build eight additional bridges in Ethiopia (following the Sebara Dildiy repair) and train two lead engineers to continue the work was $215,268. By the end of 2008, Bridges to Prosperity had constructed fifty-five bridges in twelve countries and developed newer, more cost-efficient bridge technologies, significantly reducing their costs per bridge.

A PLAN TO PUT ITSELF OUT OF BUSINESS

Bridges to Prosperity's "2020 Plan" will result in projects in twenty countries with 200 lead engineers trained by the year 2020—increasing its worldwide footbridge construction to 250 per year, and touching the lives of twenty million people. The ultimate goal of the 2020 Plan is to put Bridges to Prosperity out of business, having empowered enough people that its initiation and direction of projects is no longer needed.

A plan to provide twenty million of the world's poorest people with access to schools, health care, and markets by teaching villagers how to construct low-cost, simple, safe bridges that communities and/or local governments can build and maintain. Each bridge linking the most destitute and isolated people to three of the most crucial keys to prosperity.

In May 2007, Bridges to Prosperity taught local villagers how to construct a suspended bridge across the Santo Cruz River near the village of Mezapata in Peru. For years, villagers in Mezapata have harvested coffee beans considered some of the world's best; however, the work is labor intensive and residents sell their product for only 5 percent of the final cost to the customer who purchases it in a U.S. grocery store. Villagers earn approximately $2.70 per day—not enough to meet the basic necessities of life and certainly not enough to provide a safety net for times when the price for the beans drops or the harvest is poor. In addition, villagers were spending precious wages to repair the poorly constructed wooden bridge each time it was washed away by floods and preventing them from getting to work.

Enter Bridges to Prosperity, which helped villagers construct a 55-meter (180-foot) suspended bridge across the Santo Cruz. The bridge will withstand the annual floods and should remain viable for a minimum of twenty years. The bridge will serve approximately 3,000 people who live on either side. At a cost of $335 per meter, the bridge cost $18,425 to construct.

In 2008, a footbridge in Latin America cost $335 per meter to build, and $450 per meter in Africa—costs in Africa being higher due to high tariffs, lack of competition, high costs of materials, and poor distribution systems. That may seem like a lot. As a potential donor, you may be thinking that your small contribution won't go far in helping to build a bridge. The key is to consider the cost of the bridge to an individual user. When broken out this way, you'll see that a small contribution provides many, many crossings over an $18,000 bridge.

For instance, if you divide $18,425 by 3,000 beneficiaries, *the cost is only $6.14 per person for the lifetime of the bridge.*

If you amortize this amount over twenty years, *the cost is 31¢ per person/year*, an incredibly small investment.

You can also consider the cost per crossing: If the bridge is crossed fifty times per day (a conservative estimate), the cost per crossing is $18,425/20 years/18,250 crossings per year=*5¢ per crossing!* Remember that the men pulling travelers across the Sebara Dildiy charged 26¢ per crossing and that this consumed approximately 15 percent of a traveler's entire wages for a day. Finally, Bridges to Prosperity estimates that the boost in economic productivity resulting from one of its bridges pays for its construction within six to twelve months.

Need I say more? This is a cost-effective, high-return project that you can support with an affordable donation and help profoundly change lives.

EPILOGUE:
banchamlak at twelve years old

Despite her devastating injury, Banchamlak's story has a happy ending. In a serendipitous turn of events, Ken Frantz's nephew, Brett Hargrave, who'd accompanied Ken on the first trip to survey the bridge, met Banchamlak and her family while exploring her tiny village of Maksane. Banchamlak's father showed her injuries to Brett, Ken, and Forrest and asked if they could help his daughter. All three men were deeply saddened by Banchamlak's circumstances but did not see a way to help. They suggested she be sent to Bahir Dar, the nearest province with a hospital that could treat such a serious condition.

Even after returning to the United States, however, Brett could not forget Banchamlak. He decided to help her get the treatment she needed to improve her prospects for a better life in the remote highlands of Ethiopia. Eight months later, when Ken returned to conduct the repairs of the Sebara Dildiy, he sent for Banchamlak and her mother.

This is Ken's account of the effort to fix Banchamlak while fixing the broken bridge.

[Banchamlak sees] Dr. Mengistu in the clinic we have set up. She comes . . . with her mother to river, and this time crosses the river on a temporary gondola. . . . the rope is gone! The bridge is being repaired! Ken tells her that it was

Brett's wish to help her. Mengistu examines her and tells Ken that it might be possible to operate in Bahir Dar. We tell her mother to bring her back in about 5 days. We will take her to Bahir Dar with us to have the operation. [We] will pay and provide for her care. Banchamlak comes back on Sunday night with her oldest brother and crosses the new bridge! She is now in our care, so she and her brother sleep on Papyrus mats with us at our camp. They are also fed. They are excited and nervous of what is to come.

The next day, Ken, Banchamlak, and her brother make the 6-kilometer trek from the bridge repair camp to Mota, the nearest town. From there, they drive to Bahir Dar.

Banchamlak and her brother stay with Dr. Mengistu [the camp's physician] at his home in Bahir Dar. We meet the next day with the surgeon, a friend of Mengistu's. He examines Banchamlak's burn. She removes the blouse that we had purchased for her in Mota to further reveal that the burn extends not only across her arm, but across her breast and is pulling her breast towards her shoulder. The surgeon says he can operate Friday or Saturday. Ken asks the doctor about his experience level. Ken is worried like a father would be. Ken privately worries about the fact that there is not a single sterile operating room in the whole of Ethiopia. Ken knows that having such an operation is risky in terms of infection because the protective skin barrier is laid aside.

The price is agreed to of 200 ETB (Ethiopian Birr) for the operation, 50 for Anesthesiologist, 2 days at the clinic @ 100, 20 for 2 weeks of physical therapy, 50 for antibiotics,

50 for dressings and antibiotic creams, 10 for shoes, 120 for bus to Iste then Jara Gedu for her and brother, 30 for taxi to physical therapy, 70 miscellaneous . . . 700 ETB total . . . about US $85! It would cost 200–400 times this much in the USA. Even air fare to bring her to the USA is 20 times as much (while Ken later boards the Lufthansa flight from Addis to Cairo, he speaks with a Baptist Missionary volunteer from Atlanta who has just returned an Ethiopian child back after having plastic surgery in the USA. Ken can't help but to think of how many operations this generosity could have bought in Ethiopia! 100–500 operations can be bought in Ethiopia for the price of 1 person being taken to USA for surgery. Also, in-country operations boost the local economy and help strengthen medical facilities. However, many operations cannot be done in Ethiopia, so some charity groups have no choice but to bring them to the USA. In Africa, all help is a blessing, in spite of inefficiencies). Mengistu offers to provide and pay room and board for Banchamlak . . . Ken accepts. Banchamlak is happy at his house with a television!!!

The operation takes place on Saturday. To get Banchamlak's mind off of her upcoming operation, Ken takes her and her brother, Dr. Mengistu and his cousin to visit Tis Issat falls, an hour drive down river from Lake Tana. It is a glorious sight. It is amazing to see all the water pass over. It looks like there is so much more than there was in the river at the Sebara Didiy. The river must be much deeper than I had previously thought. I tell Banchamlak goodbye, and fly out to Addis shortly thereafter. Ken calls from Addis on Saturday. Everything went OK . . . she is just coming out of anesthesia. Ken calls again on Wednesday. Everything OK. No sign of infection. The contracture was released on both arm and breast . . . she is outside playing!!! Mengistu assisted during the surgery and there were no complications. She will, however, need to come back in 3–6 months for one last contracture release and skin graphs to her breast. Her brother returns to escort her home one week before her physical therapy is complete. He is in a hurry to return home. It is possible that her father has returned home from picking coffee in the south, and he is excited to see her. Her brother promises that Banchamlak will continue her exercises.

Banchamlak is now in high school. Life is not easy—she struggles to pay school fees that allow her to stay in a dormitory during the week, as the high school is a three-hour walk from her village. Still Banchamlak's prospects are greatly improved by the bridge that brought hope.

COMMENTS FROM OTHER VILLAGERS WHOSE LIVES HAVE BEEN TRANSFORMED BY A BRIDGE

Alem, a young woman, says: "Women from my village helped to organize and build this bridge. This has opened my eyes to what I can do."

Melaku, a village elder, says: "I am so happy, I can now die in peace."

Ayele, a young mom, says: "I can now get my baby to the Clinic when he is sick."

Tadesse, a village leader, says: "We never knew that we could accomplish so much by ourselves. We want to use what you taught us to do other projects."

Mebratu, an engineer, says: "I have been trained on two bridges. Now I will teach others to teach others."

Antihun, a young man, says: "Due to my wife and my involvement in the construction of the new bridge, both of us are village leaders now. My wife will show women what they can be. Now I understand what women leaders can do to help improve our lives."

Muhammad, a businessman, says: "I would like to help build other bridges. Since I own mules, this will allow me to expand my business, and do more trade with more people."

Beylie, a laborer, says: "I have learned to be a mason. I can now earn a much higher wage. I will now teach my son."

Kabede, a bright student, says: "I can attend middle school now. Before, reaching the middle school on the other side of the river was too dangerous."[5]

chapter 19

Potters for Peace

"Every 15 seconds, a child dies from a water-related disease."

— WATER PARTNERS INTERNATIONAL [1]

Water—it supports life, and it claims lives. It covers 70 percent of the earth's surface, but one billion people don't have safe water to drink.

You and I turn on the tap and drink, bathe, wash our clothes, brush our teeth, cook, and wash our hands without a thought. In other places, clean water is scarce and rationed with great care and used sparingly.

DID YOU KNOW? [2]

1.1 billion people lack access to an improved (safe) water supply—approximately one in six people on earth.

Less than 1 percent of the world's fresh water (or about 0.007 percent of all water on earth) is readily accessible for direct human use.

A person can live weeks without food, but only days without water.

The average American individual *uses 100 to 176 gallons of*
water at home each day.
The average African family *uses about 5 gallons of water each day.*

Millions of women and children spend several hours a day collecting
water from distant often polluted sources.

~~~~~~

WHEN A LITTLE WATER MEANS A LOT

The following news article was printed in Revistazo.com, an online magazine that conducts investigative journalism and pub-
lishes reports covering issues in Honduras in September 2002.[3]

Thousands of Families Cannot Afford
$2 for Potable Water

Martha Francisca Alvarado is a 43-year-old woman who looks
60. She lives near a ravine of dirty water where she bathes and
washes laundry for her children and grandchildren. She does not
have potable water services in her home and she does not have
the money necessary to buy the water she needs for cooking and
drinking.

She is part of the more than 2 million Hondurans who do
not have potable water in their homes and who have to work to
purchase water from the water trucks that circle the hills of the
capital city.

After Hurricane Mitch hit Honduras in 1998, the authori-
ties could not ignore the weaknesses of the water distribution
and sewer systems. Yet Martha Francisca is still living without
access to clean water.

Martha Francisca lives in Sector 2 of the neighborhood called 17 of September, a little beyond the impressive Cathedral of the Virgin of Suyapa. The area served as the municipal trash incinerator until the end of the 1960s.

Her house is near the edge of a small ravine that serves at this time of winter as the preferred playground for her three small sons and three young grandsons, despite high levels of contamination in the water. There are no services in her home for potable water, waste elimination, or electricity.

In the midst of her extreme poverty, Martha Francisca feels privileged in the winters because she does not have to walk 5 kilometers to the hill to look for water for her personal use and laundry.

"In the winter, this little ravine is a blessing from God. During the summer there is not enough water to get to us here and a person must carry water in the day and again at night. There is only a little at the foot of that little hill and we all line up and take turns," she says. They have to walk so far for water that should only be used for washing because it is not clean enough to drink.

"Now in the winter, all these little ravines run with water and we don't lack water. Now we don't suffer for water," she repeats.

Water: A Necessary Luxury

Martha Francisca is an example of the thousands of men and women in Honduras who work from sunup to sundown for the "luxury" of buying potable water, as little as twice a week.

This woman, who makes and sells tortillas, needs about four 5-gallon containers of water every 3 days to cover her basic needs, not counting bathing, waste elimination, and laundry. "The water we buy is strictly for drinking and cooking," she says.

Each jug of water is worth 15 cents, which represents a weekly investment of at least $1.20.

She earns an average daily income of $1.20, which has to cover her family's most basic needs for food and water. Nonetheless, she adds, there are days when sales are bad and "as we send out the tortillas, so they return."

"Look," she says, "I work to buy water and a little food.

"When we have too little money we only buy water for the children. Then we don't wash. We save the clothes for when we have water," she explains.

"With the money we put together we have to buy everything. We have to economize for everything, to give a little food and water to the children. We don't buy enough water, but little by little we will buy everything," she says.

This woman, thin, graying, her skin weathered by the sun, lifts her eyes to heaven to thank God because in the midst of poverty her sons and grandsons seem to be growing healthy.

"Thanks be to God because right now the children are healthy. They don't have skin diseases or diarrhea," she comments. "Thank God, because for the poor everything is difficult, don't you think?"

Economy vs. Water

A few kilometers from Martha Francisca lives Mrs. Julia Berta Aguilar, whose story is very similar. Julia is 33 years old and she works very hard to raise her six children, ages 14, 13, 11, 8, 6, and 3.

Julia's life was complicated a year and a half ago when her husband was killed while playing soccer in Nueva Suyapa.

The death of the main wage earner made the economic life of the family very difficult; they have been reduced to less than half their weekly income.

Their economic crisis has meant the cutting of basic services like water and electricity that they had been paying for with her husband's salary as a bus driver.

After her husband's death, Julia was not able to pay the approximately $2.00 for monthly water. Her debt accumulated little by little to $108 that "I did not have the capacity to pay," she says.

Julia also makes and sells tortillas to earn a daily salary of $6.00. From that money she must buy firewood, corn, and lime to make the tortillas and "after that I am only left a little to buy our food."

The lack of potable water forces her to look for alternative water sources.

Like the majority of women in the area who are united in poverty, she gets water from the ravine below the hill named Little Mountain.

"Look, in the summer I have to go to the well, there at the foot of Little Mountain, to wash clothes, especially the children's uniforms. It is near a point that is very dangerous. I go alone with the girls, risking myself," she explains.

She looks relieved when she notes that "now in the winter, I get rain water and wash here in the house."

She buys drinking water from the corner store near her house. "I buy 2 buckets of water a day (of 5 gallons each) at 15 cents," she says. "When there's no water, I feel like running away."

She laments that she cannot count on anyone for help because she has no family near. "I don't know anyone here. I don't have anyone to go to—only God."

The critical situation facing Julia Berta Aguilar is similar to that of thousands of families who live in the hills bordering the capital city. They have to find a way every day to feed their families, to send their children to school, and to obtain the water they need for drinking and bathing.

POTABLE WATER FOR ALL

The story of Potters for Peace and their work embodies everything that inspired this book. There is monumental deprivation: One billion people, or one in every six of us, lack a basic necessity for a reasonable quality of life—clean water. There is a simple, inexpensive, and brilliant tool that addresses that deprivation—a cheap and effective water filter. Finally, there are the visionaries who developed the technology as well as the organization and methodology for distributing the filters in ways that both eliminate the problem and create local opportunities for work. And, there is that rare element—the single personality who drives forward, undeterred by barriers, who by sheer force of will moves the entire engine out into the neediest, sometimes most remote, villages in order to help others realize a better life.

This story, though, has an ironic and tragic twist. The force that barreled ahead and brought Potters for Peace and clean water to so many of the world's poorest people, Ron Rivera, died in

2008 at the age of sixty. He contracted malaria while working in Nigeria to help build Potters for Peace's thirtieth factory for constructing its water filters. A single mosquito brought down a giant in the worldwide effort to eliminate extreme poverty.

Although Ron is irreplaceable, your small donation can help insure that a mosquito doesn't end his mission to provide safe water to the poor.

RIGHT PERSON, RIGHT TECHNOLOGY, RIGHT TIME

Ron Rivera referred to himself as a "sociologist, potter, and appropriate technology enthusiast." He was a gray-bearded bear of a man often sporting a tropical shirt or a T-shirt covered in clay. He dedicated his career to working in Central and South America on projects that facilitated economic development, particularly through the creation and application of "appropriate technologies" (those suitable for developing countries) and those promoting peace and social justice. In 1988, he moved to Nicaragua, where he connected with Potters for Peace and began working with rural potters, saying that one of his goals was to "meet every potter in Nicaragua."[4]

In October 1998, Hurricane Mitch caused massive destruction throughout Central America, killing nearly 11,000 people from floods and mudslides.[5] Basic infrastructure including transportation, electrical power, and safe

Photo courtesy of Potters for Peace

water was wiped out for millions of others.[6] The hurricane and the need left in its wake redefined the focus of Potters for Peace as well as Ron's life, offering him an opportunity to combine his passion for pottery and appropriate technology with his mission to work for the common good and empower the poor.

Ron's experience and skills had prepared him to help save the lives of thousands of people left without access to safe water in Nicaragua. He and Potters for Peace established a production facility to manufacture and distribute a ceramic water filter that turned contaminated water into "potable" water, which is free of coliform bacteria likely to cause potentially fatal diarrhea and is therefore safe to drink.

Years earlier while working in Ecuador where he founded the local office of the Inter American Foundation, an organization that provides grants to Latin American communities to support economic development, Ron learned of an effective water filter design, which he subsequently marketed in Ecuador. The filter was developed in 1981 by Dr. Fernando Mazariegos of the Central American Industrial Research Institute in Guatemala. Dr. Mazariegos had created a low-cost, silver-coated ceramic water filter that could be fabricated locally, employ nearby residents, and effectively purify water for the poorest people in Central America.

The Mazariegos filter was a crucial innovation as other water purification methods were not succeeding in the area. Rural communities did not embrace use of chlorine tablets, and in some cases, misuse of the chlorine caused harm. Boiling water wasn't effective when families failed to boil water long enough to purify it. By contrast, in 1994, the Family Foundation of the Americas conducted a study of the Mazariegos filter that determined its use in rural areas decreased the incidence of water-related diarrhea by 50 percent.[7]

After the hurricane, Potters for Peace set up a filter production workshop using the Mazariegos design in an existing pottery cooperative near Managua. Within six months, the facility had produced over 5,000 filters that were distributed by nongovernmental organizations. Since then, the enterprise, now known as Filtron, has become a privately owned business and produced and distributed more than 40,000 ceramic water filters through organizations such as the Red Cross, Plan International, and Doctors Without Borders.

BRINGING AN ANCIENT CRAFT INTO THE TWENTY-FIRST CENTURY

It is difficult to overstate the historical importance of the development of clay work and pottery to the advancement of civilization during the Stone Age. For approximately 12,000 years, people have used clay to create durable containers and utensils for cooking, storage, transporting, and constructing sturdier homes of brick.[8] Pottery and brick making continue to be crucial industries in developing countries.

Potters for Peace was formed in 1986 by a group of U.S. potters with a mission to help women potters in rural Nicaragua improve their livelihoods and their families' well-being by helping them build kilns, introducing time-saving methods of production, and helping them market their work worldwide. Initially, it raised funds by selling jelly in small pottery jars made by the Nicaraguan potters at street fairs in the United States.

Today, Potters for Peace continues to work intensively with potters throughout Central America, helping them combine their local artistry with enhanced methods of production and marketing that increase the profitability of their trade. Potters for Peace hosts conferences that bring potters together to share techniques, project successes, and common concerns and provides scholarships for apprenticeships that build skills.

In addition to improving the livelihoods of the potters, Potters for Peace helps reduce the impact of their work on the environment. Deforestation is a problem common to ceramics workers who use wood to fuel their kilns in developing areas around the world. This increases the price of wood fuel and causes soil erosion that can lead to devastating mudslides following heavy rain. Manny Hernandez of Northern Illinois University is a Potters for Peace technical volunteer who developed a fuel-efficient downdraft kiln that can be constructed with local bricks and labor. The kiln reduces the use of firewood fuel by as much as 50 percent. Potters for Peace is also working to develop alternative fuel burning systems that use solid agricultural waste such as rice husks, coffee husks, or sawdust to eliminate the use of firewood entirely.

SAVING LIVES WITH A POT, A BUCKET, AND A SPIGOT

The ceramic water purification filter used by Potters for Peace is elegant in its simplicity and tremendous effectiveness. Ron enthusiastically referred to the filters as "ceramic weapons of mass bacterial destruction." The system consists of a pressed clay bucket that looks much like a flowerpot 11 inches wide by

Clay filter, water collection
bucket with spigot.
Photo courtesy of Potters for Peace.

10 inches deep, made with a
mix of local terra-cotta clay
and sawdust or other combustible materials such as rice
husks. The pots are formed by
a mechanical press—the sim-
plest being a hand-operated
hydraulic jack with a two-piece
aluminum mold. When the pot is fired, the combustible ingredi-
ent burns out leaving a network of tiny pores throughout the pot.

After firing, the filter is coated with colloidal silver. This
combination of fine pore size, and the bactericidal properties of
colloidal silver produce an incredibly effective filter. Studies by
institutions including MIT, Tulane University, University of
Colorado, and University of North Carolina and field experience
have found the filter to effectively eliminate approximately 99.88
percent of most waterborne disease agents, including such
pathogens as *E. coli*, *Giardia*, and *Cryptosporidium*.[9]

The fired, treated filter pot is then placed in a five-gallon
plastic or ceramic receptacle with a lid and a spigot for drawing
filtered water from the receptacle. Water is filtered at a rate of
between 1.0 and 2.5 liters per hour. One filter will produce
enough safe drinking water each day for a family of six.

Filter units are sold for about US$15 to US$30 and include
the ceramic filter, the plastic receptacle with an instructional
sticker, and a spigot. Replacement filters cost about $4, and with

proper care, Potters for Peace recommends that the filter can be replaced every two to three years.[10] Production and transportation costs vary from country to country, and a basic shop with three or four workers can produce about fifty filters a day.

PIED PIPER FOR POTTERS FOR PEACE

For nearly ten years following Hurricane Mitch, Ron led and vastly expanded Potters for Peace's ceramic water purification project. He improved the Mazagieros design by developing the mechanical press and standardized molds to ensure a consistent product. He worked tirelessly to train and organize groups around the world that established and operated their own filter-making workshops as private enterprises. Much like PATH and its clean home delivery kits, Potters for Peace no longer operates filter-making facilities or sells filters, also known as clean water purifiers (CWPs). Instead, Potters for Peace travels and trains others to create sustainable microenterprises that manufacture the filters locally and employ nearby residents.

MARKETING, MARKETING, MARKETING

Smart businesses in the developed world know that simply offering an outstanding or innovative service or product isn't enough to succeed. No business can succeed if it doesn't have customers, and that requires marketing. Likewise, one of the most important tasks in creating a successful filter production facility is marketing the filter to those who would benefit from its use. Many filters are manufactured per orders placed for them by

NGOs such as the Red Cross, UNICEF, etc.; however, thousands more are purchased by local residents for everyday use in their homes.

Like other organizations in this book, Potters for Peace believes strongly in the importance of having end users *purchase* the filters, rather than obtaining them for free. Potters for Peace's objective is to make their product affordable,

Graphic illustration used to market filters.

but not cheap. Many other projects operate in the same manner. These organizations have found that when a family must make an effort, even sacrifice, to save the money to purchase an item like a ceramic water filter or an irrigation pump, they value the item and its usefulness more than they would otherwise. They are much more likely to use the item, use it properly, and realize its benefits.

Marketing a product like the water filter is comprised of two efforts: The first is educating the community about the important health benefits of having clean water and what clean, or potable, water really means. Many families, particularly those who are illiterate, don't have access to good public health information about disease prevention or sanitation and do not know how to truly purify water.

Second, filter manufacturers must advertise their product to residents. They must provide promotional materials to stores that sell them, brochures to distribute in villages (often in picture form for those who cannot read), and sometimes even radio or other print ads depending on the communities being served. Potters for Peace helps filter factories develop a marketing plan and materials.

MALARIA DOESN'T DISCRIMINATE

Ron Rivera.
Photo courtesy of Kathy Barnes.

Most of us think of malaria as a disease borne solely by the poor living in tropical areas of the world. Overwhelmingly, this is true, yet each year approximately 1,300 U.S. residents contract malaria overseas and are diagnosed and treated in the States.[11] Only a handful of cases treated in the United States are lethal.[12] Unfortunately, Ron Rivera was in Nicaragua when he became ill—a country where malaria is relatively common yet doesn't widely maintain the diagnostic tests or drugs necessary to combat its most lethal form.

In July 2008, Ron went to Nigeria with Professor Wole Soboyejo and a team of engineering students from Princeton University to establish a filter factory. He returned three weeks later to Managua, Nicaragua, where he lived with his wife of twenty years, Kathy McBride. His brother and niece arrived from Florida to help celebrate Ron's sixtieth birthday on Friday August 22 at Laguna de Apoyo in Nicaragua, one of Ron's favorite places. After a relaxing weekend at the lake, Ron's brother and niece returned to the States; on Wednesday, August 27, Ron and Kathy went back to work. Ron was still quite jet-lagged and seemed particularly tired, which he and Kathy attributed to the rigors of the trip to Nigeria. Thursday night, Ron developed a fever.

Over the next few days, Ron visited his doctor several times and was monitored for what appeared to be dengue fever, a virus common to the tropics and transmitted by infected mosquitoes. Ron and Kathy had both had dengue before, and Ron's symptoms seemed very typical for the disease—high fever, body aches, a general feeling of malaise, falling blood platelet counts (necessary for blood to clot), and profuse sweating. Treatment for dengue is primarily palliative—rest and fluids, although blood transfusions may be required if the illness becomes hemorrhagic, that is, if the platelet count falls low enough that blood clotting is impossible, and the patient begins to bleed internally.

By Monday, Ron's platelet count was critically low, and he was admitted to the hospital. Further testing there made it appear that Ron had dengue *and* malaria—both diseases transmitted by mosquito bites with similar symptomologies. Unfortunately, what they didn't yet know was that Ron had been infected with the most lethal form of malaria during his trip to Nigeria—the *P. falciparum* parasite, which, according to the Centers for Disease Control and Prevention, along with other classic flu-like malarial symptoms, is often complicated by serious organ failures or abnormalities in the patient's blood or metabolism.[13] Quick diagnosis and treatment are critical to preventing progressive illness and death from the infection. After forwarding blood samples to the CDC in Atlanta, Ron's infection with falciparum malaria was confirmed on Wednesday, and a drug regimen was prescribed.

Malaria occurs throughout Nicaragua, but the *P. falciparum* parasite is found almost entirely on the eastern coast, not in Managua on the west coast. As a result, the hospital treating Ron did not have the medication most effective in the rapid treatment of this strain of malaria. "Coartem" is actually a cocktail of drugs that acts quickly and effectively and stays in the blood longer than other antimalarials, helping to prevent the onset of drug resistance.

By this time, Ron was in the intensive care unit of the hospital where another family was keeping vigil over their dying grandmother. By coincidence, a friend of this family had traveled to Africa and had a medical kit containing Coartem. The recommended course of treatment for effective results is to administer the drug two times per day for three days, and Ron received the first dose at 7:00 p.m. on Wednesday, September 3.

Sadly, the good fortune of unexpectedly acquiring the most effective medication to treat *P. falciparum* was outweighed by the length of time it took to accurately diagnose Ron's illness, which had progressed beyond the reach of even this powerful drug. As the night went on, Ron's breathing became labored, and he went into cardiac arrest at 11:50 p.m.

THERE IS HOPE!

Our friends at PATH who led the development of the vaccine vial monitor and the clean home delivery kits also coordinate a global "Malaria Vaccine Initiative" that has led to the development of a vaccine showing promise in providing good protection among infants and children against malarial infection. Remember PATH the next time you take your child to the doctor for routine vaccinations. Think of Ron. Think of over one million children in Africa and Asia.

A LEGACY OF CLEAN WATER FOR MILLIONS

Ron collaborated with hundreds of others interested in bringing clean water and other appropriate technologies to the poor—sometimes establishing long-time relationships via e-mail, never having met face-to-face with many whom he'd mentored.

Before his death, Ron had made it his personal mission to establish 100 filter-making workshops in poor areas around the world. Following Hurricane Mitch, Ron and three other trainers helped create thirty factories in twenty-five countries that have produced 300,000 filters and provided safe drinking water to approximately 1.5 million people.

POTTERS FOR PEACE MAKES MIRACLES FROM MUD

Kaira Wagoner, coordinator of Ceramic Water Filter Programs for Potters for Peace, sent me the photo here, of a young girl in Nkokonjeru, Uganda, collecting what appears to be stagnant murky water in her can. The child is an AIDS orphan who has been taken in by friends of her deceased parents. She cares for their little girl and does chores such as collecting water and firewood in return for the food,

A child collects water to be purified by a Potters for Peace filter. *Photo courtesy of Potters for Peace.*

home, and family they provide for her. She collects water from a spring dug by an NGO, which, according to Kaira, works very nicely in the rainy season. Here, she is collecting water from an alternate source of standing water used when the spring runs dry.

When I received this story from Kaira, I wrote her back almost immediately. I needed to clarify: Could this possibly be the water that would be made potable by the Potters for Peace filter? Here was her reply:

> Yes, the PFP filter transforms both the muddy, still water and the clear stream water used during the dry season (which is not necessarily clean) into potable water. One of the things we found while testing the filters in Uganda is that even when the spring water is coliform free (potable), the jerrycans (like the yellow one in the picture) are not sterile, and contain a bacterial biofilm growing on the inside. Water often *becomes* contaminated while it is being transported from the source to the home. One of the benefits of the PFP filter is its provision of potable water in the home, directly before consumption. It is important to get potable water as close to the consumer as possible. Many statistics are misleading in this way, since communities with access to a communal potable water source are considered to have access to clean water. In reality, these people are often still drinking contaminated water.

The photo of the child in Nkokonjeru, Uganda, was taken during a trial of the filters, which performed very well. The community wants to construct a factory, but the project still needs funding.

The number of people worldwide who are sickened by unsafe water is staggering.

- Each year more than five million people die from water-related disease.[14]
- Diseases related to inadequate water and sanitation cause an estimated *80 percent of all sickness in the developing world*.[15]
- For children under age five, water-related diseases are the leading cause of death.[16]

Consider this fact alone: *Half of the world's hospital beds are occupied by patients suffering from a water-related disease*.[17]

Now, imagine getting filters and safe water into millions more households in developing countries and dramatically reducing the incidence of water-related illnesses. The potential to eradicate this scourge is also staggering.

HOW TO START A SAFE WATER RIPPLE

Potters for Peace maintains an incredibly lean operation, with a tiny annual budget of approximately $140,000 and a very small paid staff of three people. There are four filter production consultants who travel internationally and help establish new filter facilities. Their travel and consulting fees are negotiated with the in-country organization wishing to start a filter project. Potters for Peace covers expenses that cannot be paid by the local organizations. Approximately 45 percent of Potters for Peace's revenues come from pottery sales, 20 percent from grants, 15 percent from fees paid for consulting services, and 20 percent from individual donors.

Every day, Potters for Peace receives two to three requests for assistance in developing a water filter production site. *Your donation of any size* will help Potters for Peace continue to provide support and training to new water filter production and distribution projects throughout the developing world.

Each filter creates enough safe drinking water every day for six people. The filter lasts up to three years. So, at a purchase price of US$30, *a family of six will have enough safe water every day for just 2.7¢ per day, or 0.4¢ per person per day for three years.*

Success of the Potters for Peace model has been remarkable. Beyond creating safe water, it is providing employment opportunities for the poorest of the poor and improving the prosperity of entire communities.

A Donor's Story: Beverly Pillers

In 1997 I discovered an organization called Potters for Peace. The organization helped women potters in rural Nicaragua with technological problems, helping them to improve their work for markets outside their communities. They were offering a brigade trip to Nicaragua, to travel and meet the artisans. It was a life-changing trip, and I was able to see firsthand what small donations could accomplish.

From that point on, over the next 10 years I made small donations knowing how they would impact the lives of these artisans. I had the rare experience of seeing results before seeing the method of attaining them. At times when money was tighter, as a potter I was able to donate my work to be sold at benefit sales. I know all those small donations I made over the last 10 years changed many lives when you include the family members and the people in the communities they live in. I'm chairman of the board of directors of Potters for Peace now, and living in Nicaragua working with those same artisans. I can tell that my small donation and those from many other contributors has made a permanent social change. The potters that received the benefits of these donations are now community leaders and we're seeing their children going on to universities and choosing professions.

I feel that by participating for many years through small donations that it brought more meaning to my life, as well as helping me to set an example for my daughter.

~~~~~~~~~~~~~~

chapter 20

World Bicycle Relief
how a bike changes everything

*Mission: "Providing access to independence and
livelihood through the power of bicycles"*[1]

In 2004, F.K. Day was busy with his work as cofounder and executive vice president of SRAM (an amalgam of the founders' initials) Corporation, the world's second-largest bicycle component manufacturer. Over twenty years, F.K. had helped grow the company from a start-up to a thriving enterprise employing 2,400 people throughout the world.

When the Indian Ocean tsunami struck in December that year, F.K. had never before been involved in a program using bicycles in disaster or poverty relief, but he and his wife, Leah Missbach Day, conceived the idea to collect children's bicycles in the United States and ship them to the tsunami-hit areas. They imagined a program that recycled Western bikes, bringing joy and hope to the affected children as they rebuilt their homes and lives.

With clearance from SRAM, F.K. and Leah flew to Sri Lanka and Indonesia to collect input. F.K. had learned through his work with SRAM that "all answers reside in the field," and when he and Leah saw the devastation and destitution wrought by the tsunami, it was clear that more than children's bikes were needed: Everyone needed bikes—to get fish to the villages to sell, transport clean water, reach health clinics, and get children to schools in villages that were now far removed from their homes in resettlement camps.

A TSUNAMI OF BICYCLES HITS SRI LANKA

The people F.K. and Leah encountered said they needed bicycles immediately, and F.K. saw the opportunity to use his expertise in the bicycle industry for a good purpose. He connected with World Vision Sri Lanka, which agreed that a bicycle program in Sri Lanka could be useful. World Vision also agreed to poll their community-based aid recipient system to determine just how many bikes were needed in the tsunami-devastated regions of the island. In short order, they determined that *24,400 bicycles* were needed.

F.K. worked with a manufacturer on the island to create a bicycle that met the needs of the population. *Within about fourteen months, all 24,400 recipients had received a bicycle.*

On foot, individuals are limited to a small travel and working radius and can carry limited cargo, children, or everyday supplies. Bikes, on the other hand, vastly increase productivity, as they can haul well over 100 pounds, and individuals can travel easily

Photo courtesy of Leah Missbach Day

within a ten-mile radius. Bicycles from World Bicycle Relief provided the transportation needed to reconnect communities and commerce.

> *"I used to be a fisherman. Now I sell fish from the back of my bicycle. With this bicycle I am receiving so many benefits. There are seven members in my family. I am helping take my daughters' children to school with it."*
>
> —B. Raymond Perera, Kalutara, Sri Lanka

ROLLING OUT PROGRESS IN ZAMBIA TWO WHEELS AT A TIME

In the course of their work in Sri Lanka, F.K. and Leah learned from World Vision that the enormous death toll from the tsunami was equivalent to what happens "about every two weeks" in Africa. Silently and consistently, thousands die of disease. World Vision Zambia had volunteers helping their sick neighbors, but they were walking from house to house and community to community. What better way to empower them than through bikes? F.K. knew he could put his experience in Sri Lanka—using bikes as simple, sustainable transport—into action in Zambia.

Zambia is one of the world's poorest countries, and infrastructure challenges are a primary cause. Economic development depends on a nation's ability to conduct commerce and trade, which depends on its ability to move goods. Zambia has only 12 kilometers of roads per 100 square kilometers of land while the United States has approximately 70, and much of

Zambia's existing roads need some or major repair.[2] Located smack in the middle of the horn of Africa, Zambia is also land-locked, without access to oceanic transport of its commodities.

Poor infrastructure deprives Zambians of modern technology and services common in the United States.

Percent of roads that are paved:[3]
United States:　65 percent (2006)
Zambia:　　　22 percent (2000)

Number of vehicles per 1,000 people:[4]
United States:　774 (2000)
Zambia:　　　26 (2000)

Fixed line and mobile phone subscribers (per 100 people):[5]
United States:　139 percent (2007)
Zambia:　　　23 percent (2007)

Percent of population with a television:[6]
United States:　99 percent (2006)
Zambia:　　　26 percent (2002)

Number of personal computers per 100 people:[7]
United States:　76　(2006)
Zambia:　　　1　(2006)

Internet users (per 100 people):[8]
United States:　70　(2006)
Zambia:　　　4　(2006)

Most of us could not imagine getting through our day without these resources. In our industrialized world, caring for our families, getting an education, conducting our work, communicating with friends and relatives all require these tools and technologies.

According to Engineers Without Borders - International, "Appropriate technology for developing communities is usually characterized as being small scale, energy efficient, environmentally sound, labor-intensive, and controlled by the local community. It must be simple enough to be maintained by the people using it. Furthermore, it must match the user and the need in complexity and scale and must be designed to foster self-reliance, cooperation and responsibility. Studies by the World Bank and the United Nations have shown . . . that appropriate technology is critical to bringing more than three billion people out of poverty."[9]

World Bicycle Relief bike projects are excellent examples of appropriate and sustainable solutions to economic deprivation. The bicycles are designed to be culturally, technologically, and economically suitable. Just as Heifer International sends animals that are well-suited to their destination, World Bicycle Relief provides bicycles that are built for their specific use. For example, based on feedback from users, World Bicycle Relief doubled the capacity of rear racks and created pedals and saddles that are less prone to failure for Project Zambia. These bikes are built for hard work over rough terrain.

In order to create sustainability of the project as well as jobs within the country, over 400 field mechanics and assembly workers have been trained to produce and service World Bicycle Relief bikes throughout Zambia. Mechanics and assembly workers are well-trained to ensure quality control and earn decent wages—as much as $7.50 per day in a country where the gross national income per capita was $770 in 2007.[10] Field mechanics, who often operate as microenterprises, also receive life skills and business training that equips them to succeed.

BIKES TO FIGHT HIV/AIDS[11]

Zambia is a nation roughly the size of the U.S. state of Texas, with approximately half the population: 11.5 million people. The World Health Organization estimates life expectancy at less than 40 years, and more than 1 million people are living with HIV/AIDS. More than half the population is less than 16 years old, and one in five children have lost one or both parents to the disease.

Poverty is directly and undisputedly related to HIV/AIDS in Zambia. A parent (or parents) suffering and dying of HIV/AIDS leads to the downfall or demise of the household. The children orphaned because of HIV/AIDS are often taken in by relatives or foster families, which then leads to the overburdening of these families. Worse yet are the orphaned children forced to become the heads of households themselves. These children often turn to prostitution or theft, and sink deeper into poverty.

Remote villages, coupled with a lack of transportation, isolate patients from the growing availability of health care. Health care is then useless because it does not reach those in need. Without care and education, the disease is rampant, leaving a wake of sorrow, hopelessness, and economic devastation.

This epidemic is treatable and preventable. There are drugs and health care procedures that stop the transmission of HIV from mother to newborn. They can extend the lives of people living with HIV/AIDS and help them return to productive lives. Beyond drugs, education is effective in slowing the transmission of the disease and providing care for those who live with it. By providing bicycles, World Bicycle Relief will ensure that both health care and education reach those most in need.

In order to address the devastation wrought by HIV/AIDS in Zambia, World Bicycle Relief is working with the World Vision–led Reaching HIV/AIDS Affected People with Integrated Development and Support (RAPIDS) program to provide bicycles that allow better access to health care and education for those with HIV/AIDS, orphans, and other vulnerable children living in remote rural areas. The project's goal is to provide 23,000 bikes that will enable community-based health care volunteers and disease prevention educators to reach 500,000 individuals most in need in their communities.

According to World Bicycle Relief:[12]

> Bicycles, as tools of simple sustainable mobility, will more than quadruple the volunteers' ability to reach those in need, and allow them to travel greater distances more quickly, and with less fatigue, while carrying significantly more supplies. This results in better and more frequent health care and education for more people at a lower cost, and enables the volunteers to better care for their own needs.

Through its project in Zambia, World Bicycle Relief is actually addressing all the root causes of poverty discussed in *Give a Little*. Bicycles help the poor access health care, attend school

F.K. Day, president of World Bicycle Relief, at a meeting with RAPIDS coordinators and home-based care givers to discuss their experience in using bicycles to deliver care to remotely located patients. *Photo by Leah Missbach Day.*

and acquire an education, and get to jobs that provide income for basic necessities such as nutritious food and medications.

DOING MORE GOOD WITH A BIKE[13]

Rhoda Katite is a farmer, a shop owner, Vice Chairwoman of her community, a mother, grandmother, and sister. Somehow, she also finds time to be a volunteer caregiver, delivering help to individuals living with HIV/AIDS in and around her community, a rural village 35 kilometers northwest of Lusaka, the capital of Zambia. Felicitous Katite, her sister-in-law, is a volunteer counselor. Together, they care for about 20 patients per week. Rhoda says, "I feel from the heart to take care of patients and young children that are vulnerable. It is just a calling. I feel good because I help my family and friends."

Rhoda received a bicycle from World Bicycle Relief in April 2007. The bicycle has transformed her daily life as well as the lives of many others. Her rural village does not benefit from any public transportation. Before receiving the bicycle, Rhoda spent most of her day walking.

She is now able to get to the fields quicker and transport goods back to her shop more efficiently. She has more time to care for her own family. And she has more time and ability to

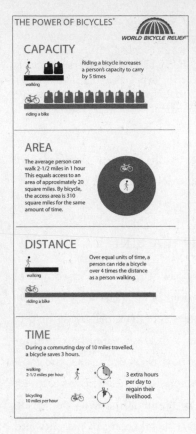

THE POWER OF BICYCLES®

WORLD BICYCLE RELIEF

CAPACITY

Riding a bicycle increases a person's capacity to carry by 5 times

walking

riding a bike

AREA

The average person can walk 2-1/2 miles in 1 hour This equals access to an area of approximately 20 square miles. By bicycle, the access area is 310 square miles for the same amount of time.

DISTANCE

Over equal units of time, a person can ride a bicycle over 4 times the distance as a person walking.

walking

riding a bike

TIME

During a commuting day of 10 miles travelled, a bicycle saves 3 hours.

walking
2-1/2 miles per hour

bicycling
10 miles per hour

3 extra hours per day to regain their livelihood.

care for her neighbors in need. She and Felicitous have been able to double their patient load while also increasing their quality of care.

Mr. Chiyokoma is one of their patients. When they [initially] learned that Mr. Chiyokoma's health was declining rapidly, Rhoda was able to transport him on her bicycle 2 kilometers to the nearest clinic, where he was tested for AIDS. He was diagnosed positive, and Felicitous was able to reach him quickly with the bicycle to counsel Mr. Chiyokoma and help him understand that HIV is not a death sentence. She patiently taught him that with time and proper medication, he will regain his health and begin farming again soon.

BIKES BRING CHANGE

Donating a bicycle is one of the highest return contributions one can make to improve a family's standard of living and well-being. According to the International Bicycle Fund, which promotes recycling used bicycles in the United States by donating them overseas, the bicycles benefit people living in developing countries in the following ways:

- Empowering people and providing them with hope and dignity
- Improving access to health care, education, and social services
- Improving economic productivity by improving transportation
- Creating opportunities for microenterprises and employment
- Empowering women and helping them achieve their potential by increasing their mobility
- Strengthening families and community by reducing travel time, thus keeping families together
- Improving the delivery of services by police, health care workers, and other extension workers by increasing their mobility

Not only does donating a bike provide many tangible gains to recipients, it is also incredibly cost-effective. When we amortize the cost of donating a World Bicycle Relief bike over ten years of ownership, the cost of the bicycle is *$34 per year* or *9¢ per day.* Consider the many, many uses of that bike every day over ten years. Can you think of a better way to use the change in your pocket? The change under your couch cushions, the coins at the bottom of your purse?

A Donor's Story: Mary Emmett

As someone who loves cycling and had most recently completed an extensive ride over the summer of 2007, it was a natural fit for me to gravitate toward the simple, yet brilliant, concept of the independence the bicycle has to offer.

I had made plans for March 2008 to travel to Lusaka, Zambia, to visit a center that was dedicated to my late husband, David Emmett, by Children International. As I was discussing these plans with a friend who works in the bike industry, he asked if I had heard of World Bicycle Relief, who just happened to have a program in Lusaka. I have done some traveling in Africa in past years and had observed the hardship that a lack of transportation affected. As I mentioned, the simplicity of this idea resonated strongly with me.

I contacted the organization to let them know I would be "in town" and would like to see what they were about. The staff was very accommodating and showed me every aspect of the business. I was given the history of how the program was initiated, the companies involved and also had the opportunity to visit the assembly site. I think the crowning moment came when I was invited to join in with the distribution of these bikes to health care workers in an out village area. This brought it all home.

I think as much as a program such as this touches the heart, it is so very important that the business be run efficiently. I found this to be very well done at WBR. I was impressed with how many support people were engaged locally and the pride they felt being associated with such an effort. I believe just giving people the tools to improve their lives allows them to find their own sense of personal pride and we can all feel good about being a part of that process.

part six

giving, lending,
AND *clicking for good*

~~~~~~~~

chapter 21

The Multi-Front Attack

"Dream no small dreams for they have no power
to move the hearts of men."

—JOHANN WOLFGANG VON GOETHE[1]

Many of the organizations in *Give a Little* are relatively small and nimble—they operate with small budgets and numbers of staff. They often focus on a specific barrier to escaping poverty; for instance, the Breathmobile addresses asthma among the urban poor; Developments in Literacy provides education where there is none; Potters for Peace creates potable water; World Bicycle Relief provides transportation.

At the same time, there are numerous large organizations that opt to take on poverty at many fronts simultaneously. This chapter of *Give a Little* offers a one-stop shopping opportunity for those who would like to support multifaceted, large-scale efforts by effective organizations.

Multilateral organizations often partner with smaller agencies like those described in this book, collaborating to leverage the tools, technology, and services developed by the newer, innovative nonprofits such as World Bicycle Relief, which partners with World Vision to distribute its bikes. Other times, larger agencies subcontract with smaller organizations to provide products or services they use in the field. For instance, UNICEF contracts with Maternal & Child Health Product in Nepal to produce clean home delivery kits, which they use around the world. These are tremendous examples of partnerships between large and small organizations to benefit those in need effectively and efficiently.

These organizations address multiple root causes of poverty. Additional information about their work can be found on their Web sites.

ACTIONAID

"Poverty is our problem." For those of you who are activist-oriented, you'll like ActionAid's two-pronged approach to eradicating poverty: developing community projects that address local needs and involve residents in their design and implementation; and improving human rights and social justice by lobbying policy makers. ActionAid provides health care, education, and food assistance. It works in areas of conflict and emergencies, and it aims to improve women's rights. ActionAid has projects in Asia, Africa, and Latin America.

ActionAid's work assists thirteen million of the most vulnerable individuals, families, and communities in forty-three countries. In Kenya alone, it stopped legislation that would have drastically increased the costs of medications for treating malaria and HIV/AIDS by at least 500 percent, making them out of reach for most citizens. Today, 40 percent of Kenyans can afford these drugs compared to just 5 percent in 2003.[2]

Worldwide, ActionAid responds to natural disasters and emergencies by getting the immediate supplies and services to

those affected, but it also takes
the longer view by helping
communities "rebuild their lives
and reduce their vulnerability
to future disasters."

Lakhia Devi sits with her
one-day-old child in Moti-   *Photo: ©Jacob Silberberg/Panos/ActionAid*
hari, East Champaran. The newborn is one of at least 102 babies delivered in the area with help from a disposable delivery
kit—blade, cotton, thread, plastic sheet, and antiseptic soap
and solution—that are being distributed by ActionAid's local
partner SSEVK.

WORLD VISION

World Vision is a Christian humanitarian organization dedicated to helping children, families, and their communities worldwide to reach their full potential by tackling the causes of
poverty and injustice. World Vision serves all people, regardless
of religion, race, ethnicity, or gender.

During the current economic crisis, World Vision is helping
struggling American families through its Storehouses that distribute items such as "clothing, diapers, blankets, household and
personal care items, and toys to strengthen families and help
provide children with a sense of hope and self-esteem."[3] Storehouses also stock items needed for home and building repair
and maintenance—often an unaffordable expense for families
during tough economic times.

Amazingly, your $25 contribution will be leveraged to pro-
vide $350 worth of these goods to families in need by paying

the shipping costs for World Vision to acquire in-kind donations from corporations and purchase additional items that are not donated. Hard to beat a 1,400 percent return on a $25 donation.

The Sauerwein family in West Virginia benefitted from just such a donation when they received building supplies from the Storehouse in Philippi, West Virginia, to help fix up their home.

Chris Sauerwein and his stepson, Justin Spurr, visited the Storehouse in Philippi, West Virginia, in early December 2007. The snow falling outside caused Justin's school to close for the day, but did not deter them from shopping for much-needed building supplies.

Chris says, "When I heard about it (the Storehouse), I thought, Oh my goodness, that would be a real blessing for us. We could save some money on remodeling our home. It's in real bad need of remodeling."

Chris runs his own floor refinishing business in the nearby town of Belington, West Virginia. He says things have been financially difficult for his family lately. "It's been real rough. My wife had to go back to work. It just seems like lately nobody's wanting to spend money on things like that because the economy around here really feels the effects of a national downturn." He explains that he has not worked for two weeks and will have another week off before he has a job scheduled. "People tighten up and business almost stops for me."

The economy of West Virginia is one of the most fragile of any U.S. state. According to U.S. Census Bureau data, West Virginia is the third lowest in per capita income, ahead of only Arkansas and Mississippi.

Chris, now forty-two, has not had medical insurance since he turned forty. He says that the rates increased dramatically at that point and he could not afford it. That lack of medical insurance, along with a slowdown in work for Chris, contributed to the need for his wife to go back to work. She works as a bank teller and gets medical benefits for herself and her son, Justin, who has physical disabilities. Doctors originally said that Justin would never walk, but after several surgeries, funded by the Shriners, Chris says, "He's just doing great."

Chris says that he moved into the family's ranch-style home about five years ago. Since then, he has been working on the house. "It's been such a long-term project for us both financially and everything. It's been a real hardship trying to get it in a comfortable condition. We're well on our way, but we have a long way to go."

He attends First Baptist Church—a World Vision partner—in Belington. Through that partnership, Chris has access to the products in the Storehouse. One of the items Chris found at the Storehouse was floor tile for his home. The house's original tile had holes in it and was coming up in places. Chris says that before, when they would get a job on the house finished, they would take any surplus they had and instead of putting it into savings, would spend the money on more supplies for the house.

Chris is very active in his community. Besides running his own business, he is president of the Belington Architectural Rehabilitation Association, whose goal is fixing up old buildings downtown. Justin pipes up hearing this organization mentioned, "I am the founder of our slogan." Chris smiles at Justin explaining that the association was searching for a slogan to explain their organization. Justin's suggestion was chosen—"Putting the Past into the Future."

"I had one employee for a while," says Chris of his business. "But now I've had to lay him off. Up until this past year, it was paying the bills and everything like that. Now we're struggling." But the Storehouse is helping this family make ends meet during this time of economic downturn. "It's just more than you know to be able to get the building materials," says Chris. "To donate these kinds of materials to people in this area, where there's no really good employment—and there isn't—it's just really indescribable what a blessing it is for people. It's like I said, it's been two or three weeks since I've been a member, and it's already been a tremendous help."

GLOBAL PARTNERS FOR DEVELOPMENT

Global Partners for Development works in the East African developing countries of Uganda, Kenya, and Tanzania helping local residents implement projects that reduce hunger, improve health, and provide education to build economic self-reliance.

A donation of just $55 to Global Partners for Development helps build a local clinic or buys medicines and supplies for an existing clinic. One small check can save so many lives.

HEALTHY, HAPPY BABIES BEGIN HERE![4]

For women in the village of Kihanda in remote southwest Uganda, the nearest health center was a day's walk away. A primitive communication system and barely passable roads almost completely isolated this rural village from health care. However, a group of village women organized to solve these most difficult problems.

Inspired by Mrs. Jane Bagye, who had lost a baby due to the distance she had to travel to receive care, the women began building the community's first health clinic. They rolled stones down the hillsides for the foundation and spent many hours working to build the walls. With Global Partners' assistance the women of Kihanda were able to finish the clinic and acquire the neces-

Photo courtesy of Global Partners for Development

sary supplies and equipment to maintain local health care. The clinic delivers not only medical care, but works to teach HIV/ AIDS prevention, nutrition, and other useful information. Not only have lives been saved, but the village people are living healthier lives.

Following the success of their first building project, the women of Kihanda went on to build a new maternity ward. Mothers can now deliver their babies safely with their families nearby.

Local clinics save the lives of thousands of people every year! Support the efforts of a village to save lives.

chapter 22

Social Investment and Fair Trade Purchasing

"People give to worthwhile programs rather than to needy institutions. The cause must catch the eye, warm the heart and stir the mind."

—HAROLD J. SEYMOUR, PHILANTHROPIST[1]

SOCIAL INVESTMENT

"Social entrepreneurship" and "microlending" are the new buzz-words in philanthropy. Many of the organizations profiled in this book were founded by social entrepreneurs—those who apply an innovative, entrepreneurial approach to solving a problem in society. Consider Nick Moon and Martin Fisher of Kick-Start, Ken Frantz of Bridges to Prosperity, F.K. Day and his wife, Leah Missbach Day, of World Bicycle Relief.

These folks applied good business principles to effectively (1) identify a need, (2) create an effective and desirable solution, (3) market the solution to those it will benefit, and (4) establish opportunities for private sector, profit-making enterprises to sustain the project.

Dr. Muhammad Yunus is another excellent example of a social entrepreneur. Yunus won the Nobel Peace Price in 2006 for his development of the Grameen Bank, an institution that provides small business loans (microloans) to poor individuals lacking collateral, so they can start a business and become self-sufficient.

Grameen Bank was created with the following objectives:[2]
- Extend banking facilities to poor men and women
- Eliminate the exploitation of the poor by money lenders
- Create opportunities for self-employment for the vast multitude of unemployed people in rural Bangladesh
- Bring the disadvantaged, mostly the women from the poorest households, within the fold of an organizational format which they can understand and manage by themselves
- Reverse the age-old vicious circle of "low income, low saving & low investment," into [a] virtuous circle of "low income, injection of credit, investment, more income, more savings, more investment, more income"

Grameen Bank began lending to the rural poor in Bangladesh in the late 1970s, and to date, has extended credit to 7.41 million borrowers,[3] 97 percent of whom are women.[4] Grameen Bank provides services in 83,343 villages,[5] through 2,481 branches,[6] covering the vast majority of villages in Bangladesh. Grameen Bank has made loans totaling $6.685 billion,[7] and *the rate of repayment of loans is 98 percent*.[8] The number of Grameen Bank borrowers living in poverty is 20 percent compared with 56 percent among nonborrowers in similar circumstances.

Grameen Bank is a portal for social investment, that is, *investment in opportunities for individuals and groups to improve their standard of living*. In this case, the investment comes in the form of microloans that help the poor move toward self-sufficiency through their own means, typically operating small businesses selling goods or services. It is not a handout; it comes with the expectation of returns in the form of loan repayment with interest and social progress. In this way, social investing is different from direct aid, which is intended to provide temporary assistance.

OPPORTUNITIES FOR SOCIAL INVESTING

Decreasing poverty around the world reduces the costs to local communities, states, nations, and the world of caring for the poor. It also diminishes all the outcomes associated with poverty, including local crime, regional wars, refugees, and spread of diseases. We're talking about a clear path to peace and well-being. Social investment is an excellent vehicle to clear that path.

In a sense, the projects already described in this book are forms of social investment as they all create or preserve individuals' opportunities to move toward self-sufficiency. The organizations that follow let you empower a specific individual or group to become economically self-sufficient.

KIVA:
"we let you loan to the working poor"

Kiva's mission is to connect people through lending for the sake of alleviating poverty. It is "the world's first person-to-person micro-lending website, empowering individuals to lend directly to unique entrepreneurs around the globe."

When you go to Kiva's Web site, you'll be able to see profiles of individual microentrepreneurs seeking loans that will allow them to start or expand their businesses. You can choose a person/project that interests you, make a loan, and expect repayment within approximately six to twelve months. During the loan period, you can receive updates on the recipient's progress and track loan payments.

Kiva works with existing microfinance institutions around the world that make loans and vet entrepreneurial candidates directly. When these institutions have more qualified candidates than they can afford to lend to, they send their profiles to Kiva. When you make a loan, Kiva directs it to its local microfinance partner, which provides the loan, conducts progress checks, tracks loan repayment, and often provides additional support to help entrepreneurs' businesses succeed.

As you can see from the following table, the average loan to an entrepreneur is approximately $400. (The information in "Latest Statistics" is continually updated.) Most loans result from multiple contributions from individuals making $10, $25, or $50 loans toward the total requested. According to Kiva, the average total amount loaned by an individual is approximately $140—that represents several small loans made to multiple entrepreneurs. This gives lenders leverage as they can spread their impact across a number of dimensions, including, for instance, female entrepreneurs, those located in a similar geographic area, funds for start-up or expansion costs, or those working in a similar industry such as construction or agriculture. Some may enjoy lending to entrepreneurs across a range of fields and needs.

LATEST STATISTICS[9]

Total value of all loans made through Kiva:	$67,491,160
Number of Kiva lenders:	475,180
Number of loans that have been funded through Kiva:	96,667
Percentage of Kiva loans that have been made to women entrepreneurs:	77.85%
Number of Kiva Field Partners (microfinance institutions Kiva partners with):	94
Number of countries Kiva Field Partners are located in:	44
Current repayment rate (all partners):	97.97%
Current default rate (all partners):	2.03%
Average loan size (This is the average amount loaned to an individual Kiva entrepreneur. Some loans—group loans—are divided between a group of borrowers.):	$422.34
Average total amount loaned per Kiva Lender (*includes reloaned* funds):	$142.32

DONORSCHOOSE.ORG

In 2000, Charles Best was a frustrated social studies teacher in a Bronx public high school. Since becoming a teacher five years earlier, he and his colleagues had grappled with the lack of access to supplies, materials, and experiences they knew would enrich their students' learning environments and draw students into lessons in more meaningful ways. Charles knew that scarcity was hindering educational opportunities throughout his school and likely much of the public school system.

At the same time, Charles believed that parents and other community members shared his frustration and that, if given the opportunity, they would gladly make affordable contributions if they knew they would directly improve their schools. He labeled this "Citizen Philanthropy" and developed DonorsChoose.org to partner community members with the teachers, projects, and students that needed them.

At DonorsChoose.org, visitors choose specific projects they'd like to support, which have already been screened by DonorsChoose.org. Often multiple donors contribute to fund single projects. Once a project is funded and carried out, donors receive thank you notes from the teacher and often the students as well. Teachers can also post photos of funded projects.

Brittany Cohen teaches at Future Leaders Institute and has had numerous projects funded through DonorsChoose.org. Here is one of her successful requests. This project is a favorite of mine because I have experienced the immense joy children get from authoring books both in the classroom and in my home, where my twin daughters are prolific writers, having begun as preschoolers dictating stories for me to write down and illustrating them themselves.

I am currently a kindergarten teacher in an underprivileged area of Harlem. I teach at one of the highest performing charter schools in the area. Despite many of the obstacles my students face, they come to school excited to learn every day. About 96 percent of the students are black, and more than 70 percent qualify for reduced or free lunch programs.

My students love writing workshop each day and love publishing parties even more. I want to give my students the opportunity to take their published pieces to the next level. By having a book-binding machine I will be able to create a professional "book" for each of them with their amazing writing work. They will be able to have this book for the publishing party and for years to come. I always encourage my students to keep their work as neat and clean as possible and by binding everything I will be able to ensure their work looks as professional as possible.

Please help me preserve my students' work for them to share with other students and family members. I will be able to hang up these bound books in my classroom and have these children take them home as keepsakes.

To be able to see my students smile during publishing parties is amazing but to see them with a bound book of all of their work would be even better![10]

Four donors contributed to fund Cohen's bookbinding machine. Their comments are posted on DonorsChoose.org along with the description and outcomes of the project.

AUDREY: "I gave to this project because a beloved friend (who recently passed away), always taught my children that to find one friend, to take a walk or to read a book will always provide comfort. Books are a passage to the world outside of our own."

STEVEN: "We gave this donation because we are so proud of what you are doing with these kids."

JULIE: "I teach second grade and know how important it is for kids to see their writing published. Good luck!"

THE PUMPKIN FOUNDATION/JOE AND CAROL REICH: "We support public education reform, specifically charter schools and services for charter schools."[11]

Cohen thanked her donors with the following note:

Thank you so much for funding my grant for a book binder. I cannot wait to compile an anthology of our poems and bind a book for each child. At the end of each writing unit we have a publishing party where kids share their work. We make a really big deal about it and invite parents, students, and other teachers to come listen. Now, my students can feel like real authors with their books! When I tell/show my students this amazing gift their smiles are going to mean everything. Thank you again.[12]

As of April 14, 2009, DonorsChoose.org had raised a total of $32,326,350 from donors in fifty states to fund projects benefitting 2,008,356 students.[13]

GLOBALGIVING:
connecting donors to doers with "a million little earth-changing ideas"

GlobalGiving is much like DonorsChoose.org, but it offers a wide range of projects from around the world. The site represents "over 450 pre-screened grassroots charity projects." You can choose where you'd like to invest by selecting from categories such as "causes," "countries," "most recently posted," and "closest to goal."

GlobalGiving begins with the dedicated, tenacious individuals who are driving change in their communities. From running orphanages and schools, to helping survivors of natural disasters, these people are do-gooders to the core. GlobalGiving connects these "good idea people" with the "generous giver people" and help projects of all sizes receive donations of all sizes.[14]

Some "generous giver people" post their reasons for giving:

I give to show my son that he should care for people and the common good of the world. Even if you have just $5, that is more than what many people have in the world. If I am willing to spend that $5 on coffee each week for myself, I think I should be more than willing to give that $5 instead to others who don't even have that much money.

If we each give a little, we all gain a lot.

Small thoughts bring about big changes. I want to make a difference to the world around me.

I know poverty and I know we need each other. Giving makes me feel rich. Sharing makes me feel our connection.

History shows that great civilizations succeed as a community, not individuals.

When I am thirsty I drink. When I am hungry I eat. When I am tired I sleep. All the while I know that many are not. I can help them. Thanks for the opportunity.

I sat down for coffee today and changed the world.

In 2004 I was deployed to Afghanistan. For some odd reason I grew to love the country and I want to see

Afghanistan do great things. The greatest hope for Afghanistan is in its children. I support education programs.

I get an incredible buzz helping others.[15]

FAIR TRADE PURCHASING

This is one of my favorite ways to make a difference. Fair trade purchasing involves buying products created by local artisans and microentrepreneurs that were paid *fair trade prices* for their merchandise. Typically, an intermediary agency (sometimes a nonprofit) purchases the products at a fair price and distributes them to a broader market than would be accessible to the artisans themselves. Fair trade market chains ensure that microentrepreneurs receive a reasonable profit from the sale of their products, rather than being exploited by intermediaries who buy their goods at rock-bottom prices then mark them up dramatically and pocket a disproportionate share of the profits. In fact fair trade market chains eliminate as many of the middlemen as possible.

Fair trade purchasing is different from buying commercially manufactured products (such as the "Red" items) where a portion of the proceeds from sales benefits a cause or program. Purchasing directly from the creators or fair trade importers and distributors empowers the original producer by increasing demand for their products and services, creating a sustainable income, and improving family and community socioeconomic well-being. When I purchase a fair trade product—and many of them can be found on grocery store shelves, including coffees, chocolate, tea, vanilla, flowers, rice, sugar, and herbs—I feel a direct connection to the craftsmen and women who labored in faraway places to create it. I have a sense of partnership with the entrepreneurs working diligently and creatively to lift themselves and their families up to better lives. I admire their efforts, and supporting them makes me feel good. I particularly love buying fair trade jewelry, garments, and artwork. Holding or wearing something created by hand by a single or small group of artisans, I imagine the people, the materials, and the travels involved in my acquiring it. I revel in my place in the global community.

When I purchase gifts, I nearly always think fair trade first. Recipients love knowing that their gift directly benefitted an individual or family. There are many portals for fair trade shopping on the Internet, and I've listed some of my favorites next.

BeadforLife: www.beadforlife.org

BeadforLife is operated by Ugandan women who turn colorful recycled paper into spectacular beaded jewelry. Members are

women with children who had been living on less than $2 a day. Many fled the war in Northern Uganda while others have HIV or other health problems. Beading provides income for food, medicine, and school fees.

Laker Fatuma.
Photo courtesy of BeadforLife.

Laker Fatuma—from Beans to Beading[16]

Fatuma, 33, has a broad smile and twinkle in her eyes that immediately creates a sense of fun and warmth. Yet she has overcome enormous difficulty. As a young teen, she was captured by the rebels who were waging war in the north. Living with them for several years she bore two children before she was able to escape and make her way to Kampala. There she moved into a slum along the railway tracks. She picked coffee beans for 40 cents a day, not enough to feed herself and her children.

"You work so hard and have nothing after a long day. If you do not get paid you do not eat," she says of that time.

Fatuma later married a man who was an "askari," a night watchman. When she was pregnant with their youngest child, her husband was killed when thieves attempted to break into the office he was guarding. Alone with four children, she did everything she could to feed them.

When she started rolling beads for BeadforLife she hoped to make about $30 a month. Instead she earned almost $100. "I was not expecting this good fortune. Everyone who bought beads has taken care of me."

When Fatuma joined BeadforLife her industrious nature came alive. She bought a popcorn machine and started earning a second stream of income. She now has built a house in Friendship Village and plans to buy a "boda boda," a motorcycle used as a taxi. She is well on her way out of poverty.

BeadforLife works to help every beader become economically independent of BeadforLife by launching their own small businesses within twenty-seven months.[17]

CraftNetwork: www.craftnetworkstore.com

CraftNetwork establishes a direct connection between consumer and craftspeople: You can choose a particular artisan whose wares you'd like to purchase and learn about his or her personal history. Its online store is an important source for sales as well as information about the artisans' cultures and backgrounds.

CraftNetwork helps artisans develop business skills and access markets to "increase their sales . . . generate employment, and improve the standard of living of its member producers." CraftNetwork represents both individual producers and organizations with many member artisans, such as KNN Cambodia.

KNN Cambodia Art & Craft was established in 2004 with the aim to develop job opportunities for the Cambodian people and increase socially responsible business. Women and handicapped persons make up 80% of the artisans of this socially responsible enterprise.

The main focus of KNN is to continue to produce handicrafts made through the traditional forms of weaving. With the development of new technologies these traditions are slowly fading and their hope is to continue on with this important part of their heritage.

KNN Cambodia produces their beautiful items combining unique traditional methods with attractive modern designs. In addition, KNN Cambodia has made a commitment to remain as a fair trade enterprise to ensure the artisans reap the benefits of their hard work.[18]

Mercado Global: www.mercadoglobal.org

"Mercado Global is a nonprofit fair trade organization that links the world's most rural and economically disadvantaged cooperatives to the U.S. market."[19]

Mercado works with cooperatives of women artisans around the world to earn a fair wage and get their products to market. With the help of grants and donations from individuals, Mercado also ensures that all artisans' children have access to educational opportunities, by constructing schools and providing scholarships. It has also provided hurricane relief and constructed water systems in local villages.

> Connecting the world's most rural and politically and socially marginalized communities to the mainstream U.S. market requires significant investments in training, support and logistical assistance. *Seventy-five percent of our artisans are illiterate,* many are widowed or experience domestic violence, and *few have more than a 2nd grade education,* let alone business training. (Italics added by author.)[20]

The return on your social investment in Mercado Global is remarkable. A donation of just $25 provides the financial literacy, advanced artisanal techniques, and business administration training of an artisan "who will then be equipped to participate in international sales opportunities."[21]

Global Exchange: www.globalexchangestore.org

Global Exchange has a dual purpose: to connect disadvantaged producers with markets around the world through its online and brick-and-mortar stores; and to increase understanding of fair trade issues among consumers. Global Exchange works with thousands of artisans in over forty countries.[22] You can choose to support particular fair trade producers from numerous countries around the world representing a wide range of social circumstances, living conditions, and products.

SUDANESE WOMEN BASKETWEAVERS

The Darfur region of Sudan has been engrossed in a complex conflict since 2003, leaving half a million people dead and over two and a half million people displaced. Those that have been displaced within Sudan are living in internally displaced persons (IDP) camps. Since 2004, NGO "CHF International" has been working with the Sudanese people living in these camps. The largest camp is located in Kalma, in Southern Darfur. Kalma is home to over 100,000 people displaced by the conflict.

Women in these camps are often left vulnerable and with no way to support their families. In response, CHF International has implemented mat and basket weaving projects to ensure that women living in the camps participate in improving their own lives, while simultaneously preserving their vibrant cultural traditions. The basket weavers come together to create their craft at the Women's Center, which is located at the center of the camp. It takes approximately one week for them to complete a single basket. The Women's Center not only offers the women of Kalma economic opportunity, but the center is also a place where the women can share their stories and begin to heal together. [23]

Ten Thousand Villages:
www.tenthousandvillages.com

About fifteen years ago, I walked into a Ten Thousand Villages store in Evanston, Illinois, and became an instant fair trade fan.

Here were beautiful wares from around the world that I would likely never have seen or accessed before without a plane ticket. Beyond the intrigue of the products themselves, was the knowledge that every purchase benefitted a small business entrepreneur in an impoverished part of the world.

Mary Njeri Njogu. *Photo courtesy of Ten Thousand Villages.*

Ten Thousand Villages grew out of the efforts of Edna Ruth Byler, also known as "the Needlework Lady." Byler traveled to Puerto Rico in 1946 and was moved by the poor living conditions there but also by the remarkable needlework being produced by talented women. She believed she could help improve their standard of living by bringing their fine work to a broader market in the United States. She began by selling their work out of the trunk of her car while educating people about the lives of the women who produced the beautiful pieces. Soon, she began importing needlework from Palestinian refugees and carved woodwork from Haiti. Thus, from the trunk of a car, was launched the global fair trade movement.

Byler had created a market-based approach to bringing sustainable economic opportunity to artisans in developing countries. Over time, her operation outgrew the trunk of her car, interested groups began holding Festival Sales, similar to art fairs, and eventually the first store, then called Self Help Crafts, opened in 1972. By 1996, when the business was renamed Ten Thousand Villages, it was selling $6.2 million worth of fair trade products.

Ten Thousand Villages now brings artisans' products to markets via multiple channels, including selling goods in its 81 brick and mortar stores as well as its online store, and by acting as wholesaler to several hundred retailers around the United States. Church, college, and community groups around the country continue to hold Festival Sales.

Ten Thousand Villages works with more than 100 artisan groups in thirty countries in Asia, Africa, and Latin America. Jacaranda Workshop, a nonprofit organization located in Nairobi, Kenya, provides employment, training, and other assistance to artisans with mental or physical disabilities.

Mary Njeri Njogu, an artisan with Jacaranda Workshop in Nairobi, Kenya, is one of 25 artisans with disabilities working with the organization. With few other opportunities, these artisans have been able to access training and a stable income through their work with Jacaranda.

Born in 1969 in Wangige village near Nairobi, Njogu was delayed in her early speech and motor development. Her parents became alarmed, and took her to a nearby hospital. They were shocked to learn that their daughter was not only intellectually challenged, but also had a physical disability affecting the entire left side of her body.

Njogu started school in 1977, dropping out in 1985 after failing to go beyond third grade. She was then enrolled at Jacaranda Special School, precursor of the Jacaranda Workshop, in 1986 and later joined the workshop in October 1992. She has been a very fast learner, reported Jacaranda Director Wycliffe Wafula, particularly in the skill of rolling ceramic beads. Njogu has now added a wide variety of skills, including shaping brass wire, assembling necklaces, and packing of products, to her repertoire.

In another field of accomplishment, Njogu represented Kenya at the Special Olympics held in the United States in 1995, competing in the 100-meter sprint and in volleyball.

Njogu has an 11-year-old son for whom she is the sole support. As a single mother, her income from Jacaranda Workshop is her only source of income. "She is always smiling, and is among the top six best artisans," said Wafula. With no formal education certificate, finding a job elsewhere has been a challenge for Njogu, and she sees Jacaranda as a wonderful opportunity to earn a living.[24]

Birthdays, holidays, teacher gifts, hostess gifts, gifts for yourself—all reasons to buy fair trade goods. When I give a fair trade gift, I often print out information about the artisan or co-op that benefitted from my purchase and tuck it in the gift box. I love watching the recipient pull out a lovely handcrafted gift along with a picture and story about its creator. Their faces transform from delight to inspiration—often followed by lots of questions about fair trade. Many of my friends now give fair trade gifts to their loved ones. And so on, and so on.

chapter 23

In a League of Its Own
greatergood network

"The noblest question in the world is What Good may I do in it?"

—BENJAMIN FRANKLIN[1]

One of the early inspirations for this book was discovering the GreaterGood Network, which operates an online portal to doing good by making direct charitable contributions, fair trade purchasing, and "clicking for charity," on behalf of a number of social causes. This site is one of the easiest, most fun and rewarding ways to help create a better world right at your computer.

> GreaterGood.org is devoted to addressing the health and well-being of people (particularly women and children), animals, and the planet.[2]

To this end, GreaterGood operates a network of Web sites that allow visitors to help a multitude of American and international charities in one of several ways. First, you can go to the Web sites and "Click to Give" by hitting "Click Here to Give—It's FREE!" at each of the Network's six sites once each day. Sponsors advertise on the site and make a contribution to

GreaterGood.org for every click. They really do—a donation for every single click. One hundred percent of the sponsors' contributions then go to nonprofit organizations working in the field. You can only click on each site once per day, but every click generates a donation to a worthy cause.

The best-known and oldest GreaterGood Network Web site is The Hunger Site, which "was founded to focus the power of the Internet on a specific humanitarian need: the eradication of world hunger."[3] The Hunger Site celebrated its tenth anniversary in 2009 and has inspired a number of similar sites, including the five additional "Click to Give" sites in the GreaterGood Network.

In addition to helping end hunger, you will find multitudes of ways to generate social good here. When you go to www.the hungersite.com, you will also see tabs that take you to sites working to fight breast cancer, address child health, improve literacy, save the rainforests, and rescue animals. Each of these sites has a "Click to Give" button.

Depending on the speed of your Internet connection, you could click on all six sites in about thirty seconds and generate donations to GreaterGood partner organizations working in each of these areas—and the results generated by the more than five million unique visitors to the sites each month are stunning.

In 2008, The Hunger Site's "Click to Give" program alone funded 66,235,889 cups of food. Other results from The Hunger Site since its inception in 1999 are equally remarkable:

On average, over 220,000 individuals from around the world visit the site each day to click the yellow "Click Here to Give—It's FREE" button.

To date, more than 300 million visitors have given more
   than *500 million cups of staple food.*
The food funded by clicks at The Hunger Site is paid for by
   sponsors who advertise on the site and distributed to
   those in need by Mercy Corps and Feeding America.
Of the sponsors' advertising fees, 100 percent goes to The
   Hunger Site's charitable partners. Funds are split
   between these organizations and go to the aid of hungry
   people in over seventy-four countries, including those in
   Africa, Asia, Eastern Europe, the Middle East, South
   America, and North America.[4]

From January through December 2008, GreaterGood.org
granted more than $3.4 million to more than fifty charities in
the United States and around the world. Significant gifts in
2008 included more than $100,000 to Mercy Corps Interna-
tional, Central Asia Institute, Feeding America, Darfur Stoves
Project, Mayo Clinic, the National Breast Cancer Foundation,
Petfinder.com Foundation, The Fund for Animals, International
Fund for Animal Welfare, and North Shore Animal League.

All of this good work created by clicking a button on your
computer! You can even sign up to receive daily e-mails remind-
ing you to go to the site and "Click to Give." I did. I click virtually every day. Pretty good use of *thirty seconds*, and you don't
even have to take out your wallet.

Once you're clicking, get one or two more people to do the
same. Your kids will love clicking to give. So will their friends.
Remember, ripples grow exponentially.

Another way you can create positive change is by *shopping in
the online store* on any of the GreaterGood Network sites. The

store sells jewelry, apparel, and gifts, many of them created by fair trade artisans and organizations. By shopping here, you generate benefits in two ways. First, your purchase supports the livelihood of the artisans and producers. Second, for every purchase, GreaterGood.org makes a donation to the partner organizations affiliated with the site. For instance, if you purchase a necklace through the store at www.thehungersite.com, Greater Good.org makes a donation to Feeding America and Mercy Corps. In 2008, purchases at The Hunger Site store funded an additional 5,845,025 cups of food. A purchase through www.thechildhealthsite.com generates a donation to the Elizabeth Glaser Pediatric AIDS Foundation, Mercy Corps, Prosthetics Outreach Foundation, and Helen Keller International.

Finally, you can make a direct contribution to charities through Gifts that Give More. You can shop for the cause you'd like to support by going to shop.thehungersite.com, a quick link to the store, and clicking on "Gifts that Give More." Here, you'll find descriptions of outstanding nonprofits improving the world every day. One hundred percent of your donation is given to the charity or project you choose. Among many other organizations, you can support Partners in Health and Feeding America through Gifts That Give More.

GreaterGood.org's partner nonprofit agencies in 2009 included the following:[5]

A Child's Right

African Wildlife Foundation

Aid to Artisans

Baal Dan

Bears Without Borders

BRAC

Camfed

Cecily's Fund

Central Asia Institute

Cree & Suena (Believe and Dream)

Darfur Stoves Project

Elizabeth Glaser Pediatric AIDS Foundation

Feeding America

First Book

Friendship Bridge

The Fund for Animals

GirlSportWorks

Haitian Health Foundation

The HALO Trust

Helen Keller International

Intelligent Mobility International (IMI)

Jungle Friends

Making Memories

Manob Sakti Unnayan Kendro (MSUK)

Mayo Clinic

Mercy Corps

The Michoacan Reforestation Fund

National Breast Cancer Foundation

The Nature Conservancy

Nepalese Youth Opportunity Foundation

Ngamba Island Chimpanzee Sanctuary

North Shore Animal League

Nyaya Health

The Ocean Foundation

Pacific Marine Mammal Center

Partners in Health

Patient Access Network (PAN) Foundation

Petfinder.com Foundation

Planet Care/Global Health Access Program

Prosthetics Outreach Foundation

Rainforest Conservation Fund

Rainforest2Reef

The Remote Area Medical (RAM) Volunteer Corps

Room to Read

Save Darfur Coalition

Save the Rain

Sit Stay Read! Inc.

Soles4Souls

SPEED Trust

Sumatran Orangutan Society (SOS)

Tibetan Healing Fund

The Vishaka Society for the Prevention of Cruelty to
    Animals (VSPCA)

The Volunteer Development Poverty Children's Association
    (VDPCA)

Womens's Education for Advancement and Empowerment
    (WEAVE)

WhizzKids United

World Bicycle Relief

World Land Trust

Zardozi

GreaterGood.org is one of the best tools I've found for everyday citizens to make a difference through affordable giving. Go to www.thehungersite.com and click, purchase, or donate. You'll be doing a world of good.

ONE FULL BOWL

Consider Imani, the child from Chapter 1, who ate only a single meager meal each day. The impact of hunger on Imani's life and her family's rippled outward, ultimately affecting her community, her nation, and the world.

Today in every one of the world's poorest countries, there are millions of Imanis. Currently, 50 of the 192 member countries of the United Nations are labeled as a "least developed country." That's more than one in every four countries around the world. These countries' gross national income per capita is $2.05 or less per day.[6] Their people suffer from hunger, poor health, lack of education, and stagnant, underdeveloped economies.

The problem is big. We know that. You've seen the numbers throughout this book.

You've also seen how small donations to any of the organizations described in this book *will make an impact*. Believe it. You can make an immediate difference in one life that over time, touches many, many lives.

Together, we will eliminate extreme poverty in developing countries and improve the lives of those living in poverty in the United States.

First, imagine that Imani's father obtained a KickStart microirrigation pump that tripled the family's crop yield, improving their diets and generating additional income. He uses a bicycle to take his larger harvests to market more regularly. Imani's bowl is filled three times each day.

Now she is healthier and stronger. Her family uses a water filter and bed nets, so she isn't getting sick from malaria or waterborne diseases, and because she is eating more, if she does get sick, her body can better fight the infection.

Her family can now enroll Imani in school as they can afford the fees for a school uniform and books. Because her health is better and her parents do not rely on her to provide labor or income for the family, Imani rarely misses school. She completes primary school and even attends secondary school because a new bridge has been constructed that reduces her daily commute to school from hours to minutes.

Imani's family is thriving and has achieved middle-class status in their community. They and their future offspring have escaped the trap of cyclical poverty.

There is peace in Imani's village because the people are employed productively in all manner of entrepreneurial enterprises, many of which were initially funded by microloans. People with reliable work, enough to eat, basic health care, and the opportunity for an education are busy improving their lives rather than fomenting violence and revolution. Peace ripples forth.

Give a little. Give once a week or once a month. Give what you can afford. Give to organizations that are making this story a reality thousands, even millions, of times over. They need you to help them do more good. If you give a little, they'll do a lot more good.

Let's fill Imani's bowl and see what happens.

chapter 24

Sixteen More Ways to Make Waves

*"Sometimes when I consider what tremendous consequences
come from little things I am tempted to think
there are no little things."*

—BRUCE BARTON[1]

These nonprofits are equally worthy of your affordable donations and will use them to help countless others improve their lives. You can get more information about them from their Web sites.

HUNGER

The Hunger Project: www.thp.org

I love The Hunger Project for its tremendous commitment to empowering local people. The Hunger Project is a global, nonprofit, strategic organization committed to the sustainable end of world hunger. They create "epicenters," which are "clusters of rural villages where women and men are mobilized to create and run their own programs to meet basic needs. After several phases over a five-year period, an epicenter becomes self-reliant, meaning it is able to fund its own activities and no longer requires further investment from The Hunger Project. "The Hunger

Project has mobilized *110 epicenter communities* in eight countries in Africa."[2]

In addition to mobilizing at the grassroots level, The Hunger Project conducts its work by empowering women as key change agents and forging effective partnerships with local government.

ECHO: www.echonet.org

"Growing Locally: Feeding Globally"—ECHO's work ripples through the technical support they provide to those working with poor people around the world. I had an "Aha! Of course" moment when I read the following story about growing vegetable gardens at HIV/AIDS hospitals and clinics. Yes, they grow the fresh veggies right on site!

Steve Bolinger is working in Senegal with the group "Development in Gardening" (DIG). He and his coworkers were introduced to ECHO at the end of 2006 when he was invited to ECHO's annual agricultural conference. At the conference, Steve presented about their experiences installing urban vegetable gardens in HIV/AIDS hospitals and clinics. They also were able to connect with other people doing similar work around the world.

Steve writes, "With the help and support of ECHO and the seeds they provide, DIG has been able to introduce many plants that were not previously known such as chaya, kale, collard greens, cranberry hibiscus, jackfruit, Indian mustard, and passion fruit. We have established all these plants in each of our clinic gardens and most of the outpatient home gardens. [The people we work with] have definitely fallen in love with the Indian mustard and their second favorite is the cranberry hibiscus.

"DIG has definitely grown over the past three years and we are now operating in Senegal, Uganda, Dominican Republic, and will be in Cambodia next year. Having the support and technical knowledge from ECHO has really helped us since each garden and each country is very different from the other. Thanks to ECHO, we have an international database of knowledge to help us solve the many problems that come our way. It is such an incredible blessing that an organization such as ECHO exists to help the people working on the ground around the world."[3]

Freedom from Hunger: www.freedomfromhunger.og
"Freedom from Hunger combines microfinance with health and life skills services to equip very poor families to improve their incomes, safeguard their health and achieve lasting food security."[4]

Rita's Story: No More "Hungry Season"[5]
Good credit. A savings account. The knowledge to use money wisely. It's the recipe for financial security.

In rural Ghana, West Africa, the recipe is the same, but the proportions are very different than the ones you and I know. It takes so little in a place like this . . . so little to make a life and death difference.

In the rural village where Rita Anohia lives with her five children, an $80 loan was the first ingredient she needed to make her family financially secure. Rita farms mangos and harvests them twice a year. Before she joined Freedom from Hunger's Credit with Education program, Rita worked hard to stretch her profits to the next harvest, but in that last month or so before the mangos ripened, her family never seemed to have enough to eat.

In Ghana, *people call this the "hungry season." It's that time each year when children grow thin and common childhood illnesses become deadly*—especially for the youngest ones. It's the time of year when having money to see a doctor and buy medicine is more important than ever. But it's also the time of year when the money just isn't there.

COURAGE TO FACE THE FUTURE

Thanks to donor support for Freedom from Hunger, we were able to bring Rita that $80 loan along with education on how to diversify her business so that money comes in year-round. Rita now farms peppers, beans, and okra in the field next to her mango grove. These crops are harvested throughout the year, ensuring a steady income. Rita also learned how to save money.

Since joining the program 5 years ago, Rita has borrowed and repaid 10 loans. The education gave her skills to manage her business, knowledge to safeguard her family's health, and courage to try new things.

Many people would have met Rita and decided she was too poor to repay a loan. Five hungry children and a couple of mango trees don't count as collateral. But Freedom from Hunger knows that women like Rita are ready to end hunger in their own families and in their communities.

Rita is one of more than a million women Freedom from Hunger serves—women who keep proving the power of credit and education in the hands of a mother. "The program has allowed me to imagine a better future—especially for my daughters," Rita tells us.

"The biggest thing for me was starting to save," says Rita. "I had never saved before. Now I have savings to tap when it's time for the school fees and for other needs, including more food. My family is better now. We eat better."

FreeRice: www.freerice.com

Visitors to www.freerice.com can play a game that tests their vocabulary, and Web site sponsors, those who advertise at the bottom of each page, donate the cost of purchasing ten grains of rice for each correct answer. All rice is distributed by the United Nations World Food Program (WFP). "It's fun, it's free, and it's real!"

FreeRice sponsors make financial contributions to the World Food Program that are unrestricted, which means WFP can use them where they are needed most. "Often WFP is able to purchase the rice in the very countries where the beneficiaries are located, cutting down on the transport time to reach the hungry and helping to stimulate local economies at the same time."

Here are some examples of where FreeRice rice has been distributed:[6]

- In Bangladesh, to feed 27,000 refugees from Myanmar for two weeks
- In Cambodia, to provide take-home rations of 4 kilograms of rice for two months to 13,500 pregnant and nursing women
- In Uganda, to feed 66,000 school children for a week
- In Nepal, to feed over 108,000 Bhutanese refugees for three days
- In Bhutan, to feed 41,000 children for eight days

- In Myanmar, to feed 750,000 cyclone affected people for three days

HEALTH

Partners In Health (PIH): www.pih.org

The work of PIH has three goals: to care for our patients, to alleviate the root causes of disease in their communities, and to share lessons learned around the world. Through long-term partnerships with our sister organizations, we bring the benefits of modern medical science to those most in need and work to alleviate the crushing economic and social burdens of poverty that exacerbate disease. PIH believes that health is a fundamental right, not a privilege. Through service, training, advocacy, and research, we seek to raise the standard of care for the poor everywhere.[7]

Denizard Wilson.
Photo courtesy of Partners in Health.

Denizard Wilson demonstrates how PIH empowers those living with disease to help themselves as well as others.

AIDS Patient in Haiti Is Also Messenger of Hope: Denizard Wilson[8]

I was on a bus on my way to Port au Prince when I heard a woman talking badly about AIDS, spreading rumors. I could not let her say those things anymore, so I said to her, "I am in-fected."

She didn't believe me. "Liar," she said.

So I took my medications from my bag and held them out in my hand for her to see. Because I have this virus in my blood, I take medicine every day. I have a community health worker who brings my medication to me every morning. Before I plan to travel anywhere, I tell my community health worker and my doctor, and they give me the pills to take with me. I explained all of this to her and the rest of the people on the bus.

"Are you lying to me?" she asked.

I replied, "You will not find one single human being who would choose to be infected by this disease. Why would I lie about this?"

Apart from the kidnapping and the political problems that we have in Haiti, there is a terrible epidemic that is sweeping through our country. Wherever I go, I try to spread this mes-sage: AIDS can touch anyone anywhere.

I am a motorcycle messenger for Partners In Health. I work in a village called Thomonde at one of their seven hospitals in Haiti's Central Plateau. I carry patient blood samples over dirt roads, and doctors send me to find patients who stop coming in for appointments, or patients who think that an HIV positive diagnosis means their life is over. I have a message for these pa-tients, and for my family, and for everyone, infected or not: as long as we are alive and have access to drugs, there is hope.

On October 4, 1993 I was diagnosed with AIDS. I had a job in an office in Port au Prince. I was making some money and advancing in my job. I started getting weak, though, and I kept getting admitted to the city hospital. I had health insurance, but it was not covering my medical expenses. Every time I began to recover my strength, I would fall ill again.

At first I tried to hide my sickness from my boss. I was afraid he would fire me if he knew that I was HIV positive. But this sickness does not know how to hide.

There came a point when I had spent all my money and could not bear this virus anymore. I finally told one of my directors that I was infected. He told me about Partners In Health—that they had a good hospital in the Central Plateau with free health care. So I moved back to Thomonde, the place I was born, to be closer to the hospital. For the 13 years that I have been with Partners In Health, I have never been sick again—not the kind of sickness I had known.

My wife is also infected. We thought that my seven-year-old was HIV positive when she was born. At that time, there was no program to prevent mothers from giving the virus to their babies.

Thanks to God, though, we know now that she is HIV negative. By the time my wife was pregnant with my second daughter, though, Partners In Health had started a program to prevent the AIDS virus from being passed from mother to child. The hospital gives us infant formula every month so that she will not be infected by her mother's breast milk.

Now she is four months old, and we are waiting for the test result to see if she is infected. There are scientists and researchers searching for drugs, and I know they will find a cure for us. That day is not far away. My community health worker used to give me three different drugs. I do not know what the medicines are called, but I know that I used to take one big pill and two small pills. Now, I only have two pills, and someday those two pills will become one. Finally, there will come a day when I will not have to take any pills at all. I know that. I feel that.

Medications have slowed the virus down, but there is no cure yet. I have a message for all the youth who are uninfected: go to school before you enter into sexual relations. It is your right to wait until you are the appropriate age to be intimate with a partner. Do not give your body to just anybody. Before you give your body to someone, ask yourself, do I know this person?

And to those of you who are infected, protect your partner. The AIDS virus is like a poison, and to give it to someone else is like a crime. I do not want to make anyone die before it is their time.

Every time you enter into sexual relations with someone, even with a condom, you are taking a chance. One decision that you make now can affect your children and their children for generations to come.

Maladi pa tonbe sou pyebwa, se sou moun li tombe. This sickness does not fall on trees, as the Haitian expression goes, but on people. I would not like for even one single living creature to become infected with this disease—not an animal, not even an insect, let alone a human being.

I want to ask all the people and organizations that are supporting Partners In Health to keep helping them so that they can give more people a chance at life, like me. I ask all the drug companies to lower the price of the medications because there are thousands and thousands of people who still do not have the chance to take medicine because they cannot even afford to buy food.

On that October day when I first learned that I was infected, there is something I had not yet realized: when a person is infected, that does not have to mean that life is over. Dr. Almazor, one of my doctors, would always encourage me when I felt depressed. He would tell me that even though I am infected, right now there is someone else who is dying, and there is someone else who is being buried at this moment. But me, I still have work to do.

Thanks to Partners In Health, and the medication they give me every day, I am alive. I have a different life, but it is life, nevertheless, and I will protect the rest of the days I have been given, thanks to God, and thanks to Partners In Health.

The only way I would be scared would be if Partners In Health did not exist. As long as they are here, I am alive. And as long as I am alive, I will have hope, and as long as I have hope, I will continue to spread this message.

The Children's Health Fund (CHF): www.childrenshealthfund.org

Aha! Much like the Breathmobile—but bringing comprehensive health care to poor children. I love it.

A DOCTOR FOR EVERY CHILD

Lack of adequate health care is a fact of life for many low-income children. According to the CHF, "problem may be transportation, insurance, or language and cultural barriers. The end result is too often the same. Children lack the essential health services to grow and thrive." In the most heartbreaking scenarios, they develop life-threatening illnesses—or lifelong conditions— needlessly, for want of decent health care."[9]

The Children's Health Fund "Blue Bus" mobile medical units draw children and families for curbside checkups and treatments. It may sound unorthodox. When necessary, it is. To ensure underserved children get the health care they need, sometimes caregivers must go to the children.[10]

CHF's patients receive comprehensive care in all areas, including complete oral health and dental treatments that are often overlooked. "We provide screening, prevention, identification and management of acute and chronic conditions; health education; and mental health and development services."[11]

CHF IN ACTION—BLUE BUS TO THE RESCUE

One of the most commonly overlooked health care issues among poor children is dental care. Poor dental health is painful, disrupts children's ability to learn, and can have long-term disastrous consequences. Fortunately for this seven-year-old, Blue Bus came to school one day.

The teachers at a school where our Blue Bus was parked brought me a seven-year-old girl whose mom had sent her to school with a swollen face. She was one of six children, ages six months to eight years. She was the oldest of the kids and had to help her single mom take care of her younger brothers and sisters. When I saw her that morning she was in severe pain and her face was so swollen her left eye was almost shut. When I examined her I found that her 1st molar was partially broken and she had several severe cavities. The infection had spread to her facial tissues. She had been complaining to her mother and teachers for some time now, but they did not pay her any mind until they saw how badly her face was swollen. She had not eaten in days due to the pain.

This was the first time she was being seen by a dental professional in her entire life. Her teeth were decayed and needed care. At this point there was very little I could do, except arrange for her to be admitted to the hospital. There she was treated with intravenous antibiotics, intravenous fluids, and adequate pain medications. A CT scan of her face was done to make sure there was no extension of the infection into her sinuses and orbits, which if was present, would mean major surgery and further complications with the possibility of blindness and brain abscess.

Luckily, the infection was limited to her tooth and the soft tissues of her face and after five days of intravenous antibiotics she was eating, pain free and smiling once again. She was seen by the dentist and me in the dental office after her discharge from the hospital. At that time, full x-rays of her mouth were done, and she was found to have two more cavities. The infected tooth was extracted and the other cavities filled. Dental cleaning with plaque removal was performed, and I educated both her and her mother about dental care. She was provided with toothbrushes, toothpaste, and written instructions on daily brushing. We also had her siblings come into the clinic for dental cleanings and checkups.

This was a good ending to a case that could have been potentially life threatening simply because the preventive maintenance on this child's teeth was not done. It is just one of the many examples of the plight that children face every day due to lack of proper health and dental maintenance.[12]

EngenderHealth: www.engenderhealth.org

EngenderHealth works to improve the health and well-being of people in the poorest communities of the world. We do this by

Mamadou Sow. In Guinea, community members come together to transport a pregnant woman to the nearest health clinic. *Photo courtesy of EngenderHealth.*

sharing our expertise in sexual and reproductive health and transforming the quality of health care. We promote gender equity, advocate for sound practices and policies, and inspire people to assert their rights to better, healthier lives. Working in partnership with local organizations, we adapt our work in response to local needs.[13]

Among its many projects, EngenderHealth addresses one of the most difficult and widespread health problems among women in developing countries: obstetric fistula. Obstetric fistula, little known and extremely rare in developed countries, occurs when tissue is ruptured during a prolonged childbirth rendering a woman incontinent, often of both urine and feces. This medical problem, easily corrected by surgery, yet unobtainable and unaffordable to most poor women, typically causes total social rejection by family and the larger community leading to isolation and destitution.

The following story portrays EngenderHealth's work to correct obstetric fistula and help women become contributing and self-sustaining members of the community.

COMMUNITIES RESPOND: WOMEN'S HEALTH FIRST![14]

Early marriage and childbirth are the norm for girls in rural Guinea, and Cire Kante was no exception. Married at age twelve, she became pregnant soon after. She spent a week in labor, with assistance from only her mother and a few elder village women. When her husband finally took her to the nearest health center in an old truck, 30 miles away and on roads muddied from heavy rains, it was too late. Cire had a stillbirth and returned home a few days later to find she was incontinent—the telltale sign of fistula.

After treatments from traditional healers failed, her family began to turn on her. "First, I was rejected by my mother-in-law, then little by little by the rest of my husband's family, and then by my husband himself," said Cire. She also was not allowed to attend religious ceremonies or community celebrations. "You cannot imagine how painful it is to work alone, eat alone, and sleep alone. The isolation was more painful and destructive than my physical handicap."

That all began to change in June 2008, when Cire met a woman whose own fistula had been surgically repaired. Cire sought treatment for herself, and before long she underwent a successful surgery at the Jean Paul II Hospital in Conakry, the capital. Slowly—after eleven years—she is getting used to being with people again.

In countries like Guinea, fistula is all too common. In many ways, it represents the challenges of improving maternal health in poor communities, where most women deliver at home, without skilled birth attendants, and many suffer long labors. Emergency obstetric care, including cesarean delivery, rarely is available and often comes too late.

Preventing fistula, a vital part of EngenderHealth's growing program, means working closely with local leaders to raise community awareness. In Guinea, *EngenderHealth's Innovations*

Fund (which provides seed money for new and promising programs) is supporting Safe Motherhood Village Committees—groups of volunteers who facilitate care for pregnant women and those living with fistula. The committees identify pregnant women and work with their families to help them get antenatal care and recognize complications and emergencies. They refer women who have obstetric emergencies—and those already living with fistula, such as Cire—to hospitals for treatment.

Through home visits, community workshops at places like local markets, and religious sermons, village committees also help men see the value in supporting their wives and accompanying them to health care facilities. And they don't shy away from tough subjects, like the consequences of early marriage and violence against women and girls. "These committees address the root causes of fistula: lack of awareness, limited access to health care, and inattention to the welfare of women and girls," said Moustapha Diallo, EngenderHealth's program manager in Guinea. "But this outreach isn't just about fistula. Everything the committees do is helping to save women's lives," he added.

At the same time, EngenderHealth is training surgeons to perform fistula repair, increasing doctors' capacity to offer high-quality obstetric care, and coordinating rehabilitation for women who have had successful surgery, making it possible for them to start new lives.

Success is already evident. In Guinea alone, more than seven hundred women received surgical repair. Experience there reinforces guiding principles in the approach: Work directly with communities, engage local leaders, and ensure that men are supportive partners. This is not only how EngenderHealth makes motherhood safer, it is also the key to bringing change that lasts—for individuals and communities alike.

The United Nations Population Fund (UNFPA): www.unfpa.org

Among many other life-saving projects, UNFPA distributes over 140,000 clean delivery kits each year.[15] At the UNFPA, a $20 donation provides twelve clean home delivery kits, which are distributed primarily through its emergency relief work with refugees of natural disasters and armed conflicts.

You can help the UNFPA support the *most vulnerable women and newborns in the world:* those living as refugees as a result of violence, hunger, natural disasters, and other forms of displacement. Can you imagine a more formidable situation than giving birth under the open sky without any means of sanitation, pain management, health care, emergency care, and possibly no food or water?

Many women have lived this experience. Many women and newborns have not survived it. With a clean delivery kit provided by the UNFPA, their odds of surviving it skyrocket.

EDUCATION

UNICEF: www.unicef.org

UNICEF provides a service close to my heart: early childhood development.

UNICEF believes that the early years of life are crucial. When well nurtured and cared for in their earliest years, children are more likely to survive, to grow in a healthy way, to have less disease and fewer illnesses, and to develop thinking, language, emotional and social skills.[16] Early Childhood Development interventions cut across all UNICEF program areas, while focusing on three areas of intervention for early childhood development: quality basic health, education and protection services; good care practices for children within the family and community; and early child development policies.[17]

First Book: www.firstbook.org

Founded in 1992, First Book provides new books to children in need, addressing one of the most important factors affecting literacy—access to books. An innovative leader in social enterprise, First Book has distributed more than 60 million free and low-cost books to disadvantaged children and the programs that serve them.[18]

FIRST BOOK—OUR IMPACT[19]

Noted pollster Louis Harris conducted an independent study to determine the effectiveness of the First Book model. This study surveyed 2,564 individuals over a 14-month period. The survey also asked mentors, teachers, and administrators to write their thoughts about First Book and its impact on their reading programs. Their comments speak for themselves:

> CONQUILLE INDIAN TRIBE: "A young boy and I taught his mother how to read and we all cried for joy together. It couldn't have happened without First Book."

> COOS COUNTY WOMEN'S CRISIS CENTER: "It's amazing. Families that have never been inside a library before are going in to get library cards. They are very proud of

them. Their kids get them, too. Suddenly, they are
proud and want to become readers."

SUNNYHILL SCHOOL: "We have a little girl in our program, a
pre-school child. She liked her book so much, she slept
with it every night under her pillow. She wouldn't part
with it for anything!"

KELSO INDIAN EDUCATION: "I had a boy whom I tutor who
almost never talked and never said how he felt. Then he
read a book we got through First Book, *Sometimes I Feel
Like A Mouse*. Suddenly he began to talk, and to talk
about how he felt."

LIVES IN TRANSITION: "A young boy with behavior
problems was taken from the foster home. We lost touch
with him, but two months later we found him and he
still had his First Book. It was his most valued
possession."

Harlem Children's Zone (HCZ): www.hcz.org

A holistic system of education, social service, and community-
building programs aimed at helping the children and families in
a 97-block area of Central Harlem.[20]

Called "one of the most ambitious social-service experiments
of our time," by the *New York Times*, the Harlem Children's
Zone® Project is a unique, holistic approach to rebuilding a community so that its children can stay on track through college and
go on to the job market.[21]

HCZ has created an oasis of success in the midst of deprivation in New York City's Central Harlem area by offering comprehensive, intensive programming that begins during a parent's
pregnancy with a nine-week parenting education workshop.

Children begin enrichment programs as preschoolers and participate in a high-quality, high-expectation education through high school. HCZ's statistics for at-risk children's performance in school are unparalleled.

Studies show that children living in homes where one or more of the following risk factors are present are much less likely to be prepared to succeed when they begin kindergarten: (1) having a mother with less than a high school education, (2) living in a family that received food stamps or cash welfare payments, (3) living in a single-parent household, and (4) having parents whose primary language is something other than English.[22] Yet, HCZ has achieved the following:

In 2008, 100 percent of HCZ preschoolers were found to be ready for school for the sixth year in a row.[23]

Nationwide, 7 percent of black eighth graders perform at grade level in math.[24] You can compare this to HCZ's results as follows:[25]

This past spring (2008), 100 percent of the third-graders at HCZ Promise Academy II scored at or above grade level in the statewide math tests. A few blocks away, 97 percent of the Promise Academy I third-graders were at or above grade level.

Many of these children have been in HCZ programs from the time their parents were in The Baby College, which highlights the effectiveness of our comprehensive model of supporting children.

TOOLS, TECHNOLOGY, AND INFRASTRUCTURE

Hippo Water Roller: www.hippowater.org

In most countries, traditional water collection involves carrying a 5-gallon (20-liter) bucket on the head. This practice puts a great burden on the body and can damage the spine, neck, and knees over time. A full Hippo Water Roller only feels like 22 pounds (10 kg) when rolled over level ground, making it possible for almost anyone to transport 24 gallons (90 liters) of water in much less time and with greater ease. Fewer trips to collect water means women and children can spend more time on productive educational and economic activities. In fact, men are proud to be seen using a Hippo Roller, and many have assumed the responsibility of collecting water for the family. Finally, the Hippo Roller also filters water, ensuring that the water collected is safe to drink.[26]

Photo courtesy of Hippo Water Roller

Margaret Mahlangu, a young mother, offers a good example of how the Hippo Roller is truly life-changing. Using traditional methods (carrying a 5-gallon bucket of water on the head), Margaret wasn't able to collect enough water to keep her children hydrated or practice basic hygiene. But thanks to support from donors, Margaret recently received a Hippo Water Roller. She can now collect 24 gallons of water much more easily and in less time. Margaret's days of making multiple trips per day to the water tap are over! Her son, Mulungisi, is benefitting too—he's attending school regularly, since he no longer needs to spend long hours each day helping his mother collect water for their family.[27]

Engineers Without Borders (EWB-USA): www.ewb-usa.org

Engineers Without Borders is in the business of capacity building. A widely adopted definition of capacity building is offered by General Henry Hatch, former Commander of the U.S. Army Corps of Engineers. "Capacity Building is the building of human, institutional, and infrastructure capacity to help societies develop secure, stable and sustainable economies, governments and other institutions through mentoring, training, education, physical projects, the infusion of financial and other resources, and most importantly, the motivation and inspiration of people to improve their lives.[28]

EWB-USA is committed to designing and implementing engineering projects in developing communities around the world. There is great need in construction, information systems, sanitation, and energy.

The following message comes from EWB-USA founder Bernard Amadei, a civil engineering professor at the University of Colorado.[29] Remember as you're reading that *Amadei's big projects can be realized with small donations.*

FOR THE WORLD'S POOR: THINK BIG

I am a civil engineer in a world where technological feats and big achievements, towering buildings, and ostentatious wonders have been the measure of our success.

The world needs no more big structures that satisfy the needs of only one billion people in the Western world. It needs a massive, sustained outpouring of compassion in action for the billions of impoverished, but resilient people asking to be seen, dreaming of a better life. The five billion whose job it is to stay alive by the end of each day.

Over the past seven years, I've had the privilege to work side-by-side with volunteers of Engineers Without Borders-USA, an organization I helped start in 2001. We work with developing-world communities to install small-scale water, renewable energy, sanitation, housing, telecommunications, and other sustainable projects.

Amazingly, that vision has spoken to and galvanized 12,000 idealistic engineers, architects, medical professionals, teachers, and students in 300 chapters around the country, now working in 47 countries around the world.

Time Magazine calls our volunteers, like those at Montana State, the "blueprint brigade." The Montana students are installing wells to bring clean water to 57 schools in western Kenya, not far from President-elect Barack Obama's families' home. So far, they've delivered on their promise for 3,000 people, and the elders look with hope to their children now in school, not miles away fetching water from contaminated streams.

Make no mistake—Engineers Without Borders-USA believes in big. We believe in big generosity, the kind that can transform our world and ease our own poverty of spirit here in America, where excessive materialism has drained our souls.

We believe in the big impacts that ripple out when we harness the talents of our best and brightest here so others can finally enjoy water, power, food, education, medicine, and jobs.

We believe in the wide-scale peace and prosperity that can come when people feel infused with hope and dignity—not bitterness and despair.

I am proud of my EWB-USA's colleagues' accomplishments the past seven years. EWB-USA volunteers work shoulder-to-shoulder with people from Ecuador to Uganda so they can finally drink a glass of clean water or turn on a solar-powered light in their hut, allowing children to study far into the night.

Have you ever witnessed the smiles of children who have clean water, light to do their homework assignments, who are able to go to school, who are no longer abused, and who stand proud of themselves as positive and healthy contributors to their communities? I have seen it in Rwanda, Afghanistan, the Middle East, and elsewhere.

As I've looked into the eyes of street children in Afghanistan desperate for a future other than terrorism, or children in Rwanda hungry for something greater than genocide, I've reached one big conclusion: we belong to one another. And children across the Earth deserve the same hopes and opportunities we give our children here.

Engineers Without Borders-USA asks you to think big with us. It's amazing what you can find inside yourself when you look for it. As Gandhi said, we need to be the change we want to see in the world. We can't wait for others to make a big-enough difference.

This month is the 60th anniversary of the UN declaration of human rights, and 1.1 billion people in the world live on less than $1 a day, 2 billion on less than $2 a day. About 1.2 billion do not have access to water, 2.4 billion do not have access to proper sanitation, and 1.6 billion do not have access to electricity. Half of the

2.2 billion children in the world live in extreme poverty and about 30,000 of them die every day for reasons that are preventable.

It's come down to us, you and me. And what a wonderful privilege that is.

America is capable of a new bigness of spirit. We are more than capable of building a more humane and equitable world where all citizens have their dignity and their basic needs met.

That's the kind of big construction project in which I can believe.

Darfur Stoves Project: www.darfurstoves.org

Every day, women living in the refugee camps of Darfur, Sudan, must walk for up to seven hours outside the safety of the camps to collect firewood for cooking, putting them at risk for violent attacks. Researchers at the Darfur Stoves Project have engineered a more efficient wood-burning stove, which is greatly reducing both the women's need for firewood and the threats against them.

The following notes come from a Berkeley-Darfur Stoves volunteer who traveled to Sudan in 2005. They are representative of many such stories that were collected.

SATURDAY, NOVEMBER 26, 2005

This mother has lived in the refugee camp for the past 18 months. She has six children with her. Her husband disappeared during the travel to the camp. She survives by keeping 4 chickens—which lay eggs but not every day. At home, she had 11 goats and several sheep.

She ran away from the Janjaweed with only the clothes on her back and the six children with her. When the Janjaweed attacked, many adults and children died in front of her eyes. The Janjaweed burnt down many houses and killed many villagers. Her uncle helped her reach the refugee camp.

She goes out to collect wood and palm leaves to weave mats to sell. She is afraid of the Janjaweed, but does not have a choice. She sells excess wood in the market for some cash for the children's needs.

THURSDAY, NOVEMBER 24, 2005

After the demonstration of cookstoves, dozens of women crowded around us, showing us their calloused, bruised and cut hands from cutting and carrying thorny desert brush wood with their bare hands. They were farmers before, not habituated to such extreme daily hardship and wanted to show the coarsening of their hands to us to illustrate the coarsening of their lives from their daily suffering and hardships. This was a very significant visible symbol to them to indicate what was happening to them.

THE BERKELEY-DARFUR ULTRA
HIGH-EFFICIENCY COOK STOVE:[30]

- Uses up to 75 percent less fuel, enabling women to minimize the dangerous seven-hour treks outside the camps to gather wood
- Can be assembled in Sudan by locals, enabling them to earn extra income and become part of the solution
- Is suited to local high-temperature and high-wind outdoor cooking methods
- Emits less smoke than other stoves, minimizing smoke inhalation

- Helps the denuded environment recover from severe overharvesting

Cosmos Ignite and One Million Lights

www.cosmosignite.com

www.onemillionlights.com

It is difficult to overstate the transformative potential of clean, affordable fuel for cooking and lighting in the developing world. Every day, millions of the world's poorest people spend hours collecting materials to use for fuel or working for wages to spend on fuel.

Cosmos Ignite Innovations is the first global social venture to sustainably address the challenges of kerosene lighting through using very efficient solar LED lighting. Cosmos Ignite's vision is "innovating to empower." Its first product, the MightyLight, is already replacing kerosene and bringing safe, affordable lighting to thousands of people in India, thanks to One Million Lights, as well as to many other developing countries.

Anna Sidana founded the Palo Alto–based nonprofit One Million Lights, which aims to distribute one million solar lights, such as MightyLights, to rural villages around the world. Cindy Workman volunteered with One Million Lights and shares her experience below, which tells how desperately the poorest people strive to attain an education, and how much clean and available light for their homes can help.

A child studies with the help of a MightyLight.

Photo courtesy of One Million Lights.

Kombo's Story[31]

Cindy Workman had been building schools and libraries for six years in the district where the village of Mnyenzeni is located in Kenya. She was familiar with the rural and almost desperate conditions of the villagers, especially the children. The villagers survive on crops of maize and a few coconut orchards scattered over the vast wasteland. They live mostly in mud huts with no access to any modern facilities. These people, including the children as they make their way to school, have to walk for several miles a day in scorching heat. The average income is 200 Kenyan Shillings or $3 per week, half of which is spent on kerosene for lighting lamps that are dim and unhealthy. When Cindy set out to distribute the MightyLights she knew how much this would change the lives of the children.

It was determined that the top students—a boy and a girl in eighth grade from each of the schools—would receive a light. Cindy interviewed the children to hear their stories and to understand their challenges. Each child had a unique story and this is the story of Kombo, a young man in high school.

Kombo gets up before dawn at 4:30 a.m. so that he can get a head start on his studies. He is a good student and has received a school scholarship that enables him to study. Without that Kombo would not be able to attend school as he has no way of paying for his education. He does not have a *Shamba*, or farm, to grow and market corn, which is the main source of income for people of this region. After two hours of studying he walks for three miles to get to school. A typical school day is from 7:00 a.m. to 4:00 p.m. After school he tends to his younger brother and sister, who are dependent on him for their livelihood. Kombo's father had died four years ago from a snake bite and his mother was driven out of the village, never to be seen again.

Kombo and his siblings have a single meal every day in the evening. Their dinner usually consists of edible weeds and *Ugali*, or finely ground corn meal. As Kombo has no land, he is not able to harvest any vegetables that would accompany the corn. By the time Kombo is done with his daily chores, it is dark and the three siblings huddle in their small and dark hut around their study table. The table nearly fills up the whole place. There is a single lonely kerosene lamp that is placed on the table. They study late into the night.

When Cindy asked Kombo what he needed most, he did not ask for books or pencils, or even food, but for kerosene. Kombo wants to study and hopes to go to the University of Kenya one day to become an engineer.

Cindy was overwhelmed at how dramatically the Mighty-Light changed the lives of the children of Mnyenzeni. She saw that the light gave them hope to be able to think beyond their dire situation and to dream of a better life. Light gave them life.

Cindy Workman is an elementary school teacher based in Utah and also an active board member of Koins for Kenya.

The charity **One Million Lights distributes solar lights** in developing countries. You can help get a solar light into a home by going to www.onemillionlights.org and making a donation.

World Toilet Organization: www.worldtoilet.org

World Toilet Organization (WTO) is a global nonprofit organization committed to improving toilet and sanitation conditions worldwide. WTO is also one of the few organizations to focus on toilets instead of water, which receives more attention and resources under the common subject of sanitation.[32]

According to the Natural Resources Defense Council, "At any one time almost half of the developing world's people are suffering from diseases associated with lack of water, sanitation, and hygiene. However, solutions are available now and are a good investment. Of the 2.5 billion people without access, nearly 1 billion are children. Approximately every 20 seconds a child dies as a direct result of a lack of access to basic sanitation—this is nearly 2 million preventable deaths each year."[33]

The World Health Organization estimates that every dollar spent on proper sanitation by governments generates on average $9 in economic benefit. WTO helps distribute the Ecosan toilet, which "utilizes a natural biological process to break down human waste into a dehydrated odourless compost-like material.[34]

ORGANIZATION CONTACT INFORMATION

ActionAid
www.actionaid.org
PostNet suite #248
Private bag X31
Saxonwold 2132
Johannesburg, South Africa
Phone: 27-11-731-4500

Action Against Hunger
(*Action Contre la Faim*, or ACF)
www.actionagainsthunger.org
Action Against Hunger - USA
247 West 37th Street, 10th Floor
New York, NY 10018
USA
Phone: 1-212-967-7800

**Asthma and Allergy
Foundation of America**
www.aafa.org
1233 20th Street NW, Suite 402
Washington, DC 20036
USA
Phone: 1-800-7ASTHMA

Baltimore Breathmobile
www.umm.edu/breathmobile
UMMS Foundation—
    Breathmobile
110 S. Paca Street, 9th Floor
Baltimore, MD 21201
USA
Phone: 1-410-328-5770

BeadforLife
www.beadforlife.org
1143 Portland Place, Ste.1
Boulder, CO 80304
USA
Phone: 1-303-554-5901

Bridges to Prosperity
www.bridgestoprosperity.org
5007 C-126 Victory Blvd.
Yorktown, VA 23693
USA
Phone: 1-757-234-6230

Build On
www.buildon.org
PO Box 16741
Stamford, CT 06905
USA
Phone: 1-203-585-5390

Chicago Mobile C.A.R.E
www.mobilecarefoundation.org
Mobile C.A.R.E. Foundation
3247 West 26th Street, Suite 2
Chicago, IL 60623
USA
Phone: 1-773-254-4030

The Children's Health Fund
www.childrenshealthfund.org
215 West 125th Street, Suite 301
New York, NY 10027
USA
Phone: 1-212-535-9400

Cosmos Ignite Innovations
www.cosmosignite.com
1421 14th Floor
Ansal Tower
Nehru Place
New Delhi 110019
India
Phone: 91-11-26425711

CraftNetwork
www.craftnetworkstore.com
91 Christopher Street, Suite 12
New York, NY 10014
USA
Phone : 1-866-326-4358

Darfur Stoves Project
www.darfurstoves.org
PO Box 856
Berkeley, CA 94701
USA
(phone not available)

Developments in Literacy
www.dil.org
12062 Valley View Street, Suite
 218
Garden Grove, CA 92845
USA
Phone: 1-714-895-5345

DonorsChoose.org
www.donorschoose.org
347 West 36th Street, Suite 503
New York, NY 10018
USA
Phone: 1-212-239-3615

ECHO
www.echonet.org
17391 Durrance Road North

Fort Myers, FL 33917
USA
Phone: 1-239-543-3246

EngenderHealth
www.engenderhealth.org
440 Ninth Avenue
New York, NY 10001
USA
Phone: 1-212-561-8000

Engineers Without Borders
http://ewb-usa.org
4665 Nautilus Court, Suite 300
Boulder, CO 80301
USA
Phone: 1-303-772-2723

Feeding America
www.feedingamerica.org
35 E. Wacker Dr., #2000
Chicago, IL 60601
USA
Phone: 1-800-771-2303

First Book
www.firstbook.org
1319 F Street, NW, Suite 1000
Washington, DC 20004
USA
Phone: 1-866-393-1222

Freedom from Hunger
www.freedomfromhunger
  .org
1644 DaVinci Court
Davis, CA 95618
USA
Phone: 1-800-708-2555

FreeRice
www.freerice.com
E-mail: WFP.Freerice@
  wfp.org
(Web site and e-mail only
  methods for contact)

Global Exchange
www.globalexchange.org
110 Capp Street, 2nd Floor
San Francisco, CA 94110
USA
Phone: 1-800-505-4410

**Global Fund to Fight AIDS,
Tuberculosis and Malaria**
www.theglobalfund.org
UN Foundation/Global Fund
PO Box 96618
Washington, DC 20090
USA
Phone: 1-415-346-4820

Global Giving

www.globalgiving.com
1816 12th Street NW
Washington, DC 20009
USA
Phone: 1-202-232-5784

Global Partners for Development

www.gpfd.org
320 Professional Center Drive,
    Suite 120
Rohnert Park, CA 94928
USA
Phone: 1-800-765-6252

Greater Chicago Food Depository

www.chicagosfoodbank.org
4100 West Ann Lurie Place
Chicago, IL 60632
USA
Phone: 1-773-247-FOOD
    (3663)

GreaterGood.com

www.greatergood.com
(only contact information
    available)

Harlem Children's Zone

http://hcz.org
35 East 125th Street
New York, NY 10035
USA
Phone: 1-212-360-3255

Heifer International

www.heifer.org
1 World Avenue
Little Rock, AR 72202
USA
Phone: 1-800-422-0474

Hippo Water Roller

www.hippowater.org
PO Box 1636
Ann Arbor, MI 48106
USA
(phone not available)

The Hunger Project

www.thp.org
5 Union Square West
New York, NY 10003
USA
Phone: 1-212-251-9100

The Hunger Site

www.thehungersite.com
One Union Square

600 University Street, Suite 1000
Seattle, WA 98101
USA
Phone: 1-206-859-5201

KickStart International
www.kickstart.org
2435 Polk Street, Suite 20
San Francisco, CA 94109-1600
USA
Phone: 1-415-346-4820

KIVA
www.kiva.org
3180 18th Street, Suite 201
San Francisco, CA 94110
USA
(phone not available)

Maternal and Child Health Product
www.mchp.org.np
MCHP Pvt., Ltd.
PO Box 7136
Anamnagar, Kathmandu
Nepal
Phone: 4-267865

Mercado Global
www.mercadoglobal.org
20 Mitchell Drive

New Haven, CT 06511
USA
Phone: 1-203-772-4292

One Million Lights
http://onemillionlights.org
PO Box 444
Palo Alto, CA 94302
USA
Phone: 1-650-740-3240

Ounce of Prevention Fund
www.ounceofprevention.org
33 West Monroe Street
Suite 2400
Chicago, IL 60603
USA
Phone: 1-312-922-3863

Partners in Health
www.pih.org
800 Boylston Street,
    47th Floor
Boston, MA 02199
USA
Phone: 1-617-432-5256

PATH
www.path.org
1455 NW Leary Way
Seattle, WA 98107

USA
Phone: 1-206-285-3500

Potters for Peace
www.pottersforpeace.org
PO Box 1043
Bisbee, AZ 85603
USA
Phone: 1-520-249-8093

Safe Passage
www.safepassage.org
PO Box 712849
Cincinnati, OH
   45271-2849
USA
Phone: 1-207-846-1188

Ten Thousand Villages
www.tenthousandvillages.com
704 Main Street
PO Box 500
Akron, PA 17501
USA
Phone: 1-877-883-8341

UNICEF
www.unicef.org
UNICEF House
3 United Nations Plaza

New York, NY 10017
USA
Phone: 1-212-326-7000

UNFPA
www.unfpa.org
220 East 42nd Street
New York, NY 10017
USA
Phone: 1-212-297-5000

World Bicycle Relief
www.worldbicyclerelief.org
1333 N. Kingsbury, 4th Floor
Chicago, IL 60642
USA
Phone: 1-312-664-3836

World Toilet Organization
www.worldtoilet.org
19 Toa Payoh West
Singapore 318876
Phone: 65-63528921

World Vision
www.worldvision.org
320 Professional Center Drive,
   Suite 120
Rohnert Park, CA 94928
USA
Phone: 1-800-765-6252

CHARITY NAVIGATOR'S APPROACH TO EVALUATING NONPROFIT FINANCIAL HEALTH

Charity Navigator measures an organization's financial *efficiency* and *capacity*. Efficiency is measured by three ratios: spending on "program services," "management," and "fund-raising costs" as a percentage of the agency's total budget. These spending categories represent how every nonprofit organization must allocate and report its expenses on its annual income tax return to the federal government. They also represent the total costs for an organization to conduct its mission.

It is important to realize that average program, management, and fund-raising costs vary between types of charities; for instance, early learning classrooms spend the majority of their revenues paying teacher salaries, which is a program cost, while museums might have higher overhead expenses involved in maintaining large and expensive facilities, grounds, and collections. Charity Navigator takes these factors into account in its rating system.

PROGRAM SERVICES

As donors, we expect charities to spend the bulk of their funding on providing programs and services. Typically, a financially efficient organization spends *a relatively high proportion of its income on program services*—most measures of effectiveness expect 70 percent or more of the budget to be directed to program costs (unless there are special circumstances, such as construction of a new facility).

OVERHEAD COSTS

Management and general expenses are another segment of the overall costs of conducting a mission. These are also known as the organization's "overhead" costs, and the general rule of thumb has been that the lower an organization's overhead, the better; the logic being that this means the agency directs more of its income toward conducting its programs. This single piece of data has informed many donors, including individuals, foundations, corporations, and government bodies and has created tremendous pressure on nonprofit agencies to keep these costs low. It turns out, however, to be a red herring.

Together, the Center on Philanthropy at Indiana University and the Center on Nonprofits and Philanthropy at the Urban Institute conducted the Nonprofit Overhead Cost Study, which examined the true meaning and role of overhead costs to a nonprofit's ability to effectively carry out its mission. Its findings rejected the long-held notion that the best nonprofits had the lowest overhead costs. The following is an excerpt from the report "Donating to Charity: a Guide."[1]

. . . the overemphasis on low overhead, far from enhancing the efficiency of charitable organizations, has reduced their effectiveness and corrupted their accounting. Let's talk about effectiveness first. Overhead pays for the organizational infrastructure that supports a program. It's the rent, electricity, heat, telephone, and furnishings. It's the management and board. It's accounting, human resources, and information technology. It's the website you visited, the annual report you read, and the time of the people who talked to you when you called. Overhead isn't waste; it's the basis for mission effectiveness. The Nonprofit Overhead Cost Project found wide variation in the adequacy of organizational infrastructure. Some charities included in the study had nice facilities, the latest computers and software, and highly experienced and sufficient staffing in supporting functions, such as accounting, information technology, and fundraising. At other charities, rain came through the roof, computers were mismatched hand-me-downs, software was makedo, and key support staff had limited training or experience for their roles, or were part-time because this was all the organization could afford.

These limitations had consequences for the effectiveness of these organizations. The mismatched computers frequently crashed and were expensive to maintain. Weak financial staff and software meant charities didn't really know where the money was going, and financial controls were often inadequate as well. Poor software meant charities didn't have good information about what they were accomplishing that they could share with donors and other supporters, or wasted money on fundraising that wasn't properly targeted. None of the organizations in this study was an extravagant spender on overhead items, and while there are undoubtedly some charities that are, by far the more common problem is spending too little on the organizational infrastructure that is the foundation for effective programs over the long term. *Lower is not better—better is better. And by and large, you get what you pay for.* (Italics added by author.)

FUND-RAISING COSTS

As donors, we don't want a large portion of our gifts being spent to raise the next ones. We expect nonprofits to *fund-raise efficiently.* Charity Navigator measures fund-raising efficiency by the ratio of fund-raising expenses to the total contributions received by the agency. This determines how much the agency spent to raise each donated dollar.

Here again, though, a caveat: There are many who believe that nonprofits would be well-served to act much more like the for-profit corporate sector. Dan Pallotta, author of *Uncharitable: How Restraints on Nonprofits Undermine Their Potential,* made the following comments about our expectations of nonprofit organizations to produce outcomes with few resources:

> We let business pay people based on value. But we don't want people making money in charity. Want to make a million as a CEO selling violent video games to kids? Go for it. Want to make a million curing kids of cancer? You're a parasite. So our top business school grads gravitate to the for-profit sector.
>
> We let business advertise until the last dollar no longer produces a penny of value, but we don't want charitable donations spent on advertising. So charities can't build demand for causes. Budweiser's all over the Super Bowl. AIDS and Darfur? Absent.

We let business make mistakes but expect charity to spend contributions cautiously. It's OK if a $100 million Disney movie flops, but if a $5 million charity walk doesn't show a 75% profit year one? Call the attorney general. So charities can't develop learning curves for revenue generation.

Amazon could forego investor returns for six years to build market dominance. But if a charity embarks on a long-term plan with no return for six years—we expect a crucifixion. Business can offer profits to attract investment capital. But there's no stock market for charity. So the for-profit sector monopolizes the multi-trillion-dollar capital markets. No competitive compensation, no advertising, no risk-taking, no long-term vision and no capital markets. A perfect storm of prohibition that puts the nonprofit sector at extreme disadvantage to the for-profit sector. We blame capitalism for the inequities of society and then refuse to let charity use the tools of capitalism to rectify them.

Maybe capitalism isn't the problem. Maybe the lack of it is. It's been banished from charity by a Puritan ethic of deprivation that considers it contaminating. Maybe an ethic that stands in the way of progress is an ethic whose time is done.[2]

ORGANIZATIONAL CAPACITY

Finally, Charity Navigator examines the overall financial health and stability of nonprofits by evaluating: (1) their history of sustaining programs and services, (2) their ability to weather financial setbacks while maintaining quality programs, and (3) their financial capacity to plan strategically and pursue long-term goals rather than surviving month-to-month. As Charity Navigator states: "Charities that show consistent growth and maintain financial stability are more likely to last for years to come."[3]

WHAT ABOUT THE REST?

Every organization in *Give a Little* that has been rated by Charity Navigator received three or four stars for its financial health and effectiveness. But some charities in *Give a Little* are not rated by Charity Navigator because they do not meet one or more of its criteria for evaluation, which include:

- Receiving a minimum of $500,000 in public support (donations from the public include individuals, government, and foundations rather than a few private donors)
- Receiving more than one-third of income from direct public support rather than government sources
- Having filed at least four federal tax returns for evaluation
- Being registered in the United States, although services can be provided globally
- Being registered with the IRS as a 501(c)(3) organization
- Filing annual federal tax returns (form 990)

From Page 26

Official Development Assistance—the 0.7 percent solution

Official Development Assistance (ODA) is an important tool for measuring contributions that help fund the Millennium Project from the twenty-two wealthy countries that are members of the Development Action Committee (DAC). The UN has requested that each DAC nation provide 0.7 percent (that's not 7 percent, that's 0.7 percent, *or seven-tenths of one penny of every $100*) of its gross national income to fund Millennium Project efforts.

In 2007, the United States had the ignoble distinction of tying with Greece for contributing the smallest percentage of its GNI to supporting developing countries by providing only 0.16 percent of GNI. This equals just $0.16 of every $100 of revenues. The only five nations to meet the Millennium Project .07 percent target were Norway, which came in first by contributing 0.95 percent, Sweden with 0.93 percent, Luxembourg with 0.90 percent, and Netherlands and Denmark, both with contributions of 0.81 percent.[1] But, other wealthy nations are making steady progress toward the 0.7 percent goal. U.S. contributions for 2001–2007 are illustrated in Table 1.[2]

Of course, in total dollars, the United States is by far the largest donor, providing $21.8 billion in 2007, fully 21 percent of total donations among member countries.[3] This $21.8 billion equals $72 in ODA per capita in the United States. At the other

Table 1
U.S. Official Development Assistance as
Percentage of Gross National Income
2001–2007

2001	2002	2003	2004	2005	2006	2007
0.11%	0.12%	0.15%	0.17%	0.23%	0.18%	0.16%

end of the scale, Norway's contribution of $3.7 billion equals a *per capita contribution of $805*.[4]

I believe that these differences illustrate one of the most important points about giving in the United States: We prefer to give *by choice* rather than by taxation, and *by choice*, we give *generously*.

From Page 54
International Fund for Agricultural Development
"Supporting Smallholders Is Crucial to Food Security,"
http://www.ifad.org/events/op/2008/g8.htm

A Paper Commissioned by FAO
"Linking Social Protection and Support to Small Farmer
Development," April 2008
www.fao.org/es/ESA/pdf/workshop_0108_social_protection
.pdf

World Food Programme
"Turning High Food Prices into Opportunities for Uganda's
Subsistence Farmers," www.wfp.org/content/development
-operation-uganda-107920-turning-high-food-prices-opportu
nities-ugandas-subsistence-farme

From Page 124
"World's Smartest Sticker"[5]

> *"Used properly, this [vaccine vial monitors] can be a miracle tool*
> *to reduce wastage and prevent the use of heat damaged stock."*
> —Dr. Umit Kartoglu,
> WHO Department of Vaccine and Biologicals,
> *GAVI Immunization Focus,* July 2003

Imagine the challenge of getting the extremely heat-sensitive polio vaccine from a high-tech pharmaceutical company in Belgium to a remote village in Ghana. The vaccine leaves by truck, is flown to Africa, and then is carried across dirt roads by truck or bicycle to eventually reach a refrigerator in a rural clinic that has sporadic electricity. The journey may take days or weeks, during which the vaccine is constantly at risk of being spoiled. Too often these vital vaccines are damaged but still used, or they're tossed out because health workers have to assume they have gone bad.

PATH found a technology originally used by the food industry to save perishable products and worked with its owners to adapt it so that it could be used to address the "cold chain" problem. The vaccine vial monitor is a small sticker, no bigger than a dime, that adheres to the vaccine vial and changes color as the vaccine is exposed to heat. The color of the sticker tells health workers whether the vaccine is bad—or can be safely used for immunization. No more uncertainty, no more waste.

Vaccine Vial Monitors Take the Heat

PATH worked with the World Health Organization (WHO) to identify a solution and then teamed up with the TEMPTIME

Photo courtesy of Dr. Umit Kartoglu, WHO

Corporation to develop vaccine vial monitors (HEATmarker™) that are printed directly on vaccine vial labels and darken with exposure to heat over time.

In 1996, the first monitors became commercially available for oral polio vaccine, adding only a few cents to the price of each vial. Today, monitors are available for all vaccines used in immunization programs in developing countries, and UNICEF requires them on all vaccines they purchase. Health workers can make informed decisions about whether vaccine vials need to be thrown away due to heat exposure and feel confident that the vaccine they use has not been damaged by the heat. PATH and WHO have developed and tested training materials for health workers that help them learn how to handle vaccines and use the monitors effectively.

During the May 2006 earthquake in Yogyakarta, Indonesia, electricity went out at health facilities for several days. Vaccine vial monitors showed that most vaccines were undamaged, despite the heat, and still usable—saving 50,000 doses of vaccine that otherwise would have been thrown away.

Saving Lives and Resources

2006 marked the tenth anniversary of the vaccine vial monitor. PATH estimates that over the *next* ten years, vaccine vial monitors will allow health workers to recognize and replace more than 230 million doses of inactive vaccine and to *deliver 1.4 billion more doses in remote settings*—actions that could save more than 140,000 lives and reduce morbidity for countless others. Thanks to the presence of the monitors, WHO was able to revise its policies to allow open vials of liquid vaccine to be used for more than a single day. That alone has saved immunization programs around the world millions of dollars. UNICEF and WHO have estimated that the use of monitors, even if only on basic vaccines, could save the global health community $5 million per year.

It's a sticky dot. Affixed to over two billion vials of life-saving vaccine, the world's smartest sticker costs between 4.5¢ and 5.5¢ per dot. PATH relied on funds from individual donors to help secure a large grant from the U.S. Agency for International Development (USAID), which led to the creation of this super sticker. Pretty good investment of an affordable donation.

ENDNOTES

introduction

1. National Geographic News, "The Deadliest Tsunami in History?" January 7, 2005, http://news.nationalgeographic.com/news/2004/12/1227_041226_tsunami.html.

2. Disaster Watch, "South Asia Tsunami 2004," http://www.disaster watch.net/TsunamiFacts_archive.html.

3. United Nations Office for the Coordination of Humanitarian Affairs, "Indian Ocean-Earthquake/Tsunami-December 2004 Table A: List of All Commitments/Contributions and Pledges as of 09 January 2009," http://www.reliefweb.int/fts (Table ref: R10).

4. America.gov, "Aid Efforts Continue Well After Devastating 2004 Tsunami," http://www.america.gov/st/washfile-english/2007/October/20071029081347AKllennoCcM0.4600946.html.

5. Center on Philanthropy at Indiana University, "New Study Finds Americans Gave More Than $3 Billion to Tsunami Relief," December 19, 2006, http://www.philanthropy.iupui.edu/News/2006/pr-Tsunami.aspx.

6. Ibid.

7. U.S. Census Bureau, "America's Family and Living Arrangements 2004," http://www.census.gov/population/projections/nation/hh-fam/table1n.txt.

8. Center on Philanthropy at Indiana University, "New Study Finds Americans Gave More Than $3 Billion to Tsunami Relief," December 19, 2006, http://www.philanthropy.iupui.edu/News/2006/pr-Tsunami.aspx.

9. David Joulfaian, "Basic Facts on Charitable Giving," (June 2005):17, OTA, http://www.treas.gov/offices/tax-policy/library/ota95.pdf in United States Department of the Treasury: Search: Charitable Giving: OTA Paper 95, http://www.ustreas.gov

chapter 1

1. American Rhetoric: Top 100 Speeches, "Edward M. Kennedy: Address at the Public Memorial Service for Robert F. Kennedy," http://www.americanrhetoric.com/speeches/ekennedytributetorfk.html (accessed May 23, 2009).

2. World Health Organization, "TB Facts and Figures," http://www.wpro.who.int/media_centre/fact_sheets/fs_20050324.htm.

3. America's Second Harvest, "How to Help," https://secure2.convio.net/a2h/site/Donation2?idb=2128549250&df_id=1560&1560.do nation=form1.

4. Laura Anderson, Central Asia Institute, communication via e-mail, February 21, 2008.

chapter 2

1. Aristotle, *The Nicomachean Ethics,* in Dwight Burlingame, *The Responsibilities of Wealth* (Indiana: Indiana University Press, 1992), 51.

2. *Giving USA*, 2008, a publication of Giving USA Foundation^{TM}, researched and written by the Center on Philanthropy at Indiana University.

3. International Monetary Fund, "World Economic Outlook Database, September 2005," http://www.imf.org/external/pubs/ft/weo/2005/02/data/dbginim.cfm in International Monetary Fund: Data and Statistics: Data: Global Data: World Economic Outlook Databases: World Economic Outlook April 2008 Database, http://www.imf.org.

4. Walmart, *2008 Annual Report*, 28, http://walmartstores.com/Investors/7666.aspx in Walmart Stores: Investors: Annual Reports, http://walmartstores.com.

5. Bill & Melinda Gates Foundation, "Grants Paid Summary," *Annual Report 2007*, http://www.gatesfoundation.org/nr/public/media/annualreports/annualreport07/AR2007GrantsPaid.html.

6. Bill & Melinda Gates Foundation, "Financials Overview," *Annual Report 2007*, http://www.gatesfoundation.org/nr/public/media/annualreports/annualreport07/AR2007Financials.html.

7. Carol J. Loomis, "Warren Buffett Gives Away His Fortune," *Fortune*, June 25, 2006, http://money.cnn.com/2006/06/25/magazines/fortune/charity1.fortune.

8. The World Health Organization, "Malaria Fact Sheet," May 2007, http://www.who.int/mediacentre/factsheets/fs094/en/index.html.

9. Rick Reilly, "Nothing but Thanks," SI.com, November 28, 2006, http://sportsillustrated.cnn.com/2006/writers/rick_reilly/11/27/reilly1204/index.html.

10. Net-O-Meter, NothingbutNets.net, August 6, 2008, http://www.nothingbutnets.net/nets-save-lives.

11. CDC, "50th Anniversary of the Polio Vaccine: Timeline," http://www.cdc.gov/vaccines/events/polio-vacc-50th/timeline.htm; CDC, "Poliomyelitis," 104, http://www.cdc.gov/vaccines/pubs/pinkbook/downloads/polio.pdf in Centers for Disease Control and Prevention, Health & Safety Topics: Diseases & Conditions: Polio (poliomyelitis): Poliomyelitis, http://www.cdc.gov (accessed June 23, 2007).

12. Sanofi Pasteur, Polio Eradication, Conquering Polio, "The March of Dimes," "http://www.polio.info/polio-eradication/front/index.jsp?code Rubrique=29&lang=EN&siteCode=POLIO.

13. Jorge Moll, Frank Krueger, Roland Zahn, Matteo Pardini, Ricardo de Oliveira-Souza, and Jordan Grafman, "Human Fronto-Mesolimbic Networks Guide Decisions About Charitable Donation," *Proceedings of the National Academy of Sciences of the USA*, October 9, 2006, http://www.pnas.org/content/103/42/15623.full.pdf+html.

14. Holly Hall, "Sex, Drugs and . . . Charity? Brain Study Finds New Links," *Chronicle of Philanthropy* (December 7, 2006), http://philanthropy.com/premium/articles/v19/i05/05001601.htm.

15. A. Knafo, S. Israel, A. Darvasi, R. Bachner-Melman, F. Uzefovsky, L. Cohen, E. Feldman, E. Lerer, E. Laiba, Y. Raz, L. Nemanov, I. Gritsenko, C. Dina, G. Agam, B. Dean, G. Bornstein, R. P. Ebstein, "TI: Individual Differences in Allocation of Funds in the Dictator Game Associated with Length of the Arginine Vasopressin 1a Receptor RS3 Promoter Region and Correlation Between RS3 Length and Hippocampal mRNA," *Genes, Brain and Behavior* (2008).

16. Richard A. Easterlin, "Will Raising the Incomes of All Increase the Happiness of All?" *Journal of Economic Behavior and Organization*, (June 1995), posted on Science Direct, http://www.sciencedirect.com/science?_ob=ArticleURL&_udi=B6V8F-3YGTSKK-T&_user=10&_rdoc=1&_fmt=&_orig=search&_sort=d&view=c&_version=1&_urlVersion=0&_userid=10&md5=75ede2e56d6778cf513148ae789732d4; E. Diener and R. Biswas-Diener, "Will Money Increase Subjective Wellbeing?" *Social Indicators Research* (February 2002), posted on ISI Web of Knowledge, Web of Science, http://cel.isiknowledge.com/InboundService.do?product=CEL&action=

retrieve&SrcApp=Highwire&UT=000174187000001&SID=
4Comi5b223J8LeGn5DF&Init=Yes&SrcAuth=Highwire&mode=
FullRecord&customersID=Highwire; Daniel Kahneman, Alan B.
Krueger, David Schkade, Norbert Schwarz, Arthur A. Stone, "Would
You Be Happier If You Were Richer? A Focusing Illusion," *Science*
(June 30, 2006), http://www.sciencemag.org/cgi/content/abstract/312/
5782/1908.

17. Elsa Youngsteadt, "The Secret to Happiness? Giving," *ScienceNow
Daily*, March 20, 2008, http://sciencenow.sciencemag.org/cgi/con
tent/full/2008/320/2.

18. World Health Organization, "Understanding Mental Health," *World
Health Report 2001*, http://www.who.int/whr/2001/chapter1/en/in
dex1.html.

19. United Nations Emergency Peace Services, "Government to Discuss
Possible Introduction of International Solidarity Levy," July 28,
2008, http://uneps-japan.blogspot.com/2008_07_01_archive.html.

20. "The Goals," *UN Millennium Development Goals Report*, http://www.un
.org/millenniumgoals in United Nations: Welcome: The UN Millennium Development Goals, http://www.un.org (accessed June 23, 2007).

21. Center for Global Prosperity, "Hudson Institute Launches Second
Annual Index of Global Philanthropy: American Private Giving
abroad exceeds U.S. government aid and proves more efficient," press
release, May 21, 2007, http://hudson.org/files/publications/PressRe
leaseIndex2007.pdf in Hudson Institute: Center for Global Prosperity: Press Release, http://gpr.hudson.org; Carol C. Adelman, "An
Executive Summary of *The Index of Global Philanthropy 2007*," http://
gpr.hudson.org/files/publications/Index2007ExecutiveSummary.pdf
in Hudson Institute: Center for Global Prosperity: Executive Summary, http://gpr.hudson.org.

22. Steven Kull, *The Federal Budget: The Public's Priorities*, (Washington,
DC: PIPA, 2005), 14.

23. Percentages calculated by dividing net ODA by total federal government on-budget receipts for each year. Annual government receipts
source is Historical Tables: Budget of the United States Government:
Fiscal Year 2007, 22, http://www.whitehouse.gov/omb/budget/fy2007/
pdf/hist.pdf in Office of Management and Budget: Budget of the
United States Government: Fiscal Year 2007, http://www.whitehouse
.gov/omb/budget/fy2007/ and the Net ODA source is ODA 1950 2006
Tab, "ODA Net," http://www.oecd.org/dataoecd/43/24/1894385.xls

in OECD: Statistics: Data by Topic: Development: Aid from DAC Members: Statistics, Data and Indicators: Reference DAC Statistical Tables: Net ODA from DAC countries from 1950 to 2006 (updated April 2007), http://www.oecd.org.

chapter 3

1. Jack Canfield, Mark Victor Hansen, Martin Rutte, Maida Rogerson, Tim Clauss, *Chicken soup for the soul at work: 101 stories of courage, compassion, and creativity in the workplace* (HCI, 1996), 59.
2. E-mail communication from Charity Navigator, August 29, 2008.

chapter 4

1. Deepa Narayan, "Global Synthesis," *Consultations with the Poor* (Washington, D.C.: World Bank, 1999).
2. Deepa Narayan, "Can Anyone Hear Us? Voices from 47 Countries" *Voice of the Poor* 1, Poverty Group, PREM, World Bank, 1999, http://siteresources.worldbank.org/INTPOVERTY/Resources/335642-1124115102975/1555199-1124115187705/vol1.pdf.
3. European Anti-Poverty Network, "What Is Poverty? Absolute Poverty," http://www.eapn.eu/content/view/59/53/lang,en.
4. European Commission, *Joint Report on Social Inclusion 2004*, http://www.eapn.eu/content/view/59/53/lang,en.
5. U.S. Department of Health and Human Services, "2008 HHS Poverty Guidelines," http://aspe.hhs.gov/poverty/08Poverty.shtml.
6. David Cay Johnston, "'04 Income in U.S. Was Below 2000 Level," *New York Times,* November 28, 2006, http://www.nytimes.com/2006/11/28/business/28tax.html.
7. Sarah Fass and Nancy K. Cauthen, "Who Are America's Poor Children?" National Center for Children in Poverty, 2007, http://www.nccp.org/publications/pub_787.html; Interview with Arthur Rolnick, "The Best Investment We Can Make," Children of the Code, http://www.childrenofthecode.org/interviews/rolnick.htm.
8. Population Reference Bureau, "2008 World Population Data Sheet," http://www.prb.org/Publications/Datasheets/2008/2008wpds.aspx.
9. Shaohua Chen and Martin Ravallion, "How Have the World's Poorest Fared Since the Early 1980's?" (World Bank Policy Research, working paper 3341, June 2004), 31, http://www-wds.worldbank.org/external/default/WDSContentServer/IW3P/IB/2004/07/22/000

112742_20040722172047/Rendered/PDF/wps3341.pdf and Population Reference Bureau, "2008 World Population Data Sheet," http://www.prb.org/Publications/Datasheets/2008/2008wpds.aspx.

10. Millennium Campaign, "Eradicate Hunger and Extreme Poverty," http://www.millenniumcampaign.org/site/pp.asp?c=grKVL2NLE& b=185518.

11. Shaohua Chen and Martin Ravallion, "How Have the World's Poorest Fared Since the Early 1980's?" (World Bank Policy Research, working paper 3341, June 2004), 31, http://www-wds.worldbank.org/external/default/WDSContentServer/IW3P/IB/2004/07/22/000112742_20040722172047/Rendered/PDF/wps3341.pdf in World Bank: Data & Research: Research: Projects & Programs: Poverty Research: Core Team: Martin Ravallion: Works by this author: 22, http://www.worldbank.org.

12. Ibid.

chapter 5

1. Eleanor Roosevelt, *Tomorrow is Now* (New York: Harper & Row, 1963), 40.

2. Deepa Narayan, *"Consultations with the Poor' from a Health Perspective," Development* 44, no. 1 (March 2001).

3. The Hunger Project, "Decline in the Number of Hunger Related Deaths," http://www.thp.org/reports/decline.htm in The Hunger Project: Learn More: Resources: Archives: Other Links: Master list of special reports: Reports on Ending World Hunger, http://www.thp.org (accessed July 3, 2007).

4. Mark Nord, Margaret Andrews, and Steven Carlson, "Household Food Security in the United States, 2005," 4–5, http://www.ers.usda.gov/Publications/ERR29/ERR29.pdf in United States Department of Agriculture: Economic Research Service: Food & Nutrition Assistance: Food Security & Hunger: Household Food Security in the United States, 2005: Household Food Security, http://www.ers.usda.gov.

5. Howard Berkes, "Hunger in America: A Rural Struggle to Keep the Family Fed," *NPR: All Things Considered*, November 21, 2005, National Public Radio, http://www.npr.org/templates/story/story.php?storyId=5018670.

6. World Food Programme, "Introduction: Hunger Glossary: Nutrition-Related Terms and Definitions," http://www.wfp.org/aboutwfp/intro

duction/hunger_what.asp?section=1&sub_section=1 in World Food Program: Who We Are: Introduction: What is Hunger, http://www.wfp.org (accessed July 3, 2007).

7. Ibid.

8. Deepa Narayan, "Can Anyone Hear Us? Voices from 47 Countries" *Voice of the Poor*, Poverty Group, PREM, World Bank, 1999, http://site resources.worldbank.org/INTPOVERTY/Resources/335642-112 4115102975/1555199-1124115187705/vol1.pdf.

9. Action Against Hunger, "Ending Malnutrition: How New Tools are Reshaping Our Options on Hunger," http://www.actionagainsthunger .org/pressroom/features/ending-malnutrition-how-new-tools-are-re shaping-our-options-hunger.

chapter 6

1. "2009 Annual Letter from Bill Gates: Agriculture," http://www.gates foundation.org/annual-letter/Pages/2009-agricultural-development -africa-asia.aspx.

2. The World Bank Group, "Kenya Data Profile," http://devdata.worldbank .org/external/CPProfile.asp?PTYPE=CP&CCODE=KEN in World Bank: Data & Research: Data: Key Statistics: Data By Country: Country Profiles: Kenya, http://web.worldbank.org (accessed July 5, 2007).

3. "Tracking Poverty in Kenya: Methods and Measures," World Bank presentation at Nairobi national poverty workshop, March 21, 2005, http://www.worldbank.org/afr/padi/tracking_poverty_kenya.pdf.

4. Foodnet: Marketing and Postharvest Research in Eastern and Central Africa, "Market Information," http://www.foodnet.cgiar.org/market/ Kenya/Kenya.htm#agric_economy in Foodnet: Country Profiles: Kenya: About Kenya: Agriculture and Economy, http://www.food net.cgiar.org.

5. UN Data, "Nutrition, Undernourished as Percentage of Total Population (FAO Estimates)," http://data.un.org/Data.aspx?d=FAO&f=sr ID%3A3690.

6. World Economic Forum on Africa, "Reengineering Growth," comments by Namanga Ngongi, president of the Alliance for a Green Revolution in Africa (AGRA) in Kenya, June 2008, http://www .weforum.org/pdf/summitreports/africa2008/growth.htm.

7. *KickStart Annual Report, 2006.*

8. Lennart Båge, "Supporting Smallholders Is Crucial to Food Security," as published in the G8 Summit special report of the *Financial Times*, July 7, 2008, http://www.ifad.org/events/op/2008/g8.htm.

9. World Bank, "Environment at a Glance 2004 Kenya," http://web.worldbank.org/servlets/ECR?contentMDK=20856313&sitePK=407255.

10. Ibid.

11. KickStart, "Micro-Irrigation Technologies," http://www.kickstart.org/tech/technologies/micro-irrigation.html in KickStart: The Technologies: Micro-Irrigation Technologies, http://www.kickstart.org/home/index.html (accessed July 5, 2007).

12. Martin Fisher, KickStart International, "Identify Opportunities," http://www.kickstart.org/what-we-do/step-01.php (accessed May 23, 2009)

13. Story provided by KickStart International via e-mail communication with author.

chapter 7

1. Heifer International, "Our History," http://www.heifer.org/site/c.ed JRKONiFiG/b.201520/ (accessed May 23, 2009).

2. Joe Eaton and Ron Sullivan, "Getting Poverty's Goat," *Earth Island Journal* 20, no. 2 (Summer 2005), http://www.earthisland.org/eijournal/new_articles.cfm?articleID=962&journalID=83 in Earth Island Journal: Earth Island Journal: More: Archives: volume 20 no. 2, http://www.earthisland.org.

3. Heifer International, "Goats: The Most Giving Animals Around," http://www.heifer.org/site/apps/ka/ec/product.asp?c=edJRKQNiFiG&b=477887&ProductID=164806 in Heifer International: Give: Online Gift Catalog: Goat, http://www.heifer.org (accessed July 5, 2007).

4. Heifer International, "Goat Breeding Development on Family Farms in Stoczek Lukowski." http://www.heifer.org/site/apps/nl/content3.asp?c=edJRKQNiFiG&b=718989&ct=913969 in Heifer International: Our Work: Our Projects: Poland, http://www.heifer.org (accessed June 23, 2007).

5. Heifer International, "Goats: The Most Giving Animals Around."

6. The World's Healthiest Foods, "Milk, Goat," http://www.whfoods.com/genpage.php?tname=foodspice&dbid=131 in Whole Foods: The

World's Healthiest Foods: Eating Healthy: The World's Healthiest Foods: Low Fat Dairy: Milk, goat, http://www.whfoods.com (accessed July 5, 2007).

7. Barbara Justus, "Weaving a Hopeful Future," Heifer International http://www.heifer.org/site/c.edJRKQNiFiG/b.201600.

8. Heifer International, communication via e-mail, April 26, 2007.

9. Heifer International, "Thailand Tribes Find Self-Reliance in Their Own Backyards," http://www.heifer.org/site/c.edJRKQNiFiG/b.1331245.

chapter 8

1. Pearl Bailey, *Pearl's Kitchen: An Extraordinary Cookbook* (New York: Harcourt, 1973).

2. FIVIMS, "Food Security," http://www.fivims.net/glossary.jspx?show_result=true?lang=en#F in Food and Agriculture Organization of the United Nations: International Partners: Food Insecurity and Vulnerability Information and Mapping Systems: Glossary: F, http://www.fao.org.

3. United States Department of Agriculture, "Household Food Security in the United States, 2007," http://www.ers.usda.gov/Publications/ERR66.

4. Ibid.

5. Brandeis University, Heller School for Social Policy and Management, Center on Hunger and Poverty, "The Consequences of Hunger and Food Insecurity for Children: Evidence from Recent Scientific Studies," June, 2002, 3, http://www.centeronhunger.org/pdf/ConsequencesofHunger.pdf in Center on Hunger and Poverty: News: more news: What's New: News from 2002, http://www.centeronhunger.org.

6. America's Second Harvest, "How We Work: Kids Cafe," http://www.secondharvest.org/how_we_work/programs_we_support/kids_cafe.html in America's Second Harvest: How We Work: Programs We Support: Kids Cafe, http://www.secondharvest.org (accessed July 7, 2007).

7. Ross Fraser, Media Relations Manager, America's Second Harvest, e-mail to author, February 7, 2007.

8. Roger Thurow, "Meal Plan For Hungry Kids, 'Backpack Clubs' Try to Fill a Gap," *Wall Street Journal Online*, June 14, 2006, A1, http://online.wsj.com/public/article/SB114909067247767572-nc8dj8a55ka HNZgo3rY4MDtqjxU_20060627.html?mod=blogs.

9. Arkansas Rice Depot, "A Hungry Child Can't Learn," http://www
.ricedepot.org/food_for_kids1.htm in Arkansas Rice Depot: Food
For Kids, http://www.ricedepot.org (accessed July 17, 2007).

10. America's Second Harvest, "How We Work: BackPack Program,"
http://www.secondharvest.org/how_we_work/programs_we_sup
port/back_pack_program.html in America's Second Harvest: How
We Work: Programs We Support: BackPack Program, http://www
.secondharvest.org (accessed July 7, 2007).

11. Roger Thurow, "For Hungry Kids, 'Backpack Clubs' Try to Fill a
Gap," *Wall Street Journal*, June 14, 2006.

12. Mark Nord, "Household food security in the United States, 2004,"
Economic research report, United States Department of Agriculture,
Economic Research Service, no. 11, http://www.ers.usda.gov/publica
tions/err11.pdf (accessed May 23, 2009).

13. Roger Thurow, "For Hungry Kids, 'Backpack Clubs' Try to Fill a
Gap," *Wall Street Journal*, June 14, 2006.

chapter 9

1. World Health Organization and World Bank, "Dying for Change,"
http://www.who.int/hdp/publications/dying_change.pdf.

2. Deepa Narayan, "Can Anyone Hear Us? Voices from 47 Countries,"
Voice of the Poor 1, Poverty Group, PREM, World Bank, 1999, http://
siteresources.worldbank.org/INTPOVERTY/Resources/335642-
1124115102975/1555199-1124115187705/vol1.pdf.

3. The Global Fund to Fight Aids, Tuberculosis and Malaria, "The Global
Malaria Epidemic," http://www.theglobalfund.org/en/about/malaria.

4. World Health Organization, "Malaria: Socioeconomic Impact,"
http://www.who.int/mediacentre/factsheets/fs094/en/index.html.

5. United Nations Department of Economic and Social Affairs News,
"The Inequality Predicament," (Vol. 9, no. 5, September–October 2005),
http://www.un.org/esa/desa/desaNews/desa95.html.

6. United Nations Population Fund, "State of World Population 2002:
People, Poverty, and Possibilities," 2002, http://www.unfpa.org/swp/
2002/english/ch5/index.htm.

7. Deepa Narayan, "Consultations with the Poor from a Health Perspective," *Development*, 44, no. 1 (March 2001): 15–21, http://econpapers
.repec.org/article/paldevelp/v_3a44_3ay_3a2001_3ai_3a1_3ap_3a15-
21.htm

8. Deepa Narayan, "Can Anyone Hear Us? Voices from 47 Countries," *Voice of the Poor*, Poverty Group, PREM, World Bank, 1999, http:// siteresources.worldbank.org/INTPOVERTY/Resources/335642- 1124115102975/1555199-1124115187705/vol1.pdf.

9. World Bank Group, "World Development Indicators," http://web .worldbank.org/WBSITE/EXTERNAL/DATASTATISTICS/0,, contentMDK:21725423~pagePK:64133150~piPK:64133175~the SitePK:239419,00.html.

10. Ibid.

11. World Health Organization, "Fact Sheet: Top Ten Causes of Death," 2002, www.who.int/entity/mediacentre/factsheets/fs310.pdf.

chapter 10

1. Partners Asthma Center, "Breath of Fresh Air: Poverty and Asthma," http://www.asthma.partners.org/NewFiles/BoFAChapter15.html.

2. Massachusetts Senate, "Attacking Asthma: Combating an Epidemic Among Our Children, A Report of the Senate Committee on Post Audit and Oversight," December 2002, http://www.mass.gov/legis/ senate/asthma.htm#_ftnref5.

3. Centers for Disease Control and Prevention, "Healthy Youth! Health Topics: Asthma," http://www.cdc.gov/Features/SchoolAsthma.

4. Asthma and Allergy Foundation of America, "Asthma Facts and Figures," http://aafa.org/display.cfm?id=8&sub=42#_ftn12.

5. American Lung Association, "Search LungUSA," http://www.lungusa .org/site/c.dvLUK9O0E/b.4061173/apps/s/content.asp?ct=3227479.

6. Ibid, Asthma Facts and Figures, AAFA.

7. F. J. Malveaux and S. A. Fletcher-Vincent, "Environmental Risk Fac tors of Childhood Asthma in Urban Centers," *Environmental Health Perspectives* 103(Suppl 6) (September 1995): 59–62, http://www.pub medcentral.nih.gov/articlerender.fcgi?artid=1518936.

8. Ibid.

9. Anita Manning, "Asthma Patients Struggle with Financial Bills," August 31, 2008, http://www.usatoday.com/money/industries/health/ 2005-08-31-health-care-crunch-asthma_x.htm.

10. Ibid.

11. Ibid, Centers for Disease Control and Prevention, "Healthy Youth! Health Topics: Asthma."

12. Massachusetts Senate, December 2002.

13. Asthma and Allergy Foundation of America, "History," http://www .aafa.org/display.cfm?id=10&sub=36.

14. University of Maryland Medical Center, "Breathmobile," http:// www.umm.edu/breathmobile.

15. University of Maryland Medical Center, "Become a Donor," http:// www.umm.edu/breathmobile/donor.htm.

16. Story provided by Breathmobile via e-mail communication with author.

17. Mary Beth Bollinger, "Impact of the Breathmobile on Underserved Children with Asthma," University of Maryland School of Medicine, 2008.

18. Mobile C.A.R.E., "Reduced Resource Utilization," http://www.mo bilecarefoundation.org/8stats.html (accessed May 23, 2009).

19. Mobile C.A.R.E., "Better School and Work Attendance," http:// www.mobilecarefoundation.org/8stats.html (accessed May 23, 2009).

20. Ibid; Bollinger, "Impact of the Breathmobile."

chapter 11

1. Earth Institute at Columbia University, "Improving Global Health in the Developing World: An Interview with Jeffrey Sachs," http://www .earth.columbia.edu/sitefiles/file/about/director/2009/Brown%20 Journal%20of%20World%20Affairs%20interview_AD(1).pdf.

2. World Health Organization: Media Center: Fact sheet No. 104, "Tu- berculosis: Infection and Transmission," (Revised March 2007), http:// www.who.int/mediacentre/factsheets/fs104/en/ in World Health Or- ganization: Health Center: Tuberculosis: Fact Sheet on Tuberculosis, http://www.who.int/en.

3. Brenda Wilson, "Groups Take Aim at Tuberculosis," *NPR: Morning Edition*, March 8, 2006, http://www.npr.org/templates/story/story .php?storyId=5250984 in NPR: National Public Radio: Programs: Morning Edition: Past Shows: March 2006 8: Global Health, http:// www.npr.org.

4. Centers for Disease Control and Prevention, "National Center for HIV/AIDS, Viral Hepatitis, STD, and TB Prevention, Division of Tuberculosis Elimination, "Questions and Answers about TB, 2009, http://www.cdc.gov/TB/faqs/qa_introduction.htm.

5. The Global Fund to Fight AIDS, Tuberculosis and Malaria, "Fight- ing AIDS," http://www.theglobalfund.org/en/about/aids.

6. Ibid.

7. Ibid.

8. Ibid.

9. World Health Organization, "2008 Tuberculosis Facts," http://www .who.int/tb/publications/2008/factsheet_april08.pdf; Laura Gammaitoni and Maria Clara Nucci, "Using a Mathematical Model to Evaluate the Efficacy of TB Control Measures," in Centers for Disease Control and Prevention, National Center for Infectious Diseases, *Emerging Infectious Diseases* 3, no. 3 (July–September 1997), http:// www.cdc.gov/ncidod/EID/vol3no3/nucci.htm.

10. Ibid.

11. Ibid.

12. The Global Fund to Fight AIDS, Tuberculosis and Malaria, "Fighting Tuberculosis," http://www.theglobalfund.org/en/about/tuberculosis/default.asp.

13. Christian Auer, Claudia Kessler-Bodiang, and Manfred Zahorka, "The Worldwide Battle Against Tuberculosis," Swiss Centre for International Health, Swiss Agency for Development and Cooperation, October 2002.

14. Centers for Disease Control, "Malaria Facts: Malaria Worldwide," http://www.cdc.gov/malaria/facts.htm.

15. Ibid.

16. Malaria Foundation International, "Economic Costs and Barriers to Development," http://www.malaria.org/index.php?option=com_content&task=view&id=131&Itemid=32.

17. The Global Fund to Fight AIDS, Tuberculosis and Malaria, "How the Global Fund Works: Resource Needs: 2006–2007," http://www.theglobalfund.org/en/about/how.

18. The Global Fund to Fight AIDS, Tuberculosis and Malaria, "Focus on Nepal: AIDS Widows Band Together for Support," http://www .theglobalfund.org/en/savinglives/nepal/hiv3.

19. World Health Organization, "Pakistan: Mortality and Burden of Disease, Tuberculosis," http://www.who.int/countries/pak/en.

20. Greenstar Social Marketing, "Success Story: Abdul Ghaffar," http:// www.greenstar.org.pk/success-stories-TB.htm.

21. USAID, "Telling Our Story: Saving Lives Through Improving Children's Nutrition," http://www.usaid.gov/stories/cambodia/ss_cambodia _volunteer.html.

22. Partners for Development, "Where We Work: Cambodia," http:// www.pfd.org/whereWeWorkCambodia.htm.

23. USAID, "Saving Lives Through Improving Children's Nutrition," http://www.usaid.gov/stories/cambodia/ss_cambodia_volunteer.html.

24. The Global Fund to Fight AIDS, Tuberculosis and Malaria, http://www.theglobalfund.org/en.

25. The Global Fund to Fight AIDS, Tuberculosis and Malaria, "Fighting AIDS," http://www.theglobalfund.org/en/about/aids/default.asp.

26. The Global Fund to Fight AIDS, Tuberculosis and Malaria, "Fighting Tuberculosis," http://www.theglobalfund.org/en/about/tuberculosis/default.asp.

27. The Global Fund to Fight AIDS, Tuberculosis and Malaria, "Fighting Malaria," http://www.theglobalfund.org/en/about/malaria/default.asp.

28. The Global Fund to Fight AIDS, Tuberculosis and Malaria, "Funding the Global Fight Against HIV/AIDS, Tuberculosis and Malaria: Resource Needs 2008–2010," http://www.theglobalfund.org/documents/publications/replenishment/oslo/ResourceNeeds2008-2010_en.pdf.

29. Ibid.

30. The Global Fund to Fight AIDS, Tuberculosis and Malaria, "Pledges," http://209.85.173.132/search?q=cache:T2u2UV1mOT4J:www.theglobalfund.org/documents/pledges%26contributions.xls+global+fund+commitments+2008-2010+bill+gates&hl=en&ct=clnk&cd=2&gl=us.

chapter 12

1. UNFPA, "Maternal Mortality Update 2002: A Focus on Emergency Obstetric Care," http://www.unfpa.org/upload/lib_pub_file/201_filename_mmupdate-2002.pdf.

2. World Health Organization and World Bank, "Dying for Change," http://www.who.int/hdp/publications/dying_change.pdf.

3. M. Kamrul Islam and Ulf-G. Gerdtham, "The Costs of Maternal-Newborn Illness and Mortality," World Health Organization, 2006, "http://who.int/reproductive-health/universal_coverage/issue2/consequences.htm.

4. USAID, "Maternal and Child Health: Disabilities as a Result of Pregnancy or Childbirth," http://www.usaid.gov/our_work/global_health/mch/mh/disability.html.

5. Islam and Gerdtham, "The Costs of Maternal-Newborn Illness and Mortality."

6. Ibid.

7. Ibid.

8. Joint Learning Initiative on Children and HIV/AIDS, "Can a Developing Country Support the Welfare Needs of Children Affected by AIDS?" www.jlica.org/debate/shanta.pdf.

9. World Health Organization, "Neonatal and Perinatal Mortality: Country, Regional and Global Estimates," WHO, 2006, http://www.who.int/whosis/indicators/2007MortNeoBoth/en/index.html.

10. PATH, "About PATH," http://www.path.org/about.php.

11. World Health Organization, "Maternal Mortality," http://www.who.int/making_pregnancy_safer/topics/maternal_mortality/en/index.html.

12. Ibid.

13. Lale Say and Mie Inoue of The World Health Organization (WHO), and Samuel Mills and Emi Suzuki of The World Bank, "Maternal Mortality in 2005 Estimates Developed by WHO, UNICEF, UNFPA and The World Bank," World Health Organization, 2007, http://www.who.int/reproductive-health/publications/maternal_mortality_2005/index.html.

14. World Bank, "World Development Indicators," http://ddp-ext.worldbank.org/ext/DDPQQ/member.do?method=getMembers.

15. World Health Organization, "Why Do So Many Women Still Die in Pregnancy or Childbirth?" http://www.who.int/features/qa/12/en/index.html.

16. International Centre for Diarrheal Disease Research, Bangladesh, "Evidence for Interventions Included in the Minimum Package of Maternal and Newborn Interventions," http://www.icddrb.org/pub/publication.jsp?classificationID=68&pubID=8469.

17. PATH, "Final Research Report: Evaluation of a Clean Delivery Kit Intervention in Preventing Cord Infection and Puerperal Sepsis in Mwanza, Tanzania," July 2005, http://www.path.org/publications/details.php?i=1011.

18. PATH, "Clean-Delivery Kits: Guidelines for Use in Programmatic Settings," http://www.path.org/files/RH_dk_fs.pdf.

19. Ibid.

20. PATH, "Delivery Kit," http://www.path.org/files/TS_update_delivery_kit.pdf.

21. PATH, "Funding Innovation: PATH's Use of Flexible Funding in 2007," http://www.path.org/files/ER_innv_fund_rpt_2007.pdf.

22. Ibid.

chapter 13

1. Shantayanan Devarajan, Margaret J. Miller, and Eric V. Swanson, "Goals for Development: History, Prospects, and Costs," The World Bank Human Development Network, Office of the Vice President and Development Data Group, Policy Research Working Paper, April 2002, http://www-wds.worldbank.org/external/default/WDSContent Server/IW3P/IB/2002/04/26/000094946_02041804272578/Ren dered/PDF/multi0page.pdf; According to the International Dairy Foods Association, in 2006, Americans spent nearly $23 billion on ice cream and frozen desserts, http://www.idfa.org/facts/icmonth/page2.cfm.

2. USAID, Equip 2, "Financial Issues," http://www.equip123.net/we barticles/anmviewer.asp?a=564.

3. UN News Centre, "Ban Calls for Boosting Reading Skills as Part of Efforts to Tackle Health Concerns," September 8, 2008, http://www .un.org/apps/news/story.asp?NewsID=27964&Cr=literacy&Cr1=: According to the United Nations' report "World Population Prospects: Population Age Composition," found at www.un.org/esa/pop ulation/publications/WPP2004/WPP2004_Vol3_Final/Chapter2 .pdf, in 2005, 28.2 percent of the world's population was comprised of children under age fifteen. The author calculated the ratio of illiterate adults by multiplying the 2008 total world population (as determined by the World Population Clock at www.census.gov/main/www/pop clock.html) by 0.818 (the percentage of the population in 2005 comprised of people age fifteen and older) to determine the total number of adults in 2008. The author then divided the total number of illiterate adults (774 million) by the total number of adults.

4. The World Bank, "EdStats Query," http://ddp-ext.worldbank.org/ext/ DDPQQ/member.do?method=getMembers&userid=1&queryId= 189.

5. The World Bank Group, "You Think, but Do You Know? Education, What Is It?" http://youthink.worldbank.org/issues/education.

6. World Bank, http://web.worldbank.org/WBSITE/EXTERNAL/ DATASTATISTICS/0,,contentMDK:20394704~isCURL:Y~me

nuPK:1192714~pagePK:64133150~piPK:64133175~theSitePK: 239419,00.html.

7. UNDP, "Human Development Reports, Ethiopia," http://hdrstats .undp.org/countries/country_fact_sheets/cty_fs_ETH.html.

8. UNICEF, "Real Life Stories: Awatif's Story," http://www.unicef.org/ voy/explore/education/explore_224.html.

chapter 14

1. EndPoverty 2015: Millennium Campaign, "Universal Education," http://www.endpoverty2015.org/goals/universal-education.

2. Central Intelligence Agency, "The World Factbook, 2008," https:// www.cia.gov/library/publications/the-world-factbook/print/xx.html.

3. EndPoverty 2015: Millennium Campaign, "Universal Education," http://www.endpoverty2015.org/goals/universal-education.

4. Save the Children, "In My Own Words," May 2004, http://www.sa vethechildren.org/publications/technical-resources/health/reproduc tive-health/In_My_Own_Words.pdf.

5. Lawrence H. Summers, *Investing in All the People: Educating Women in Developing Countries* (Washington, D.C.: World Bank, 1994).

6. Ibid.

7. Ibid.

8. Developments in Literacy, "About Us," http://www.dil.org/about.htm.

9. Developments in Literacy, "Our Vision," http://www.dil.org/about-us.html (accessed May 23, 2009).

10. World Bank, "Gross National Income Per Capita 2007, Atlas Method and PPP," http://siteresources.worldbank.org/DATASTATISTICS/ Resources/GNIPC.pdf.

11. Developments in Literacy, "Home," http://www.dil.org.

12. World Bank, "EdStats Query," http://web.worldbank.org/WBSITE/ EXTERNAL/TOPICS/EXTEDUCATION/EXTDATASTA TISTICS/EXTEDSTATS/0,,contentMDK:21528247~menu PK:3409442~pagePK:64168445~piPK:64168309~theSitePK: 3232764,00.html.

13. Developments in Literacy, "Stories," http://www.dil.org/stories-zur iat.html (accessed May 23, 2009).

chapter 15

1. Leslie Iwerks and Mike Glad, *Recycled Life,* documentary film about the Guatemalan City Dump.
2. World Bank, "World Development Indicators Quick Query," http://ddp-ext.worldbank.org/ext/DDPQQ/member.do?method=get Members&userid=1&queryId=135.
3. Ibid.
4. United Nations Human Development Programme, "Human Development Reports," http://hdrstats.undp.org/indicators/indicators_table.cfm.
5. *Recycled Life,* DVD Documentary produced by Mike Glad and directed by Leslie Iwerks.
6. Safe Passage, "Educational Reinforcement," http://www.safepassage.org/about-the-program/educationalreinforcement.html.

chapter 16

1. National Center for Children in Poverty, "Child Poverty," http://www.nccp.org/topics/childpoverty.html.
2. J. Bernstein, C. Brocht, and M. Spade-Aguilar, *How Much Is Enough? Basic Family Budgets for Working Families* (Washington, D.C.: Economic Policy Institute, 2000).
3. R. Kotulak, "Reshaping Brain for Better Future," *Chicago Tribune,* April 15, 1993, section 1.
4. Ibid.
5. Art Rolnick, "Early Childhood Development: Economic Development with a High Public Return," *Fedgazette,* March 2003, http://www.minneapolisfed.org/pubs/fedgaz/03-03/earlychild.cfm.
6. Interview with Arthur Rolnick, "The Best Investment We Can Make," Children of the Code, http://www.childrenofthecode.org/interviews/rolnick.htm.
7. High Scope Perry Preschool Study, "Long-Term Study of Adults Who Received High-Quality Early Childhood Care and Education Shows Economic and Social Gains, Less Crime," press release, November 2004, http://www.highscope.org/Content.asp?ContentId=282.
8. Chicago Public Schools Office of Research, Evaluation and Accountability, "School Query Tool," http://research.cps.k12.il.us/resweb/qt.
9. Ounce of Prevention Fund, "Early Returns of Educare of Chicago: A Report to Investors," http://www.ounceofprevention.org/includes/

tiny_mce/plugins/filemanager/files/Early%20Returns%20on
%20Educare%20of%20Chicago.pdf.

10. Ounce of Prevention Fund, "About Us," http://www.ounceofpreven
tion.org/aboutus.php.

11. Ounce of Prevention Fund, *Annual Report 2007*, http://www.ounceof
prevention.org/includes/tiny_mce/plugins/filemanager/files/2007
%20Annual%20Report–FINAL.pdf.

chapter 17

1. Deepa Narayan, "Can Anyone Hear Us? Voices from 47 Countries,"
Voice of the Poor, Poverty Group, PREM, World Bank, 1999, http://
siteresources.worldbank.org/INTPOVERTY/Resources/335642
-1124115102975/1555199-1124115187705/vol1.pdf.

2. World Bank, "World Development Indicators," http://web.world
bank.org/WBSITE/EXTERNAL/DATASTATISTICS/0,,con
tentMDK:21725423~pagePK:64133150~piPK:64133175~theSite
PK:239419,00.html and "Data by Topic: Infrastructure," http://web
.worldbank.org/WBSITE/EXTERNAL/DATASTATISTICS/0,
,contentMDK:20415471~menuPK:1192714~pagePK:64133150
~piPK:64133175~theSitePK:239419,00.html; International Energy
Agency, "Electricity/Heat in Cambodia in 2005," http://www.iea
.org/Textbase/stats/electricitydata.asp?COUNTRY_CODE=KH;
Measure DHS STATcompiler, http://www.measuredhs.com; Human
Development Reports, "Human and Income Poverty: Developing
Countries, 2004," http://hdrstats.undp.org/indicators/21.html; Umesh
D. Parashar, Erik G. Hummelman, Joseph S. Bresee, Mark A. Miller,
and Roger I. Glass, "Global Illness and Deaths Caused by Rotavirus
Disease in Children," *Emerging Infectious Diseases*, posted June 9,
2003. http://www.medscape.com/viewarticle/453675_5.

chapter 18

1. Bridges to Prosperity, "Miracles in Ethiopia and Peru!" http://www
.bridgestoprosperity.org/stories.htm.

2. World Bank, "Gross National Income per Capita 2007, Atlas Method
and PPP," http://siteresources.worldbank.org/DATASTATISTICS/
Resources/GNIPC.pdf.

3. The Rotarian, "Bridging Worlds," August 2008.

4. From Ken Frantz's journal.

5. Bridges to Prosperity, "Miracles in Ethiopia and Peru!" http://www .bridgestoprosperity.org/stories.htm (accessed May 23, 2009).

chapter 19

1. Water Partners International, "Water Facts," http://www.water.org/ waterpartners.aspx?pgID=916.

2. Ibid.

3. Revistazo.com, "Thousands of Families Cannot Afford $2 for Potable Water," http://www.revistazo.com/english/sept.

4. Potters for Peace, "Potters," http://pottersforpeace.org/?page_id=7.

5. National Climate and Data Center, "Mitch: the Deadliest Atlantic Hurricane Since 1780," http://lwf.ncdc.noaa.gov/oa/reports/mitch/ mitch.html#DAMAGE.

6. Ibid.

7. Potters for Peace, "Filters," http://s189535770.onlinehome.us/pot tersforpeace/?page_id=9.

8. Emmanuel Cooper, *Ten Thousand Years of Pottery* (University of Penn- sylvania Press, 2000).

9. Ibid.

10. Ibid. Potters for Peace, "Study on Life Span of Ceramic Filter Col- loidal Silver Pot Shaped (CSP) Model," http://pottersforpeace.org/ wp-content/uploads/filter-longevity-study.pdf.

11. Centers for Disease Control and Prevention, "Malaria," http://www .cdc.gov/malaria/faq.htm.

12. Centers for Disease Control and Prevention, "Malaria Surveillance, United States 2004," http://www.cdc.gov/mmwr/preview/mmwrhtml/ ss5504a2.htm.

13. Centers for Disease Control and Prevention, "Malaria," http://www .cdc.gov/malaria/disease.htm.

14. Water Partners International, "Water Facts," http://www.water.org/ waterpartners.aspx?pgID=916.

15. Potters for Peace, "Filters," http://s189535770.onlinehome.us/potters forpeace/?page_id=9.

16. Water Partners International, "Water Facts," http://www.water.org/ waterpartners.aspx?pgID=916.

17. Ibid.

chapter 20

1. World Bicycle Relief, "Our Work," http://www.worldbicyclerelief .org/our_work/index.php (accessed May 23, 2009).

2. Vijaya Ramachandran, Alan Gelb, and Manju Kedia Shah, *Africa's Private Sector: What's Wrong with the Business Environment and What to Do About It* (Washington, D.C.: Center for Global Development, February 2009).

3. World Bank, Data and Statistics, "Private Sector at a Glance," http://web.worldbank.org/WBSITE/EXTERNAL/DATASTATISTICS/0,,contentMDK:21323532~menuPK:1192714~pagePK:64133150~piPK:64133175~theSitePK:239419,00.html.

4. Population Reference Bureau, "Number of Vehicles per 1,000 People: 2000," http://www.prb.org/Datafinder/Topic/Bar.aspx?sort=v&order=d&variable=99.

5. World Bank, Data and Statistics, "Information Technology," http://web.worldbank.org/WBSITE/EXTERNAL/DATASTATISTICS/0,,contentMDK:20394827~menuPK:1192714~pagePK:64133150~piPK:64133175~theSitePK:239419~isCURL:Y,00.html.

6. World Bank, "Information and Communications for Development 2006: Global Trends and Policies," http://web.worldbank.org/WBSITE/EXTERNAL/DATASTATISTICS/0,,contentMDK:20459133~menuPK:1192714~pagePK:64133150~piPK:64133175~theSitePK:239419,00.html.

7. Ibid.

8. Ibid.

9. Engineers Without Borders, "Solution of the Month," http://www.ewb-international.org/solutionofmonth.htm.

10. The World Bank, "Gross National Income per Capita 2007, Atlas Method and PPP," http://siteresources.worldbank.org/DATASTATISTICS/Resources/GNIPC.pdf.

11. World Bicycle Relief, "Project Zambia," http://www.worldbicyclerelief.org/projects/zambia/#thepower.

12. Ibid.

13. World Bicycle Relief, "The Power of Bicycles Stories: Rhoda Katite," http://www.worldbicyclerelief.org/stories/story_rhoda.php.

chapter 21

1. World of Quotes, "Johann Wolfgang von Goethe," http://www.worl dofquotes.com/author/Johann-Wolfgang-von-Goethe/1/index.html (accessed May 23, 2009).
2. ActionAid, "Our Work," http://actionaidusa.org/who/overview.
3. World Vision, "Giving Center, Donate, By Category, US Programs," http://donate.worldvision.org/OA_HTML/xxwv2ibeCCtpItmD spRte.jsp?section=10369&item=1115331.
4. Global Partners for Development, "Success Stories: Healthy, Happy Babies Begin Here!" http://www.gpfd.org/global_pages/global_stories .html#health.

chapter 22

1. Harold Seymour, *Designs for Fund Raising*, 2nd ed. (Detroit: The Taft Group, 1988).
2. Grameen Bank, "A Short History of Grameen Bank," http://www .grameen-info.org/index.php?option=com_content&task=view&id= 19&Itemid=114.
3. Grameen Bank, "Key Information of Grameen Bank in US Dollars," http://www.grameen-info.org/index.php?option=com_content&task =view&id=37&Itemid=428.
4. Grameen Bank, "Grameen Bank at a Glance: October 2008," http:// www.grameen-info.org/index.php?option=com_content&task=view &id=26&Itemid=175.
5. Grameen Bank, "Key Information of Grameen Bank in US Dollars," http://www.grameen-info.org/index.php?option=com_content&task =view&id=37&Itemid=428.
6. Ibid.
7. Ibid.
8. Grameen Bank, "Grameen Bank at a Glance: October 2008," http:// www.grameen-info.org/index.php?option=com_content&task=view &id=26&Itemid=175.
9. Kiva, "Latest Statistics," http://www.kiva.org/about/facts.
10. DonorsChoose.org, "Completed Projects, Here's Your Work!" http:// www.donorschoose.org/donors/proposal.html?id=240149&zone=0 (accessed May 23, 2009).
11. Ibid.
12. Ibid.

13. DonorsChoose.org, "About Us: Impact to Date," http://www.donors choose.org/about/impact.html?zone=0.

14. Global Giving, "How GlobalGiving Works," http://www.globalgiving.com/howitworks.html.

15. GlobalGiving, "GlobalGivers: See why they give," http://www.global giving.com/givers.html (accessed May 23, 2009).

16. BeadforLife, "Meet Laker Fatuma," http://www.beadforlife.org/2bead ersLaker.html.

17. BeadforLife, "About BeadforLife," http://www.beadforlife.org/1about .html.

18. CraftNetwork, "KNN Cambodia," http://www.craftnetwork.com/knn-cambodia.

19. Mercado Global, "About Us," http://www.mercadoglobal.org/index .php?section=2 (accessed May 23, 2009).

20. Mercado Global, "Donate Now," http://www.mercadoglobal.org/index .php?section=10 (accessed May 23, 2009).

21. Mercado Global, "Donate Now," http://www.mercadoglobal.org/index .php?section=10.

22. Global Exchange, "About Us," http://www.gxonlinestore.org/aboutus .html.

23. Global Exchange, "Fair Trade Producers: Sudan," http://www.gxon linestore.org/sudan1.html.

24. Ten Thousand Villages, "Support System," http://www.tenthousand villages.com/catalog/story.detail.php?story_id=140.

chapter 23

1. Benjamin Franklin, *Poor Richard's Almanac, 1737.*

2. GreaterGood.org, "Our Mission," http://www.greatergood.org/mis sion.html (accessed May 23, 2009).

3. The Hunger Site, "How You're Helping," http://shop.thehungersite .com/store/royaltytotals.do?siteId=220.

4. Ibid.

5. GreaterGood, "Charitable Partners," http://www.greatergood.org/part ners.html.

6. U.N. Office of the High Representative for the Least Developed Countries, Landlocked Developing Countries, and Small Island Developing States, "The Criteria for the Identification of the LDCs," http://www.un.org/special-rep/ohrlls/ldc/ldc criteria.htm

chapter 24

1. Forbes, Inc., *The Forbes Scrapbook of Thoughts on the Business of Life* (Triumph Books, 1995).
2. The Hunger Project, "Community Centers for Meeting Basic Needs," http://www.thp.org/what_we_do/key_initiatives/community_centers/overview (accessed May 23, 2009).
3. ECHO, "Growing Locally, Feeding Globally," *ECHO Annual Report*, 2007/2008, http://www.echonet.org/documents/annualreport0708.pdf.zip.
4. Freedom from Hunger, "Worldwide Programs," http://www.freedomfromhunger.org/programs/ (accessed May 23, 2009).
5. Freedom from Hunger, "Rita's Story: No More 'Hungry Season.'" Story sent by Christine Dodson, Manager, Donor Communications, Freedom from Hunger.
6. FreeRice.com, "Frequently Asked Questions," http://www.freerice.com/faq.html.
7. Partners In Health, "The PIH Model of Care—Partnering with Poor Communities to Combat Disease and Poverty," http://www.pih.org/what/PIHmodel.html.
8. Global Health Council, "AIDS Patient Is Messenger of Hope: Denizard Wilson," http://www.globalhealth.org/publications.
9. Children's Health Fund, "Child Health Care," http://www.childrenshealthfund.org/child-health-care (accessed May 23, 2009).
10. Ibid.
11. Children's Health Fund, "Medical," http://www.childrenshealthfund.org/child-health-care/enhanced-medical-home/medical (accessed May 23, 2009).
12. Children's Health Project, story provided by Gabrielle Schang, Vice President, External Affairs.
13. EngenderHealth, "Our Mission," http://www.engenderhealth.org/about/mission.php (accessed May 23, 2009).
14. EngenderHealth, "Communities Respond: Women's Health First!" Story provided by Carey Meyers, MPH, Manager, Communications and Marketing, EngenderHealth.
15. Per UNFPA Procurement Division, September 2008.
16. UNICEF, "Early Childhood: The Big Picture," http://www.unicef.org/earlychildhoo/index_bigpicture.html (accessed May 23, 2009).
17. UNICEF, "UNICEF in Action," http://www.unicef.org/earlychildhood/index_action.html (accessed May 23, 2009).

18. First Book, "FAQ," http://www.firstbook.org/site/c.lwKYJ8NVJvF/b.677523/ (accessed May 23, 2009).

19. First Book, "Our Impact," http://www.firstbook.org/site/c.lwKYJ8NVJvF/b.674339.

20. Harlem Children's Zone, "Programs," http://www.hcz.org/programs/overview (accessed May 23, 2009).

21. Harlem Children's Zone, "The Harlem Children's Zone Project," http://www.hcz.org/programs/the-hcz-project (accessed May 23, 2009).

22. U.S. Department of Education, National Center for Education Statistics, "Entering Kindergarten: A Portrait of American Children When They Begin School: Findings from The Condition of Education 2000," Nicholas Zill and Jerry West, NCES 2001–035 (Washington, D.C.: U.S. Government Printing Office, 2001), http://nces.ed.gov/pubs 2001/2001035.pdf.

23. Harlem Children's Zone, "How Our Work Is Succeeding for Poor Children and Families," http://hcz.org/our-results.

24. Harlem Children's Zone, "Home," http://hcz.org/home.

25. Harlem Children's Zone, "How Our Work Is Succeeding for Poor Children and Families," http://www.hcz.org/our-results.

26. Hippo Water Roller, www.hipporoller.org.

27. Story contributed by Cynthia Koenig, Hippo Water Roller, January 15, 2009.

28. Henry J. Hatch, "Capacity Building: Opportunity for Enduring Peace," American Physical Society, Forum on International Physics, *International Newsletter*, July 2007, http://74.125.95.132/search?q=cache: IQ0RNE2od7UJ:www.aps.org/units/fip/newsletters/upload/july07 .pdf+Henry+Hatch,+2004+capacity+building&cd=3&hl=en&ct= clnk&gl=us (accessed May 23, 2009).

29. Engineers Without Borders, "For the World's Poor: Think Big," http:// www.ewb-usa.org/news.php?ID=65.

30. The Hunger Site, "High Efficiency Stoves for Darfur Refugees," https:// shop.thehungersite.com/store/item.do?itemId=31012&siteId=220& sourceId=46&sourceClass=Category&index=2.

31. One Million Lights, "Current Stories," http://www.onemillionlights .org/currentprogramsAfrica.html.

32. World Toilet Organization, "Who We Are," http://www.worldtoilet .org/aboutus.asp (accessed May 23, 2009).

33. Natural Resources Defense Council, "World Toilet Day Recognizes

2.5 Billion People Without Proper Sanitation," http://www.nrdc.org/media/2008/081119d.asp.

34. Ecosan, "Ecosan Waterless Toilet: Product Information," http://www.ecosan.co.za/product_info.html.

Appendix B

1. The Center on Philanthropy at Indiana University, National Center for Charitable Statistics and the Urban Institute, "Donating to Charity: A Guide," 2004, http://nccsdataweb.urban.org/kbfiles/541/Donor%20Guide.pdf.

2. National Public Radio, *Marketplace*, commentary by Dan Pallotta, *Use Capitalism to do Good Works*, December 11, 2008, http://marketplace.publicradio.org/display/web/2008/12/11/pm_post_puritan_philanthropy.

3. Charity Navigator, "How Do We Rate Charities?" http://www.charitynavigator.org/index.cfm?bay=content.view&cpid=35.

Author's Notes

1. Organization for Economic Cooperation and Development, "Debt Relief Is Down: Other ODA Rises Slightly," April 2008, http://www.oecd.org/document/8/0,3343,en_2649_34447_40381960_1_1_1_1,00.html.

2. Organization for Economic Development and Cooperation, "Table 1: Net Official Development Assistance in 2002," http://www.oecd.org/dataoecd/43/56/2507734.pdf; Organization for Economic Development and Cooperation, "Statistical Annex of the 2008 Development Co-operation Report," http://www.oecd.org/dac/stats/dac/dcrannex.

3. Ibid.

4. Per capita numbers derived by dividing Net ODA in Tab34e, "Table 34. Share of Debt Relief in DAC Members' Total Net ODA in 2005" by 2005 Population in Tab38e, "Table 38. Gross National Income and Population of DAC Member Countries," http://www.oecd.org/dataoecd/52/10/1893151.xls in OECD: Statistics: Data by Topic: Development: Aid from DAC Members: Statistics, Data and Indicators: Statistical Annex of the 2006 Development Co-operation Report: Tables 33 to 38, http://www.oecd.org.

5. PATH, "World's Smartest Sticker," http://www.path.org/projects/vaccine_vial_monitor.php.

ACKNOWLEDGMENTS

Give a Little was transformed from an idea into a book as a result of numerous acts of encouragement and generosity from people I am fortunate to call my friends, mentors, and family.

I am forever grateful to Brad Hoak, who gladly gave me all the time I needed to be a stay-at-home mom while working out an idea for a book in our basement office. He believed in and backed me 100 percent—even putting in over 200 hours double-checking and formatting footnotes. Our daughters, Rosa and Grace, patiently tolerated their mom's long hours in the basement and, at one point, created a list of affirmations that kept me going. They provided large doses of much-needed comic relief, joy, and fun throughout this project.

My dear friend Bonnie Braverman cheered me on and stuck by me through many highs and lows over the past several years. She also read at least two drafts of the manuscript. Everyone needs a Bonnie. Other wonderful friends, including Kim Sterling, Judy and Dick Lester, Jami and Steve Kessler, Marylee Swiatowiec, Buket Ozer, Robin Byster, Mary Jane Chainski, Sue Berger, Erica Anderson, Joan Pendleton, Joan Lancaster, and Adrienne Walker-Heller encouraged and buoyed me along the way. I'd never have survived the deadlines and pressures without Wendy Selene.

Anna Lvovsky and Julie Moscow at the Marly Rusoff Literary Agency first noted the potential buried in my long book proposal, and agent extraordinaire, Marly Rusoff, shared her time and wisdom with me over a cup of tea and turned an academic treatise into the book I really wanted to write. She has been a wonderful mentor and advocate and I owe her a tremendous debt of gratitude.

Hyperion Books' Barbara Jones, Ellen Archer, and Will Balliett believed in the project and showed me how a first-rate publisher takes an idea from good to great. Sarah Landis, my editor at Hyperion, made my book a better read and me a better writer. I've never felt in more capable hands. Production editor Kevin MacDonald added technical sophistication that pulled it all together.

To my mom and dad, Lloyd and Suzy Smith, I owe my dogged determination and belief that I can accomplish anything I set my mind to. It doesn't get any better than that. My sister, Nicole Kinner, and brother, Scott Smith, provided enthusiastic support.

To my research assistants, Nancy McGourty and Laurel Konopacki, I'd never have made my submission deadline without your hours of phone-calling, e-mailing, and general persistence. Many days, you kept me two steps back from the edge of insanity.

Jerome McDonald's radio program *Worldview*, which I listen to religiously on WBEZ Chicago Public Radio, planted the initial seeds for this book, particularly his "Global Activism Thursday" series. His 2006 interview with Paul Barker, then country director for CARE International in Afghanistan, convinced me that individuals were the answer to many of the world's most urgent social crises.

Finally, I want to thank the dozens of folks in the nonprofit sector around the world who provided me with time they didn't have as well as information, feedback, insight, background, obscure data, stories, explanations, and re-explanations.

These folks include Ken Weimar, Nick Moon, and Martin Fisher from KickStart International; Ray White, Judith Valesco, and Jo Luck from Heifer International; Ross Fraser at Feeding America; Robert Dolgan and Shannon Stubblefield of the Greater Chicago Food Depository; Adrianna Logalbo of the United Nations Foundation; Stephen Samuelson of Chicago's Mobile C.A.R.E.; Michelle Foster of Baltimore's Breathmobile; Siri Wood of PATH: a Catalyst for Global Health; Renu Munankarmi at Maternal and Child Health Products; Dr. Jeffrey Sachs and Margaret Buchanan of the Earth Institute at Columbia University; Beatrice Bernescut and Katy Anderson of the Global Fund to Fight AIDS, Tuberculosis and Malaria; Rachel Meyn and Karen Bolmer of Safe Passage; Fiza Shaw and Annie Field of Developments in Literacy; Barbara Hoffman and Angela Walker of the Ounce of Prevention; Ken Frantz at Bridges to Prosperity; Janice Chambers of The Rotarian; Kaira Wagoner and Reynaldo Diaz of Potters for Peace and Claysure; Beverly Pillers of Potters for Peace; Kathy McBride; Chris Strout and Jill Reid of World Bicycle Relief; Danielle Flood of ECHO; Chris Dodson of Freedom from Hunger; Andrew Marx of Partners in Health; Gabrielle Schang of the Children's Health Fund; Carey Meyers of Engender Health; Katie Brown of First Book; Marty Lipp of the Harlem Children's Zone; Cynthia Koenig of Hippo Water Roller; Josh Dick; Susan Skog of Engineers Without Borders; Amy Callis of the Darfur Stoves Project; Anna Sidana of One Million Lights; Matthew Scott of Mighty Light; Maia Ruefa of World Toilet Organization; Rachel Wolff and Karen Kartes of World Vision; Robin Bell of Save the Children; Catherine Kirby at Global Partners for Development; Charles Best at DonorsChoose.org; Joan Ochi at GlobalGiving; Torkin Wakefield at Bead for Life; Kristen Jenkins at Ten Thousand Villages; Rosemary Jones of GreaterGood.org; and Melissa Brown at Giving USA.

COPYRIGHT JOVANKA NOVAKOVIC/BAUWERKS.COM

Wendy Smith has worked in the nonprofit sector for the past twenty years. She has extensive knowledge of how the nonprofit sector operates, what makes programs effective, and what motivates donors to give. She is inspired by the generosity of everyday citizens and passionate about informing them of the power of their giving. Wendy lives in a suburb of Chicago with her twin daughters.